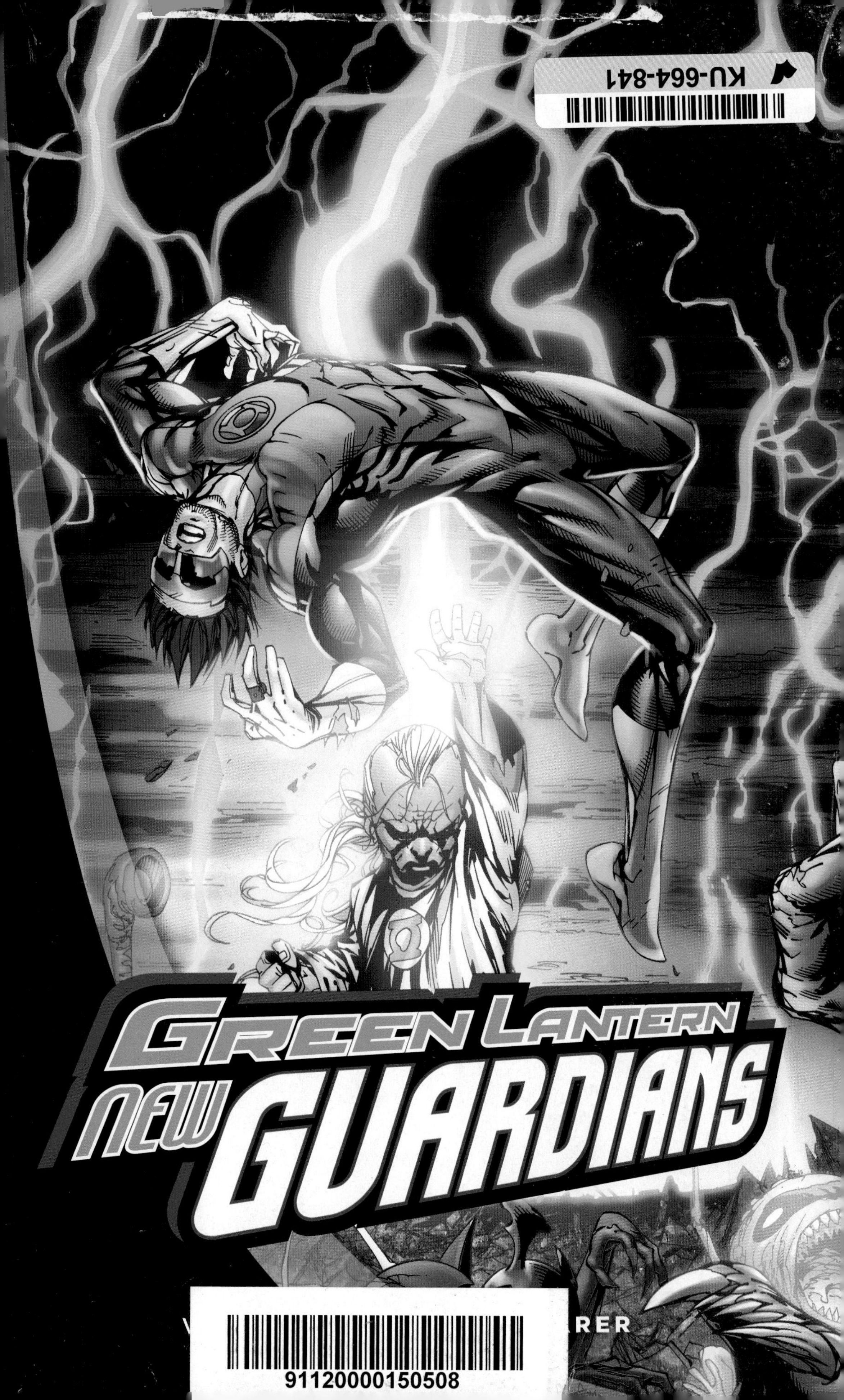
GREEN LANTERN
NEW GUARDIANS

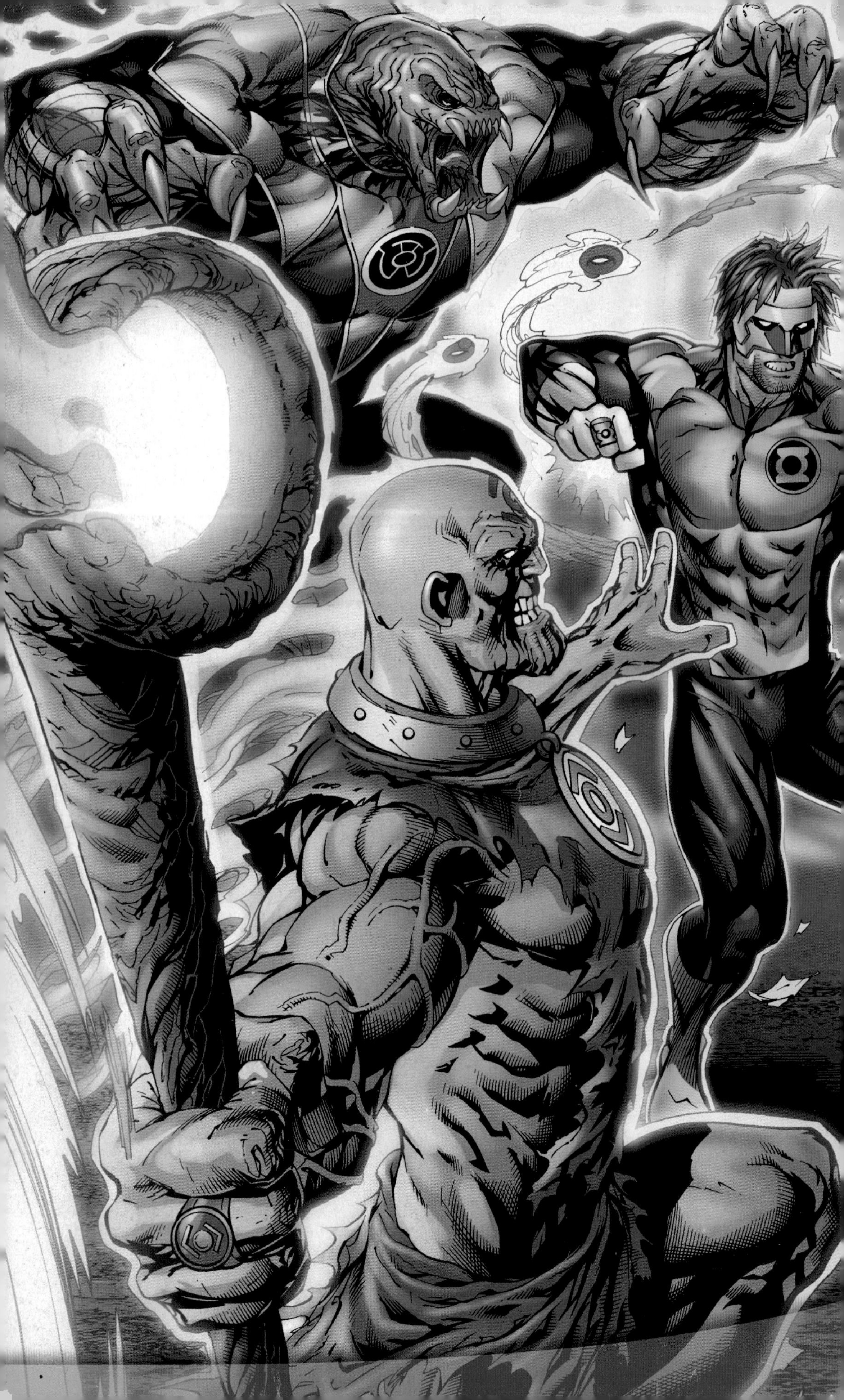

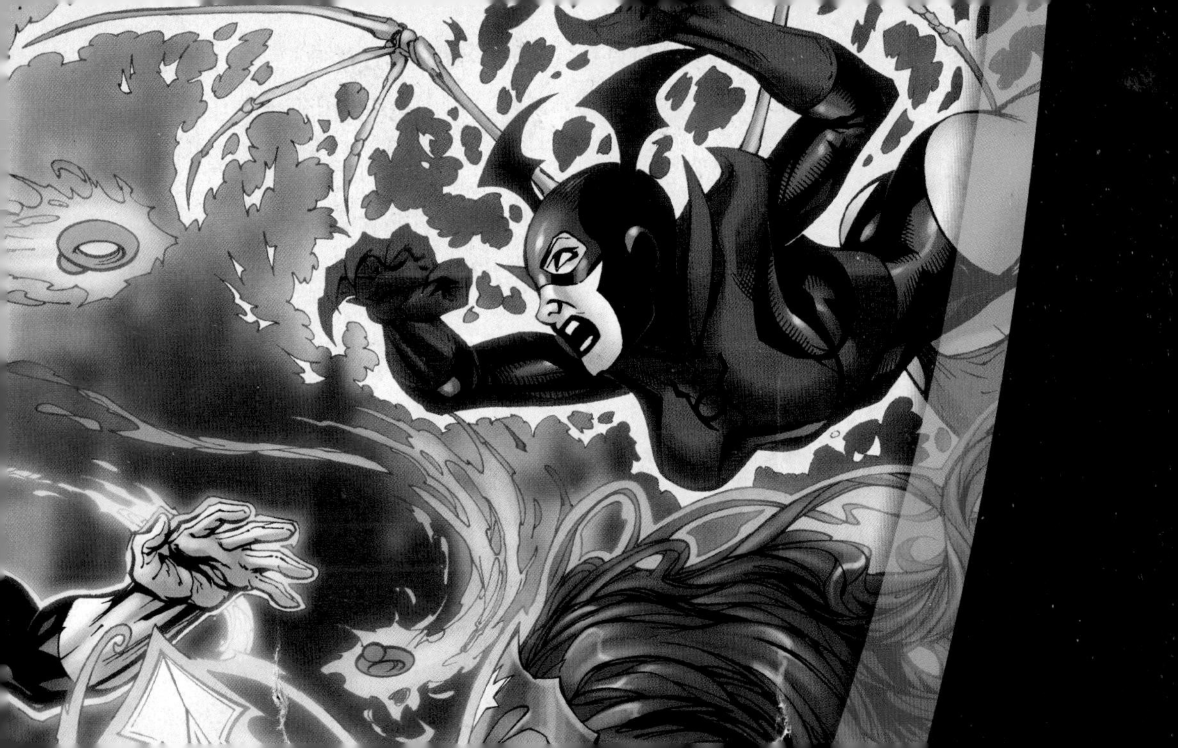

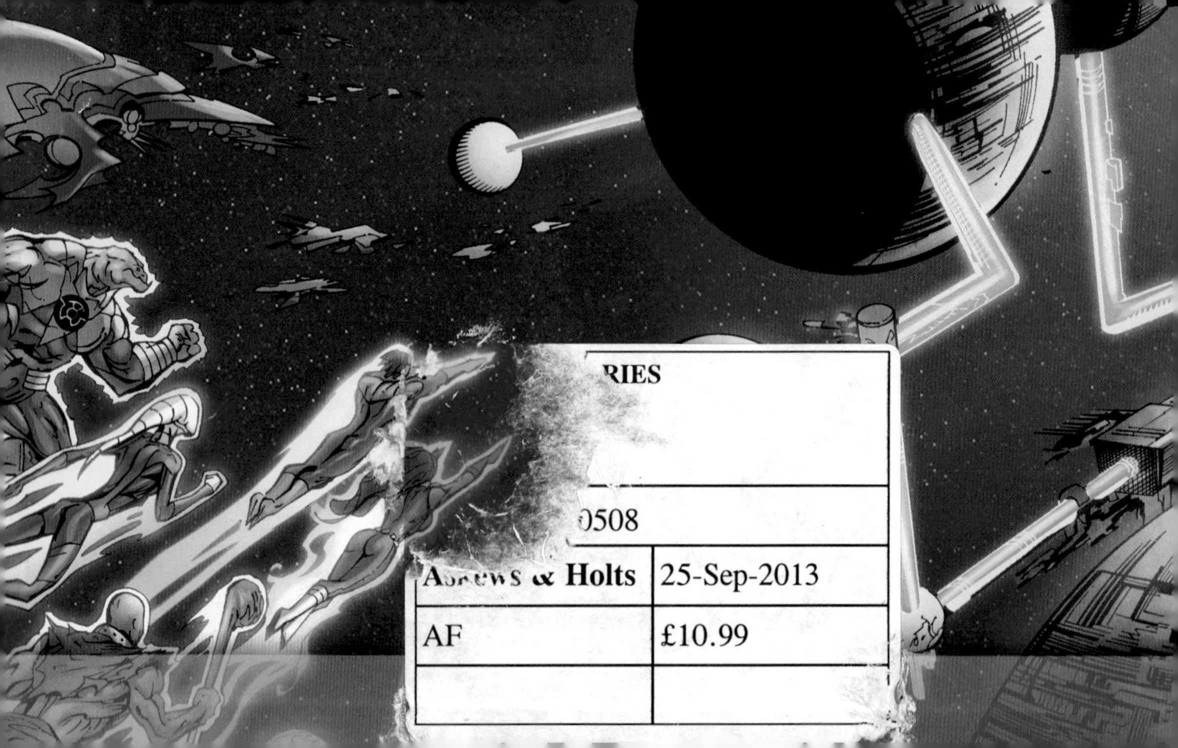

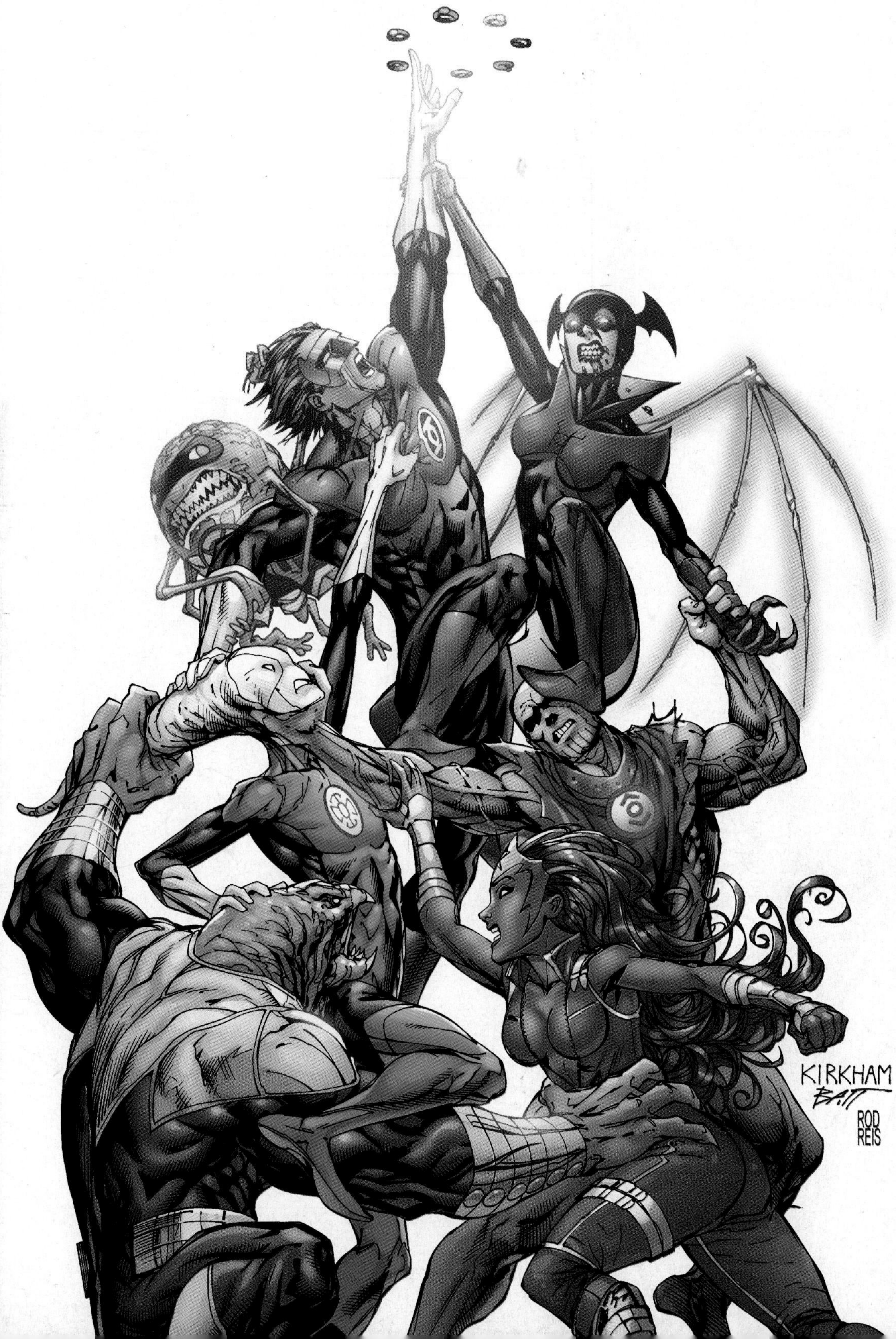
KIRKHAM
BATT
ROD
REIS

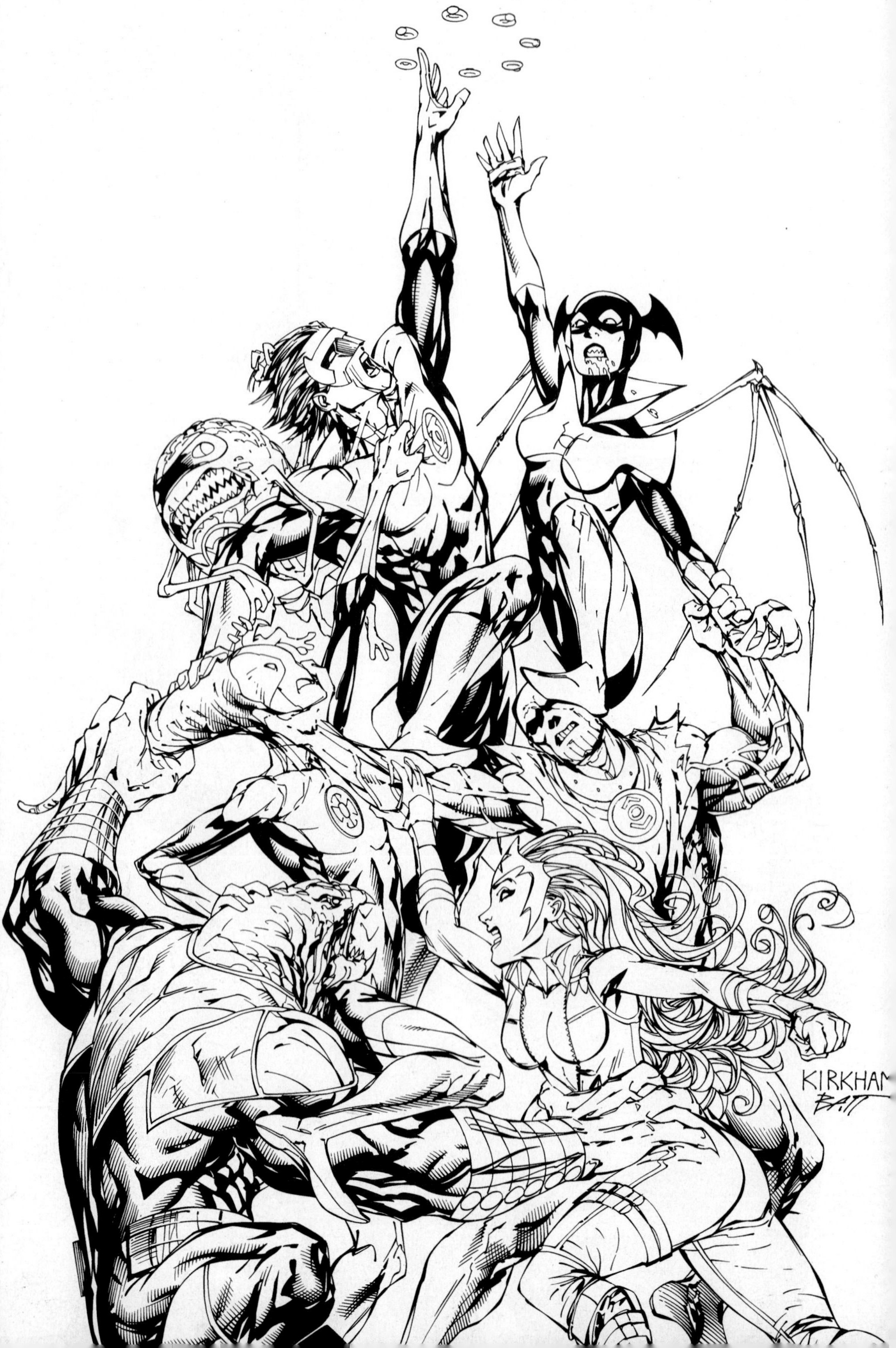
KIRKHAM

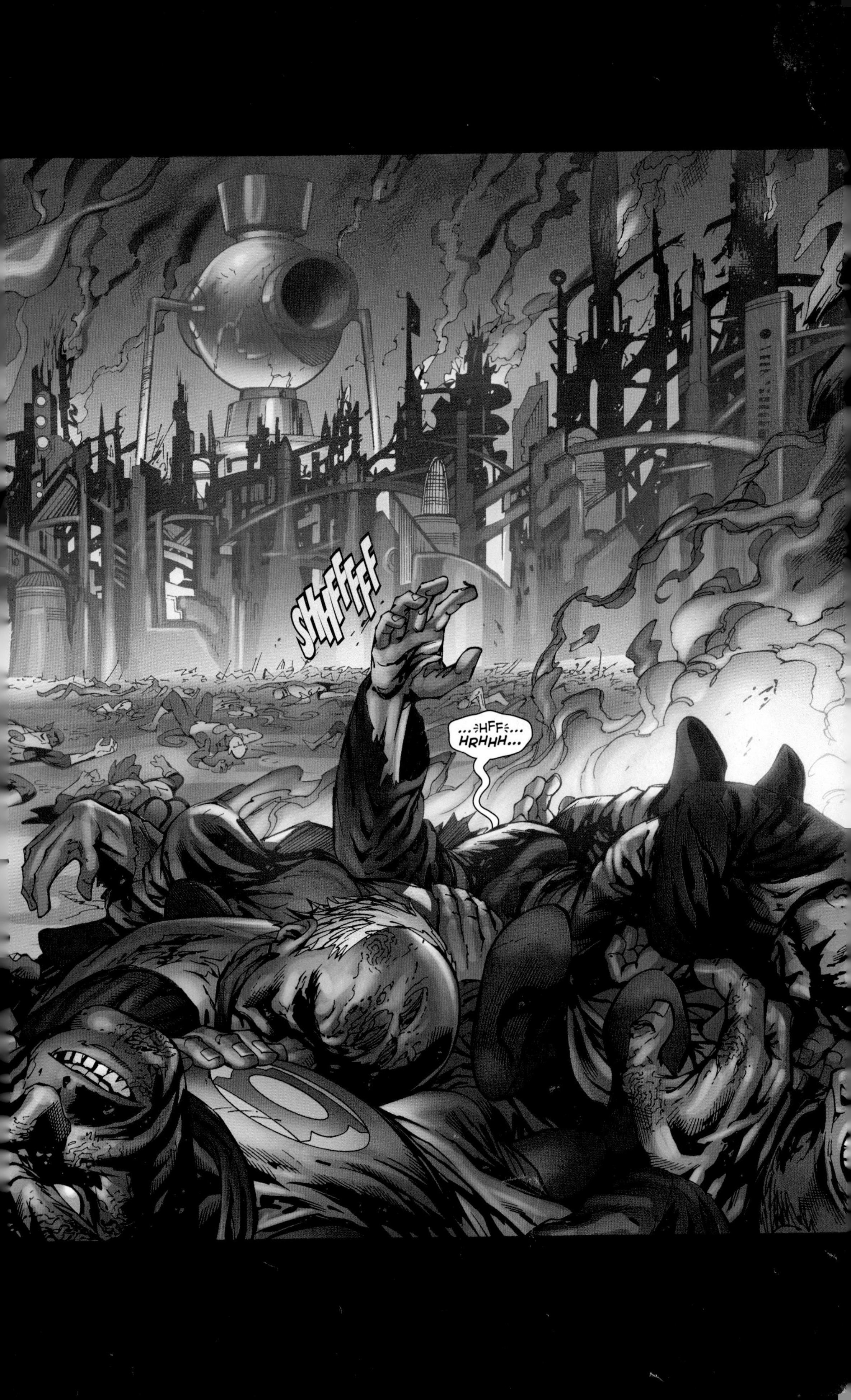
SHFFFFF
...HFF... HRHHH...

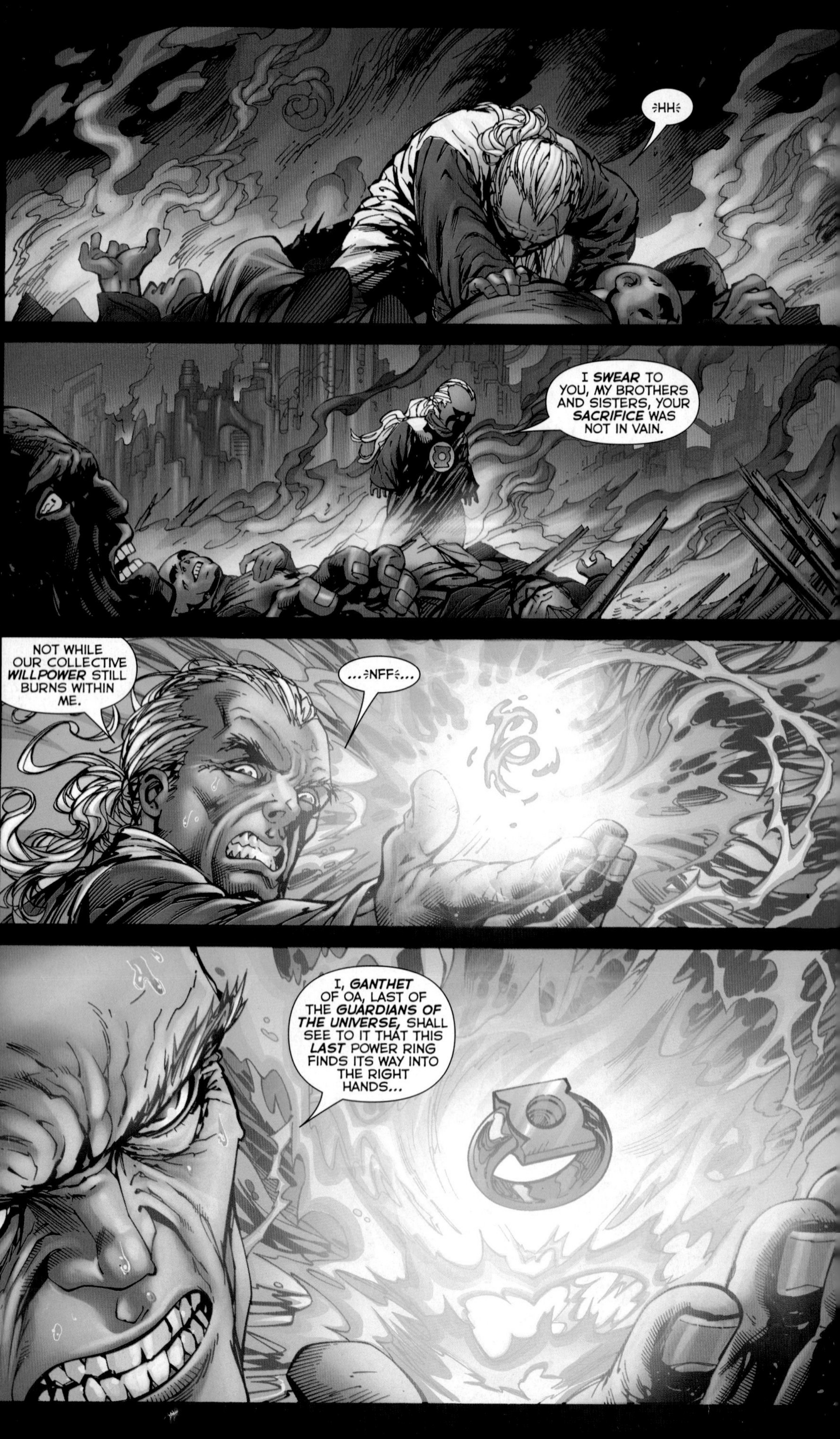
HH
I SWEAR TO YOU, MY BROTHERS AND SISTERS, YOUR SACRIFICE WAS NOT IN VAIN.
NOT WHILE OUR COLLECTIVE WILLPOWER STILL BURNS WITHIN ME.
...NFF...
I, GANTHET OF OA, LAST OF THE GUARDIANS OF THE UNIVERSE, SHALL SEE TO IT THAT THIS LAST POWER RING FINDS ITS WAY INTO THE RIGHT HANDS...

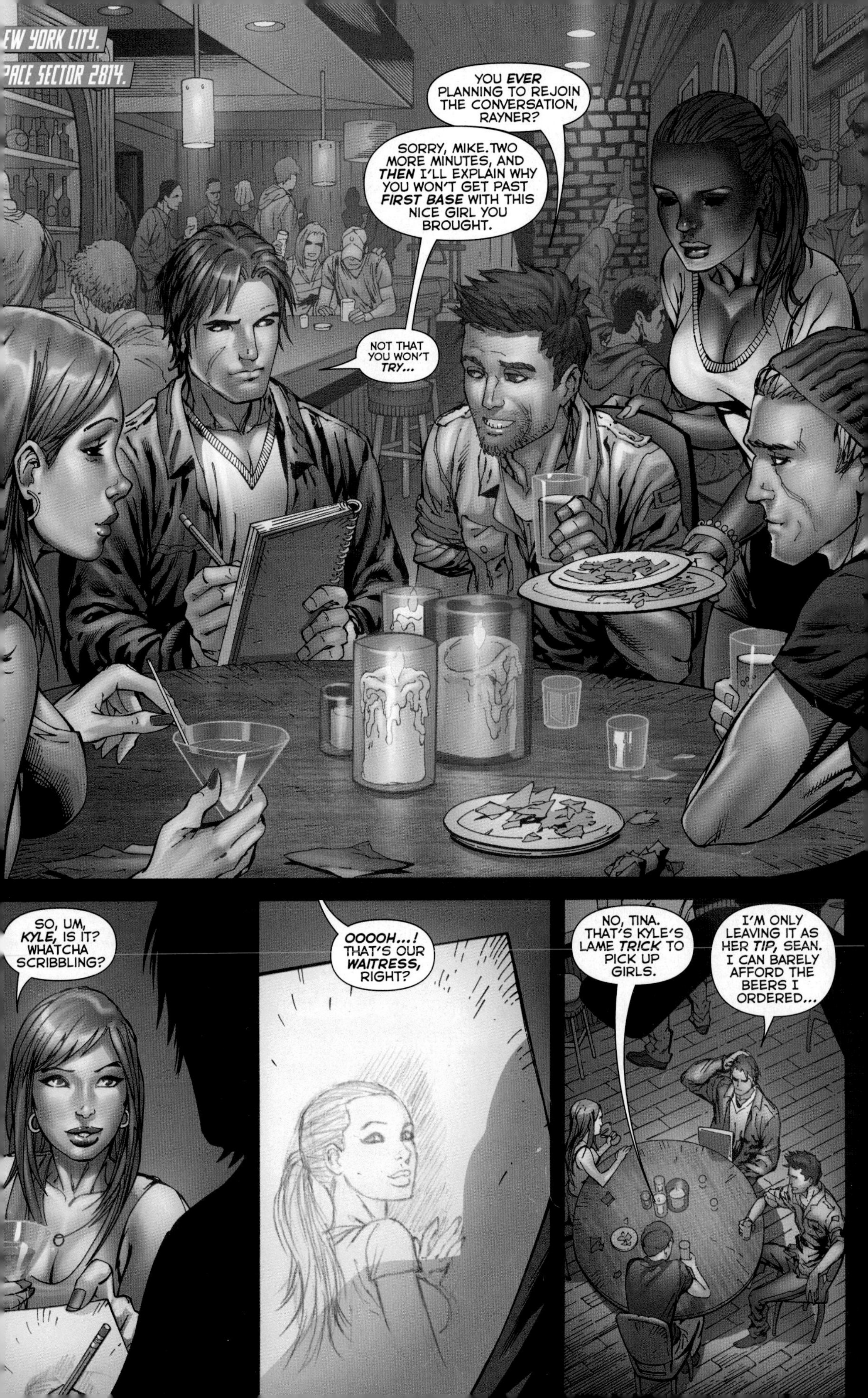

EW YORK CITY.
PACE SECTOR 2814.
YOU EVER PLANNING TO REJOIN THE CONVERSATION, RAYNER?
SORRY, MIKE. TWO MORE MINUTES, AND THEN I'LL EXPLAIN WHY YOU WON'T GET PAST FIRST BASE WITH THIS NICE GIRL YOU BROUGHT.
NOT THAT YOU WON'T TRY...
SO, UM, KYLE, IS IT? WHATCHA SCRIBBLING?
OOOOH...! THAT'S OUR WAITRESS, RIGHT?
NO, TINA. THAT'S KYLE'S LAME TRICK TO PICK UP GIRLS.
I'M ONLY LEAVING IT AS HER TIP, SEAN. I CAN BARELY AFFORD THE BEERS I ORDERED...

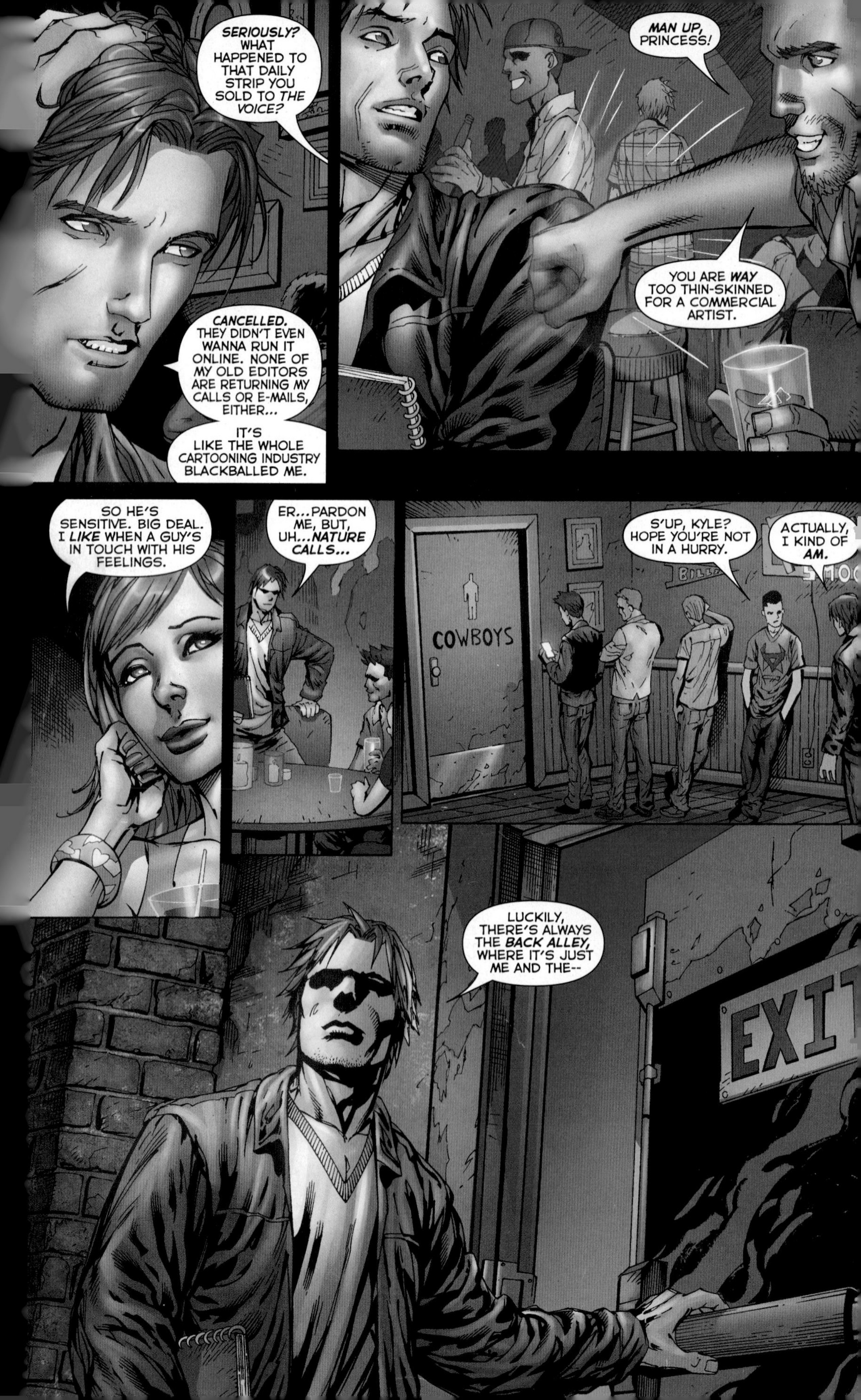
SERIOUSLY? WHAT HAPPENED TO THAT DAILY STRIP YOU SOLD TO THE VOICE?
CANCELLED. THEY DIDN'T EVEN WANNA RUN IT ONLINE. NONE OF MY OLD EDITORS ARE RETURNING MY CALLS OR E-MAILS, EITHER...
IT'S LIKE THE WHOLE CARTOONING INDUSTRY BLACKBALLED ME.
MAN UP, PRINCESS!
YOU ARE WAY TOO THIN-SKINNED FOR A COMMERCIAL ARTIST.
SO HE'S SENSITIVE. BIG DEAL. I LIKE WHEN A GUY'S IN TOUCH WITH HIS FEELINGS.
ER...PARDON ME, BUT, UH...NATURE CALLS...
COWBOYS
S'UP, KYLE? HOPE YOU'RE NOT IN A HURRY.
ACTUALLY, I KIND OF AM.
LUCKILY, THERE'S ALWAYS THE BACK ALLEY, WHERE IT'S JUST ME AND THE--
EXIT

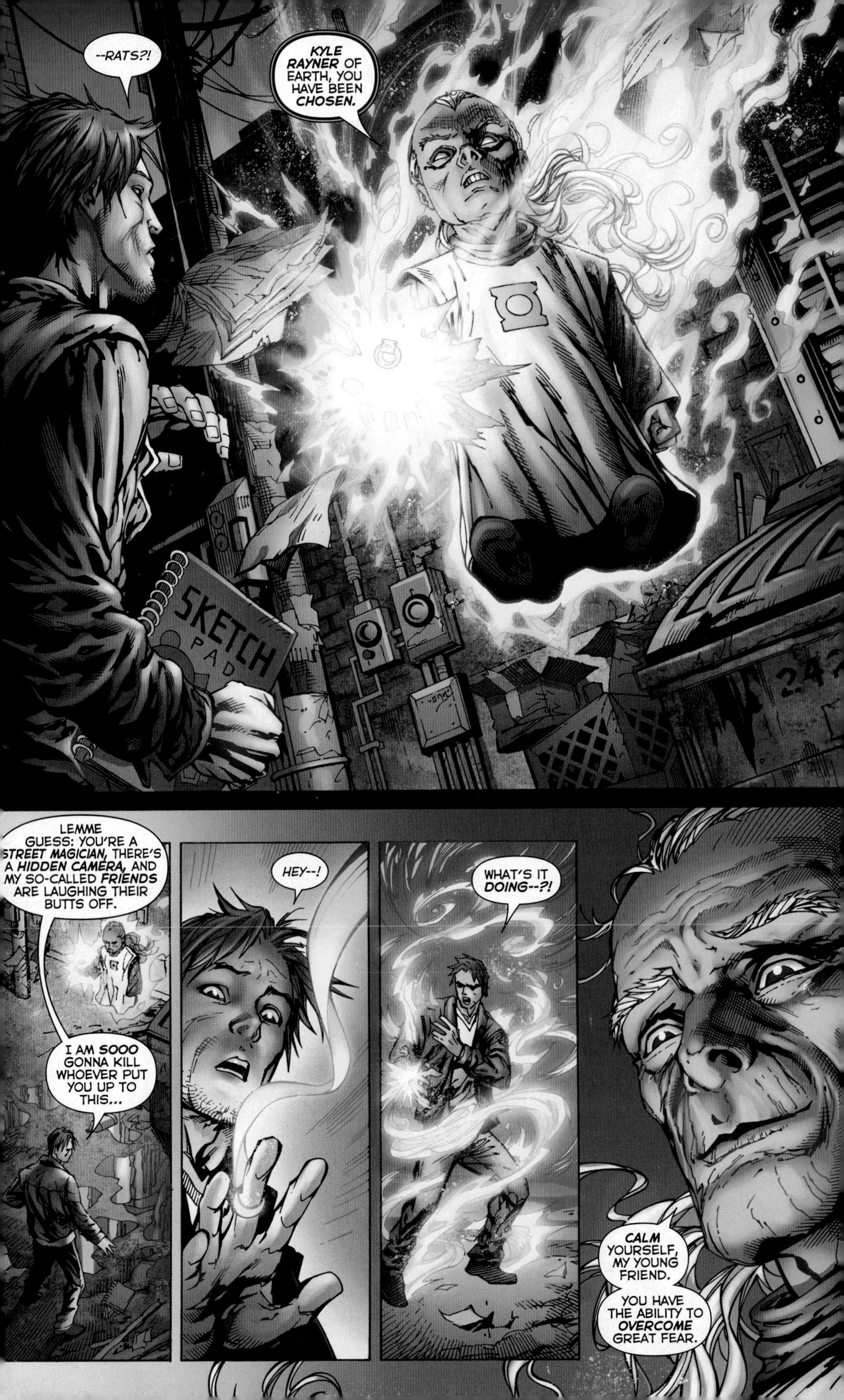
--RATS?!
KYLE RAYNER OF EARTH, YOU HAVE BEEN CHOSEN.
SKETCH PAD
LEMME GUESS: YOU'RE A STREET MAGICIAN, THERE'S A HIDDEN CAMERA, AND MY SO-CALLED FRIENDS ARE LAUGHING THEIR BUTTS OFF.
I AM SOOO GONNA KILL WHOEVER PUT YOU UP TO THIS...
HEY--!
WHAT'S IT DOING--?!
CALM YOURSELF, MY YOUNG FRIEND.
YOU HAVE THE ABILITY TO OVERCOME GREAT FEAR.

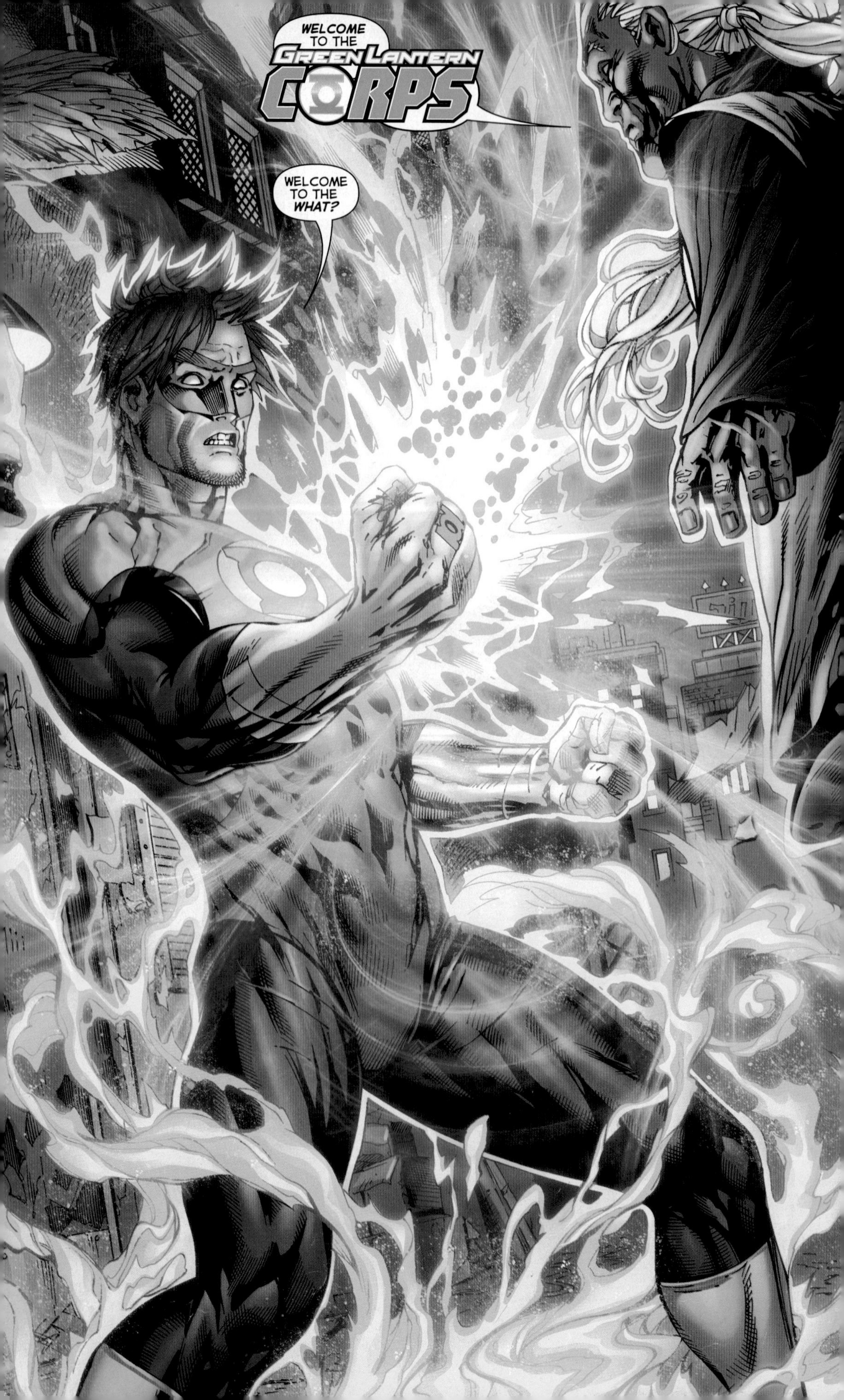
WELCOME TO THE
GREEN LANTERN CORPS
WELCOME TO THE WHAT?

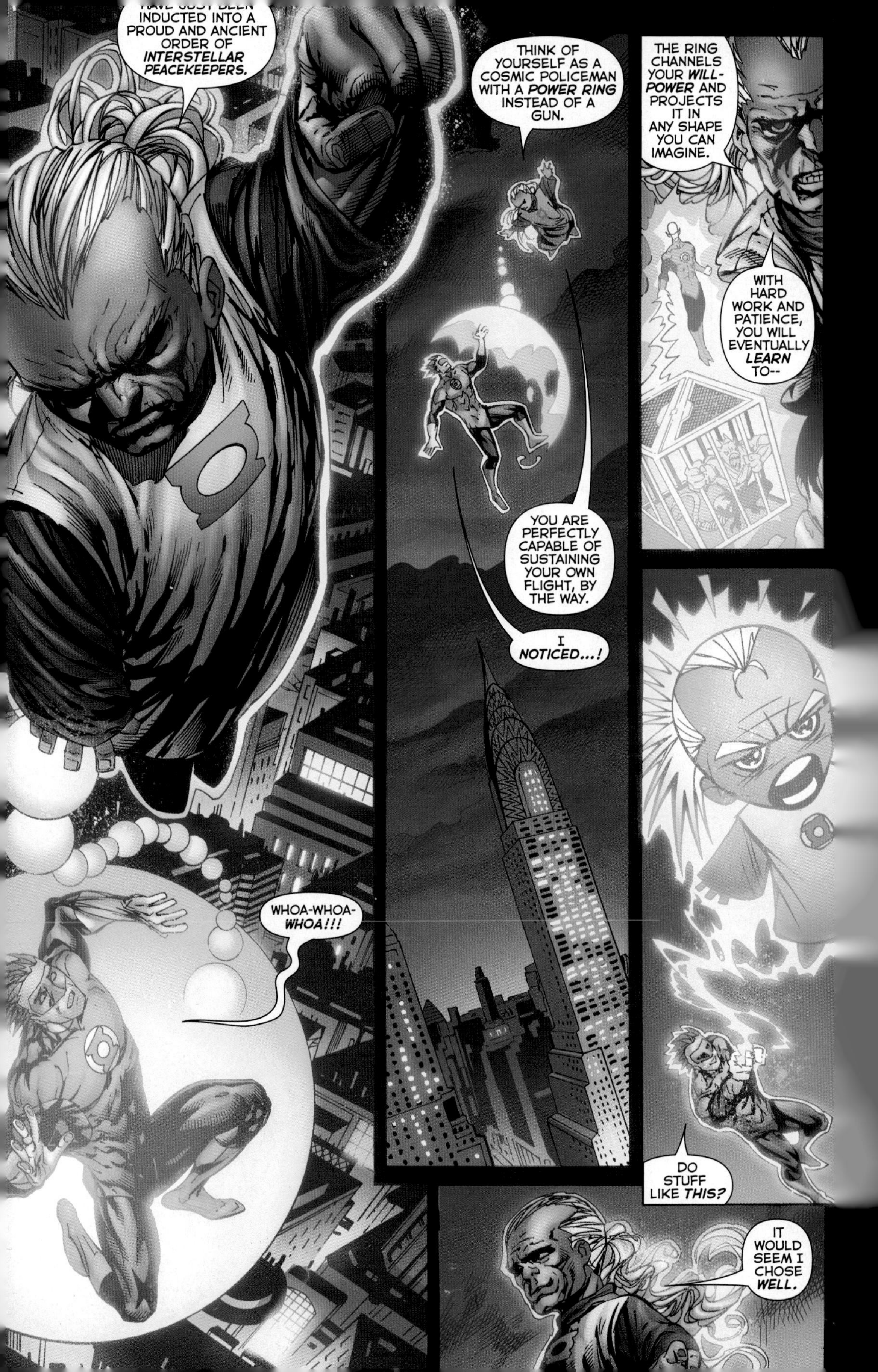
INDUCTED INTO A PROUD AND ANCIENT ORDER OF *INTERSTELLAR PEACEKEEPERS.*
WHOA-WHOA-*WHOA!!!*
THINK OF YOURSELF AS A COSMIC POLICEMAN WITH A *POWER RING* INSTEAD OF A GUN.
YOU ARE PERFECTLY CAPABLE OF SUSTAINING YOUR OWN FLIGHT, BY THE WAY.
I *NOTICED...!*
THE RING CHANNELS YOUR *WILL-POWER* AND PROJECTS IT IN ANY SHAPE YOU CAN IMAGINE.
WITH HARD WORK AND PATIENCE, YOU WILL EVENTUALLY *LEARN* TO--
DO STUFF LIKE *THIS?*
IT WOULD SEEM I CHOSE *WELL.*

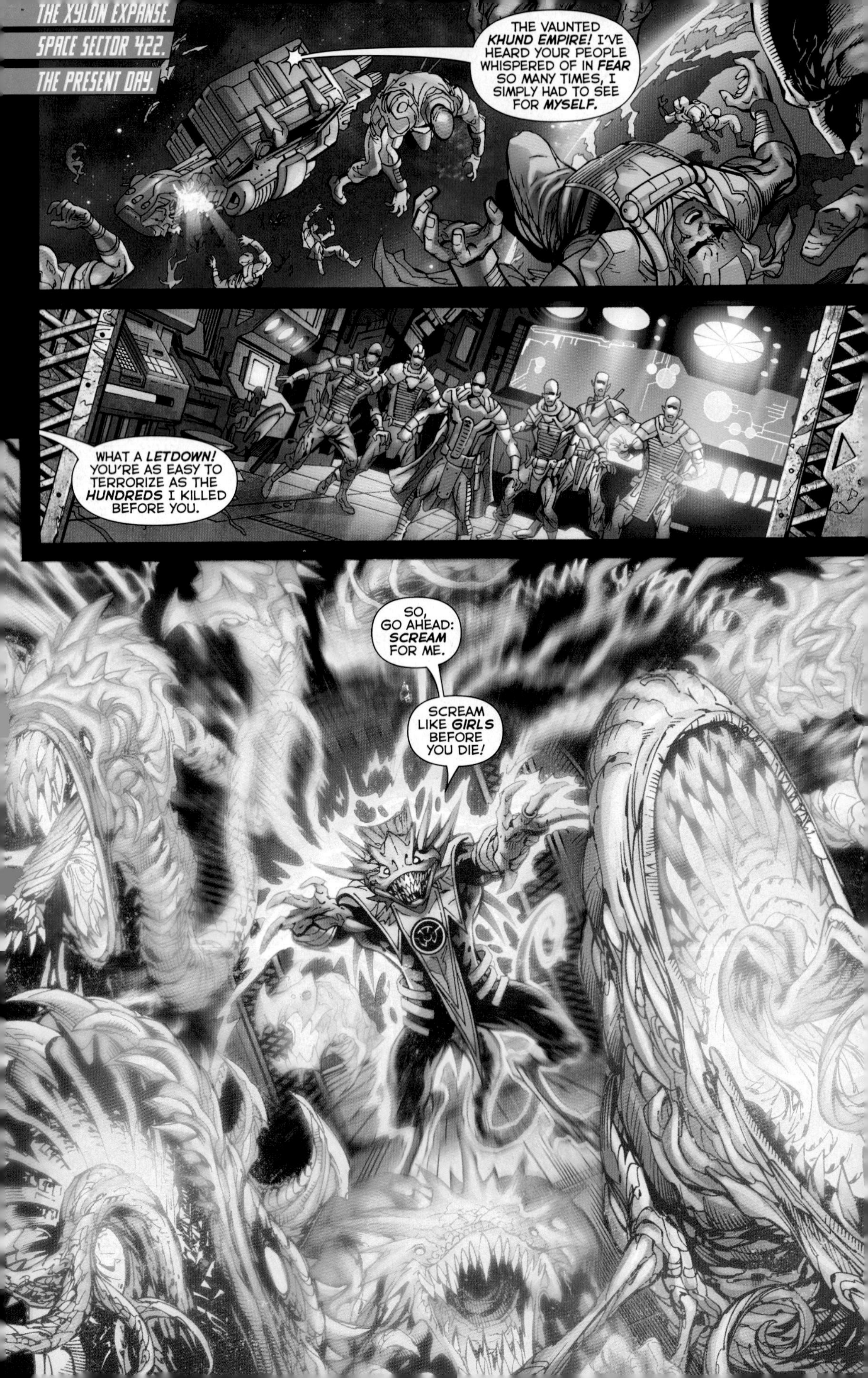
THE XYLON EXPANSE.
SPACE SECTOR 422.
THE PRESENT DAY.
THE VAUNTED KHUND EMPIRE! I'VE HEARD YOUR PEOPLE WHISPERED OF IN FEAR SO MANY TIMES, I SIMPLY HAD TO SEE FOR MYSELF.
WHAT A LETDOWN! YOU'RE AS EASY TO TERRORIZE AS THE HUNDREDS I KILLED BEFORE YOU.
SO, GO AHEAD: SCREAM FOR ME.
SCREAM LIKE GIRLS BEFORE YOU DIE!

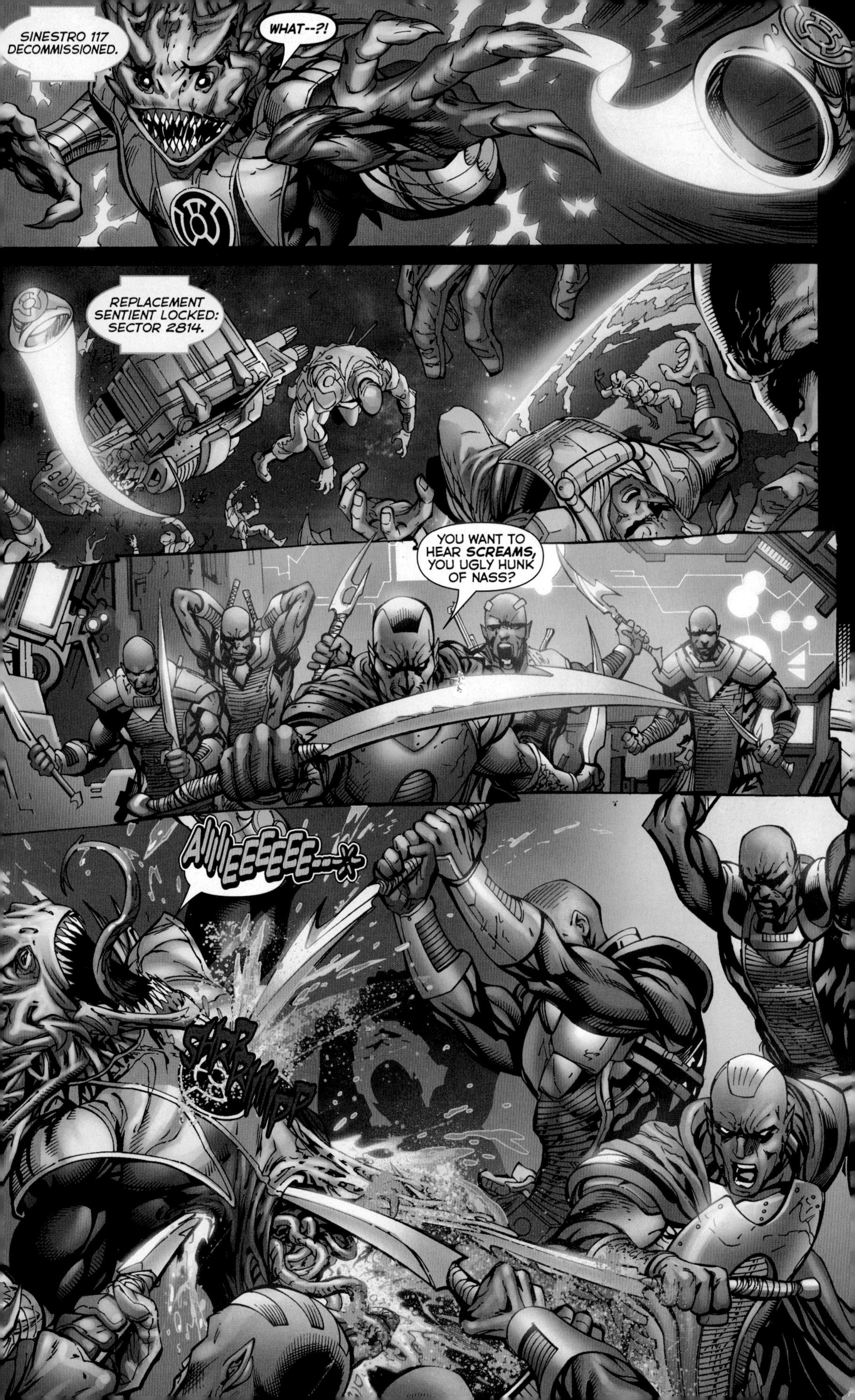
SINESTRO 117 DECOMMISSIONED.
WHAT--?!
REPLACEMENT SENTIENT LOCKED: SECTOR 2814.
YOU WANT TO HEAR SCREAMS, YOU UGLY HUNK OF NASS?
AIIIEEEEEE---

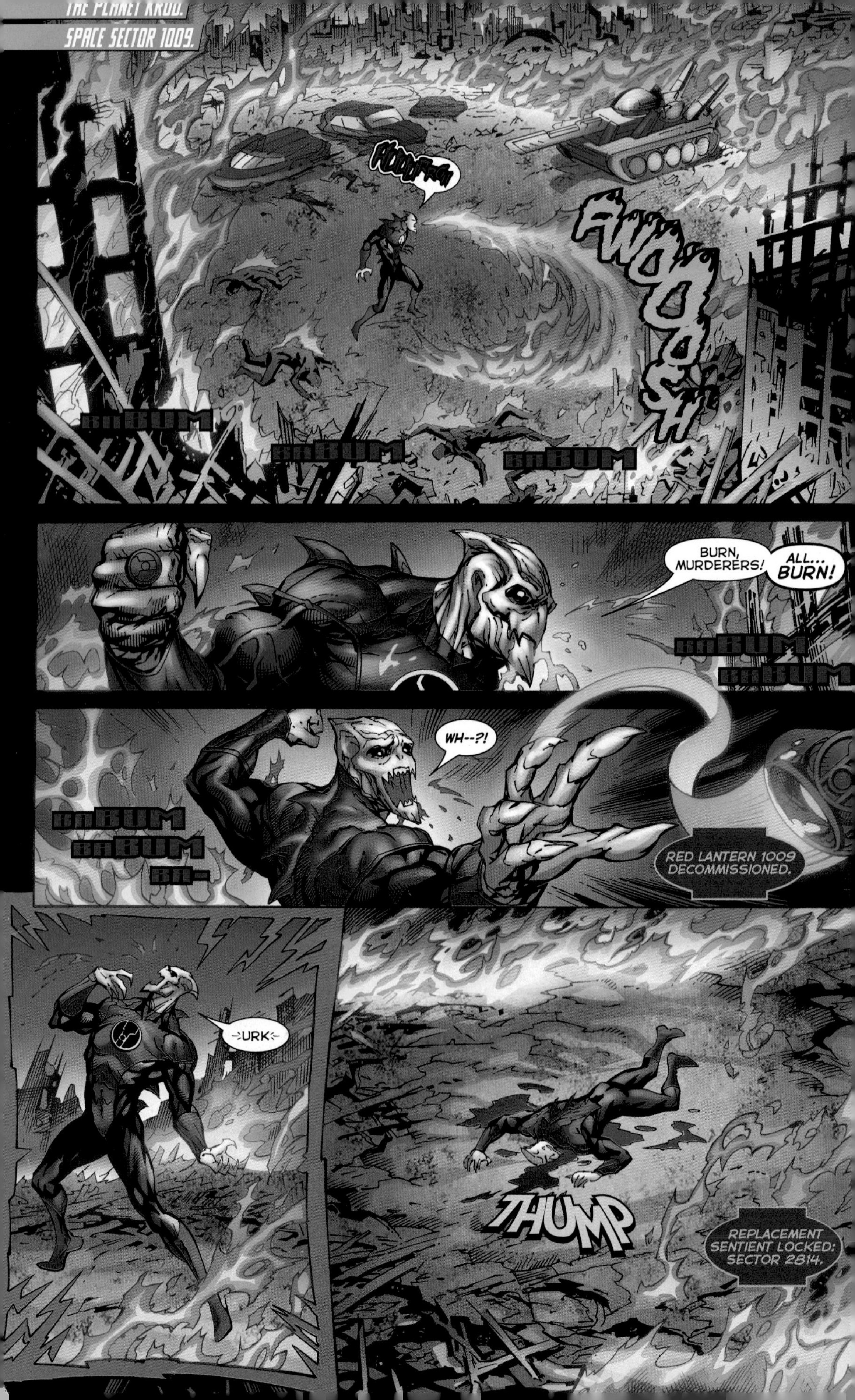
THE PLANET KROD.
SPACE SECTOR 1009.
FWOOOSH
BRBUM
BRBUM
BRBUM
BURN, MURDERERS!
ALL... BURN!
BRBUM
BRBUM
WH--?!
BRBUM
BRBUM
BR-
RED LANTERN 1009 DECOMMISSIONED.
URK
THUMP
REPLACEMENT SENTIENT LOCKED: SECTOR 2814.

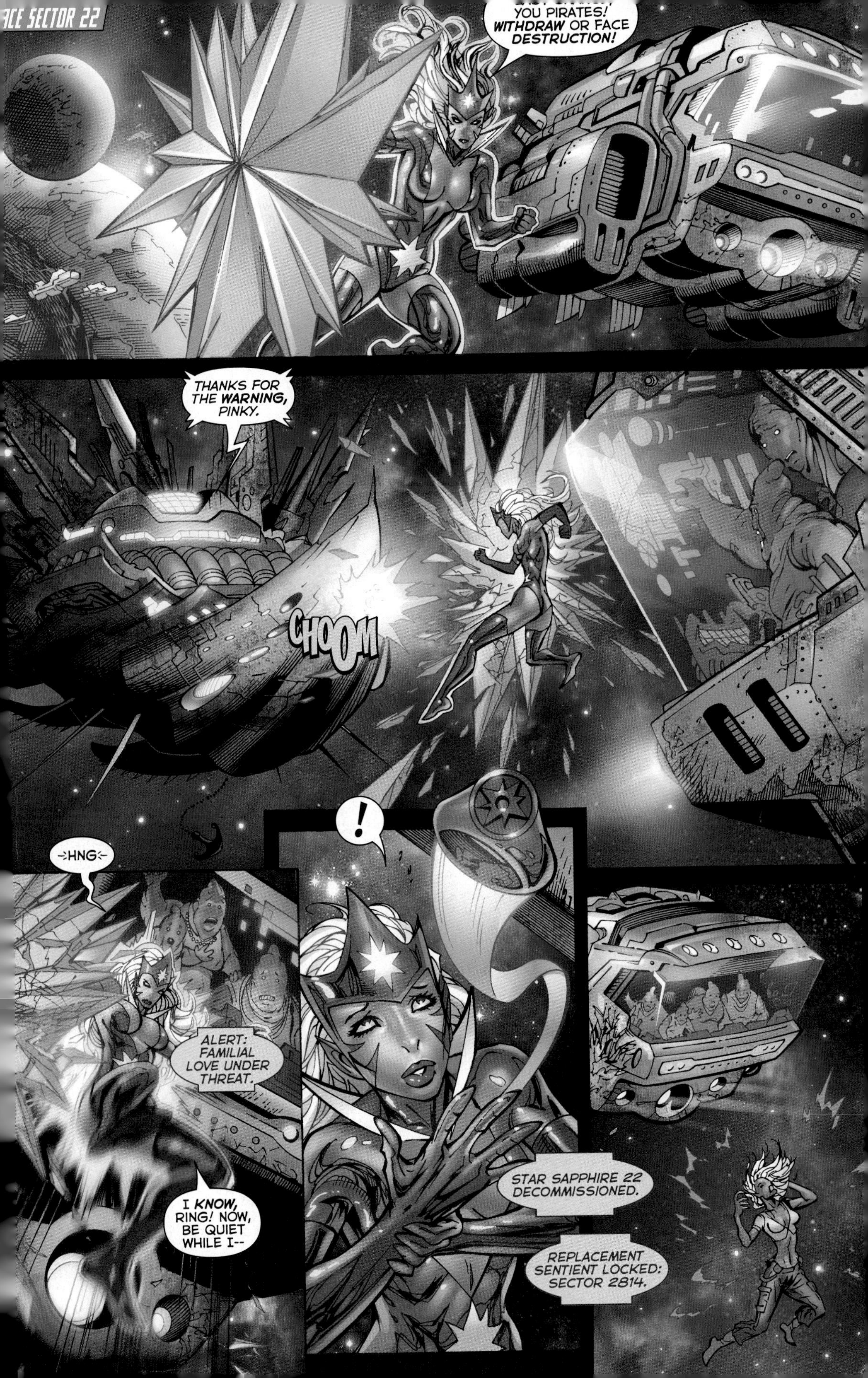
ACE SECTOR 22
YOU PIRATES! WITHDRAW OR FACE DESTRUCTION!
THANKS FOR THE WARNING, PINKY.
CHOOM
-HNG-
!
ALERT: FAMILIAL LOVE UNDER THREAT.
I KNOW, RING! NOW, BE QUIET WHILE I--
STAR SAPPHIRE 22 DECOMMISSIONED.
REPLACEMENT SENTIENT LOCKED: SECTOR 2814.

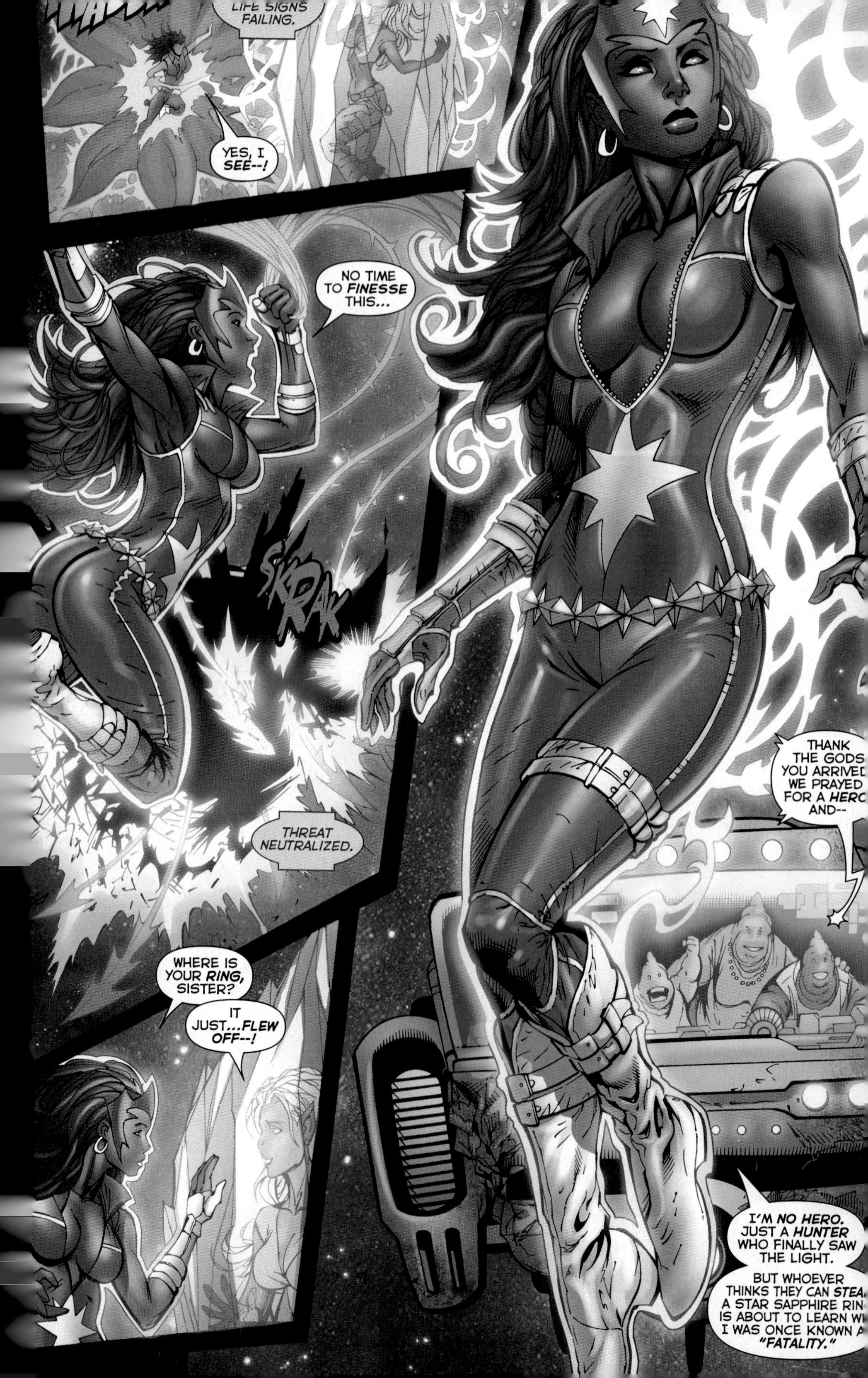

LIFE SIGNS FAILING.
YES, I SEE--!
NO TIME TO *FINESSE* THIS...
SKRAK
THREAT NEUTRALIZED.
THANK THE GODS YOU ARRIVED WE PRAYED FOR A HERC AND--
WHERE IS YOUR *RING,* SISTER?
IT JUST...*FLEW OFF*--!
I'M *NO HERO.* JUST A *HUNTER* WHO FINALLY SAW THE LIGHT.
BUT WHOEVER THINKS THEY CAN *STEA* A STAR SAPPHIRE RIN IS ABOUT TO LEARN WH I WAS ONCE KNOWN A *"FATALITY."*

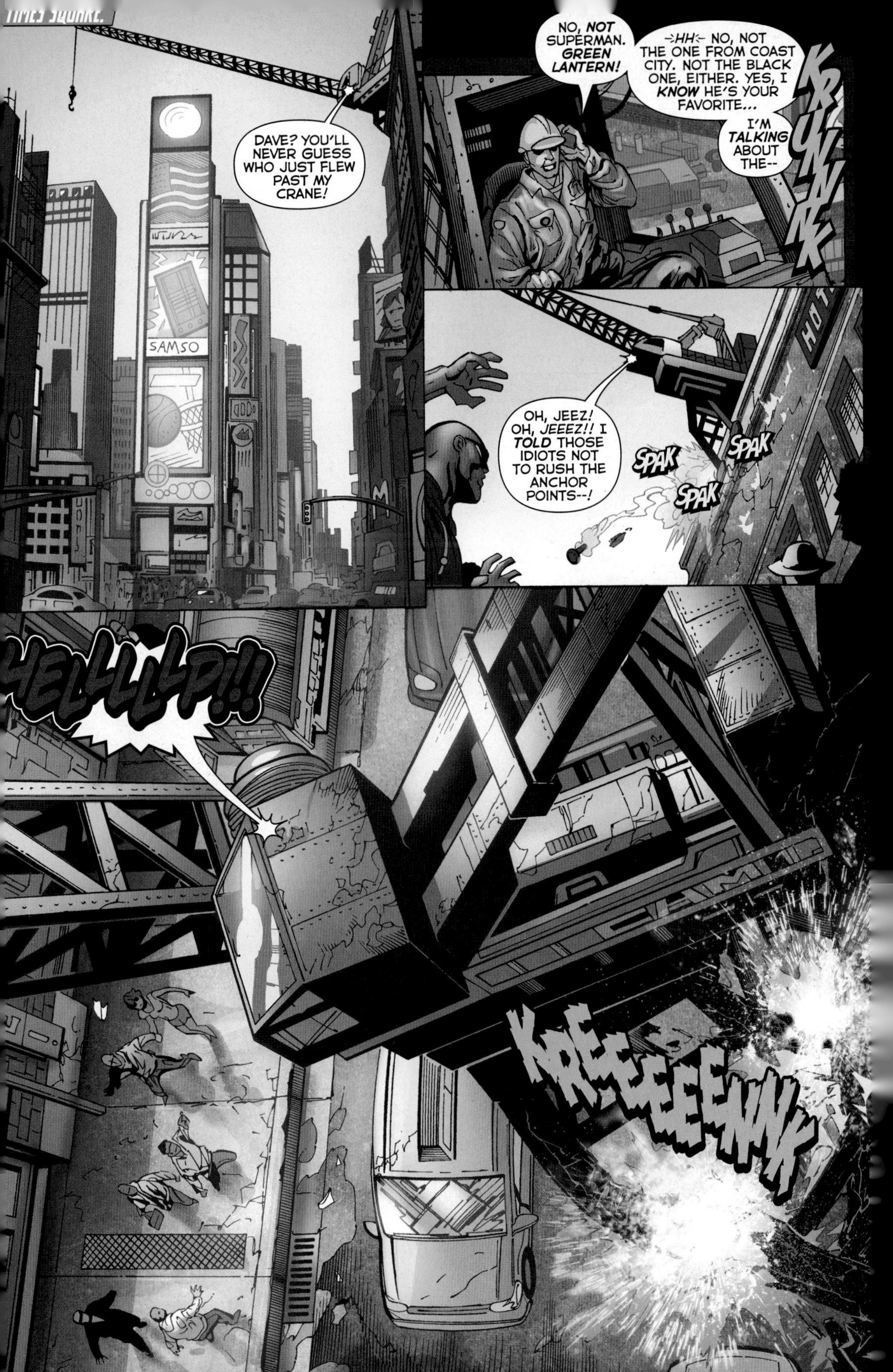
TIMES SQUARE.
DAVE? YOU'LL NEVER GUESS WHO JUST FLEW PAST MY CRANE!
SAMSO
NO, NOT SUPERMAN. GREEN LANTERN!
-HH- NO, NOT THE ONE FROM COAST CITY. NOT THE BLACK ONE, EITHER. YES, I KNOW HE'S YOUR FAVORITE...
I'M TALKING ABOUT THE--
KRUNNNK
OH, JEEZ! OH, JEEEZ!! I TOLD THOSE IDIOTS NOT TO RUSH THE ANCHOR POINTS--!
SPAK
SPAK
SPAK
HELLLLP!!
KREEEEEENNK

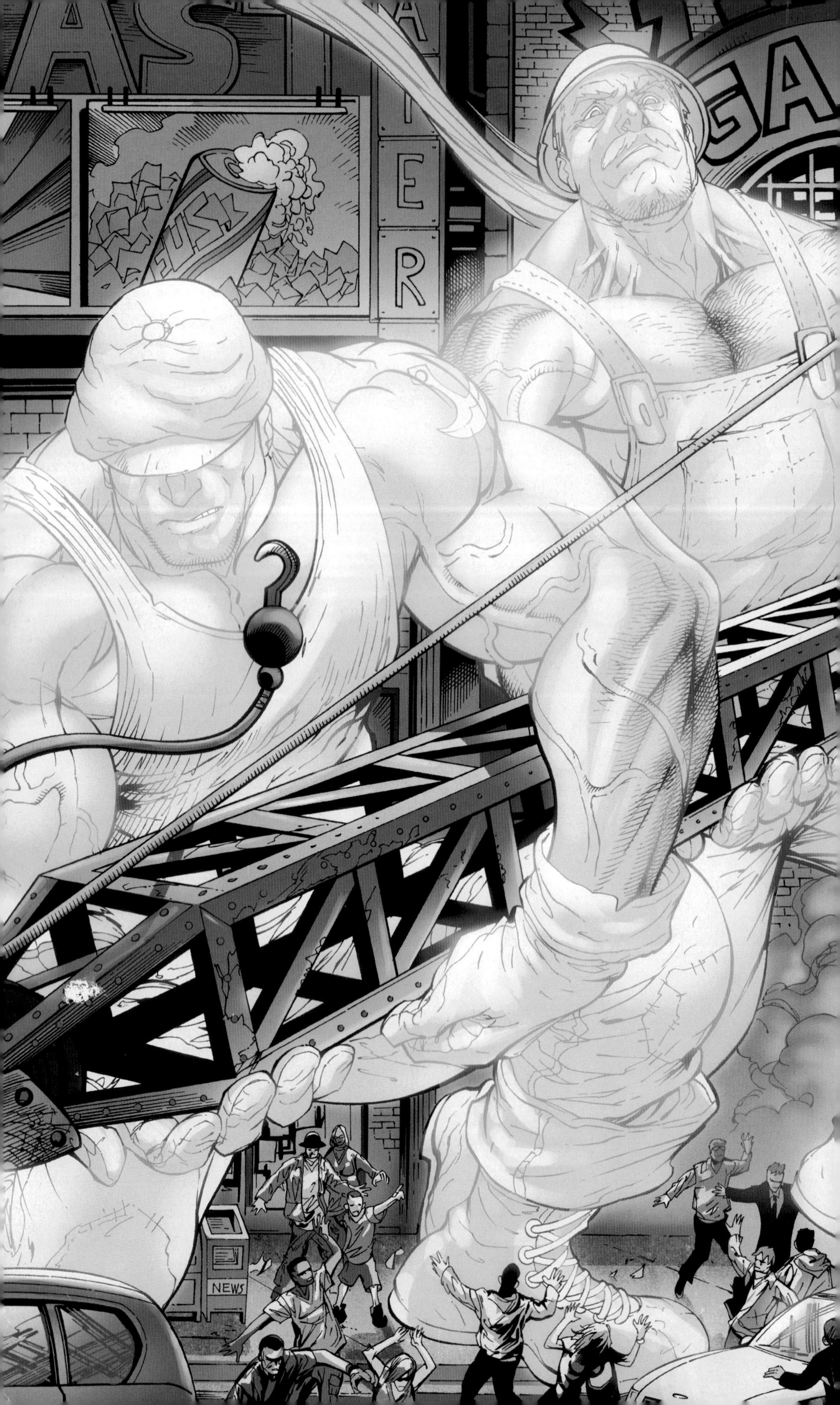
NEWS

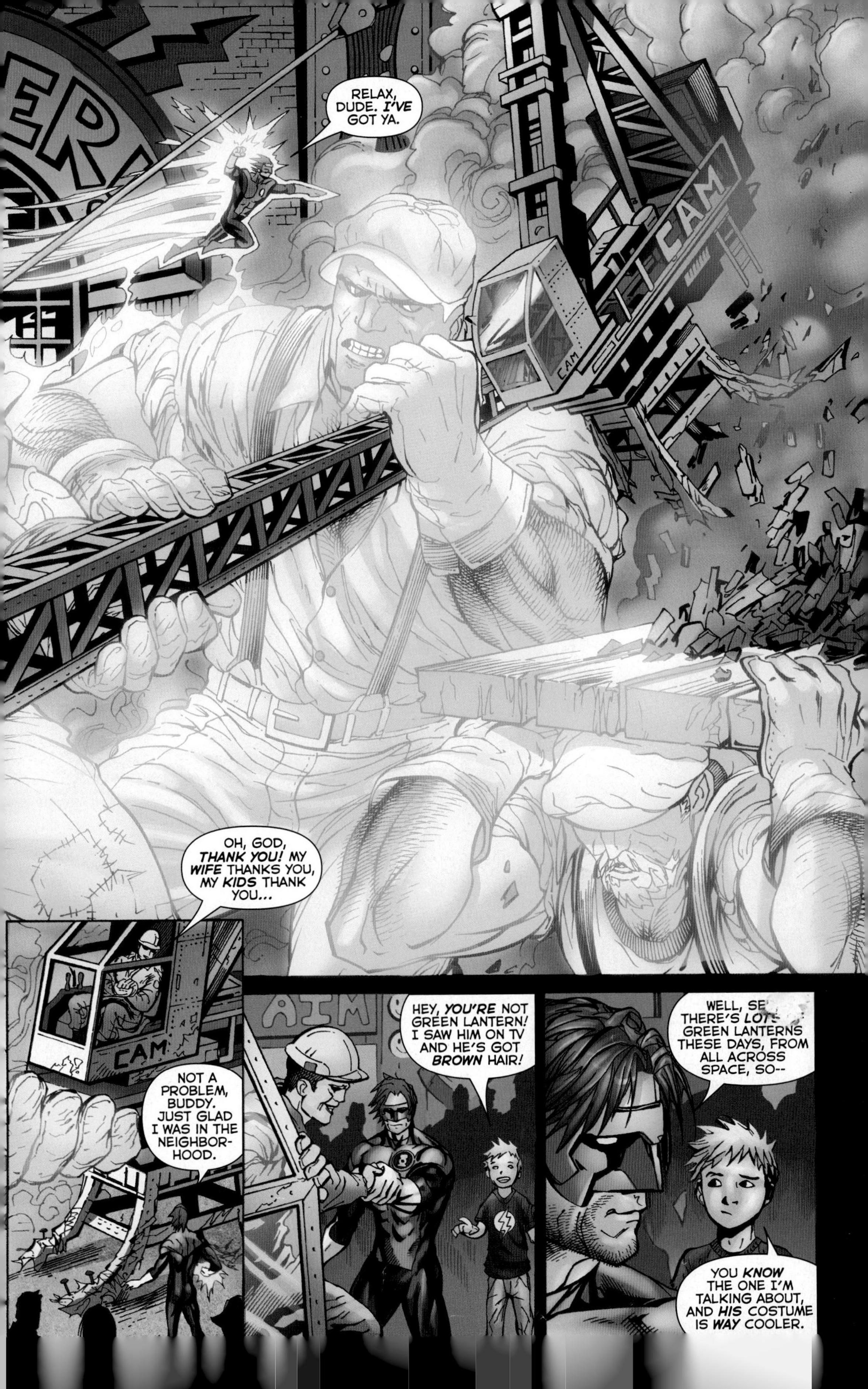
RELAX, DUDE. I'VE GOT YA.
OH, GOD, THANK YOU! MY WIFE THANKS YOU, MY KIDS THANK YOU...
NOT A PROBLEM, BUDDY. JUST GLAD I WAS IN THE NEIGHBOR-HOOD.
CAM
HEY, YOU'RE NOT GREEN LANTERN! I SAW HIM ON TV AND HE'S GOT BROWN HAIR!
WELL, SE THERE'S LOTS GREEN LANTERNS THESE DAYS, FROM ALL ACROSS SPACE, SO--
YOU KNOW THE ONE I'M TALKING ABOUT, AND HIS COSTUME IS WAY COOLER.

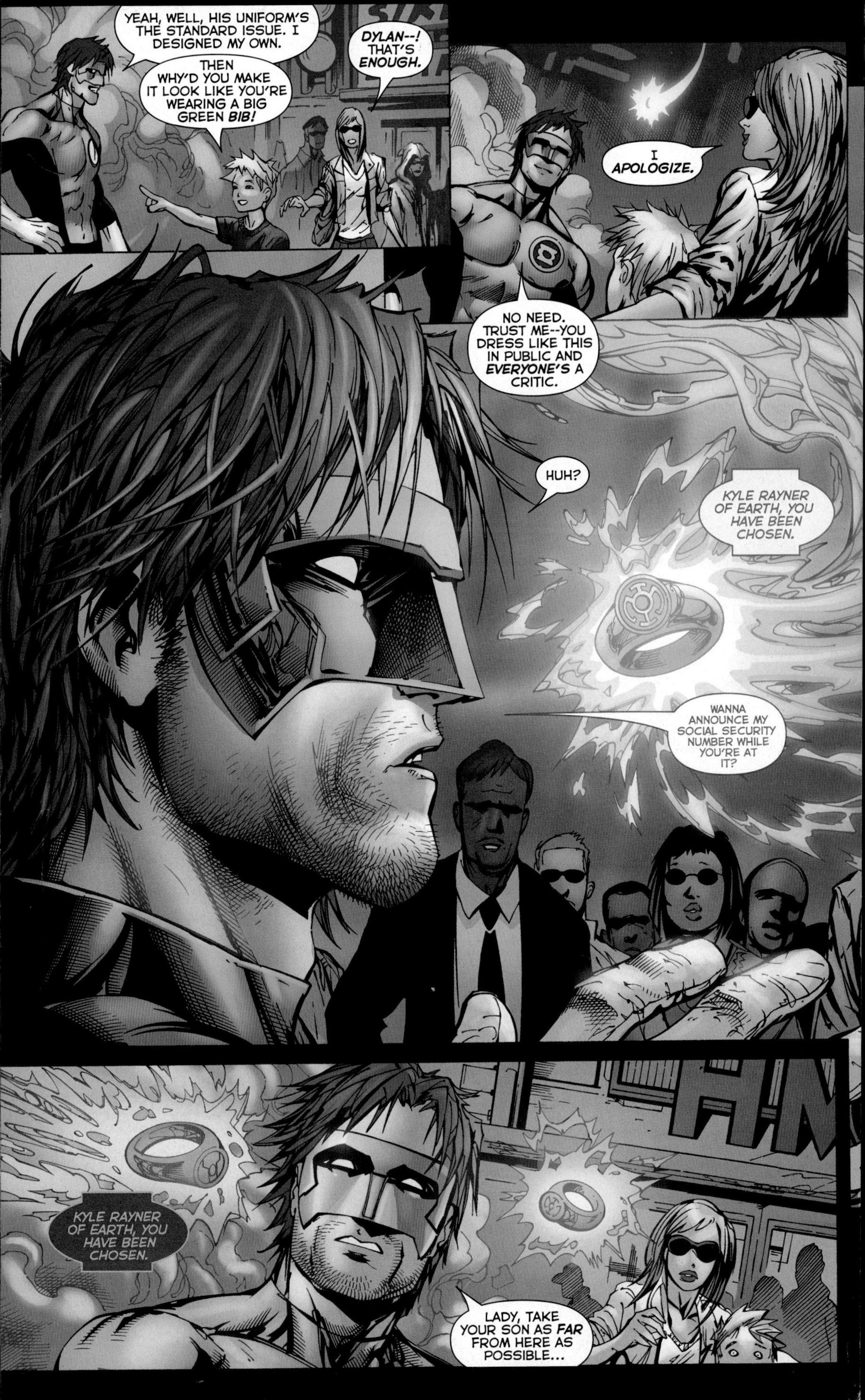

YEAH, WELL, HIS UNIFORM'S THE STANDARD ISSUE. I DESIGNED MY OWN.
THEN WHY'D YOU MAKE IT LOOK LIKE YOU'RE WEARING A BIG GREEN BIB!
DYLAN--! THAT'S ENOUGH.
I APOLOGIZE.
NO NEED. TRUST ME--YOU DRESS LIKE THIS IN PUBLIC AND EVERYONE'S A CRITIC.
HUH?
KYLE RAYNER OF EARTH, YOU HAVE BEEN CHOSEN.
WANNA ANNOUNCE MY SOCIAL SECURITY NUMBER WHILE YOU'RE AT IT?
KYLE RAYNER OF EARTH, YOU HAVE BEEN CHOSEN.
LADY, TAKE YOUR SON AS FAR FROM HERE AS POSSIBLE...

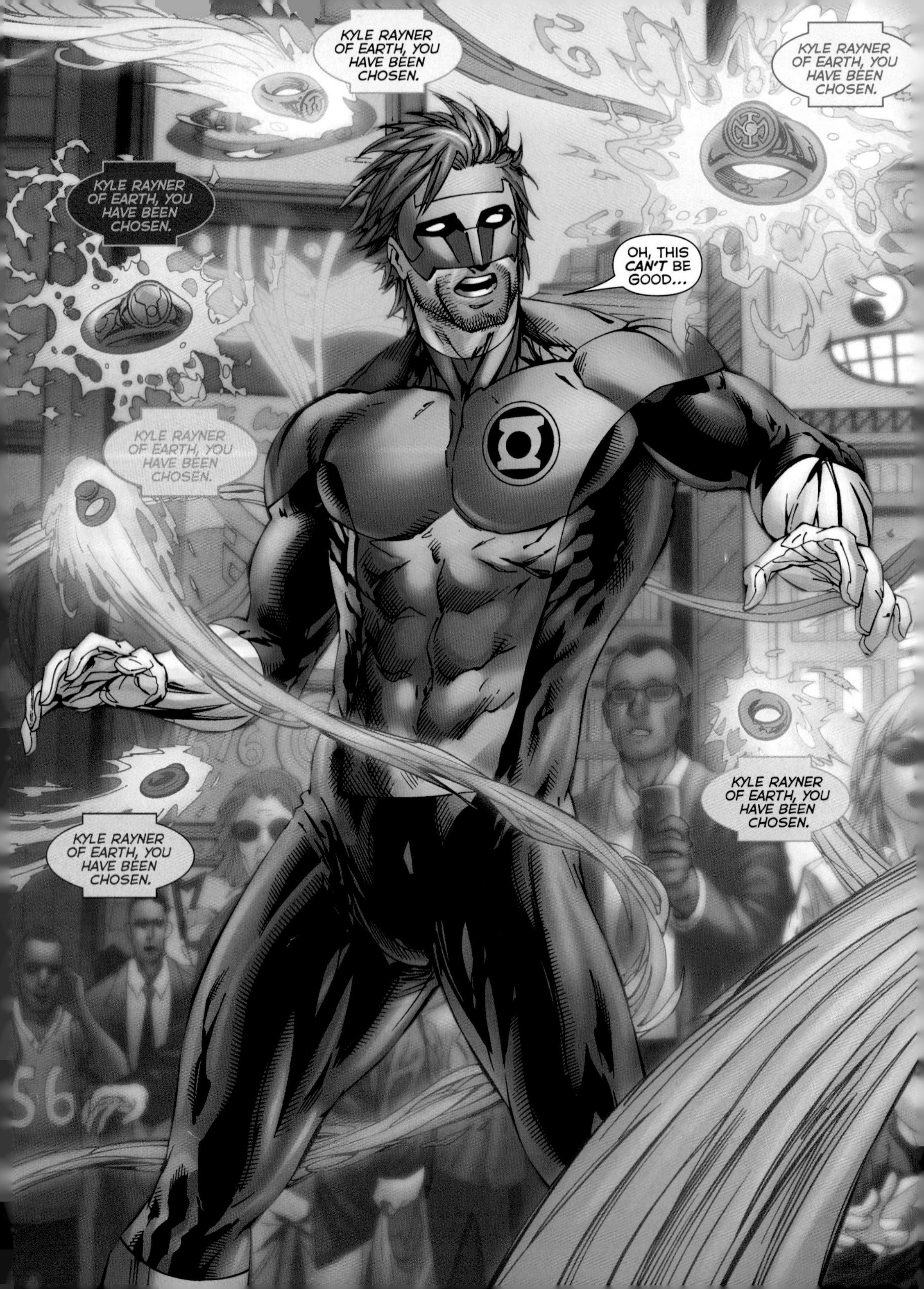
KYLE RAYNER OF EARTH, YOU HAVE BEEN CHOSEN.
KYLE RAYNER OF EARTH, YOU HAVE BEEN CHOSEN.
KYLE RAYNER OF EARTH, YOU HAVE BEEN CHOSEN.
OH, THIS CAN'T BE GOOD...
KYLE RAYNER OF EARTH, YOU HAVE BEEN CHOSEN.
KYLE RAYNER OF EARTH, YOU HAVE BEEN CHOSEN.
KYLE RAYNER OF EARTH, YOU HAVE BEEN CHOSEN.

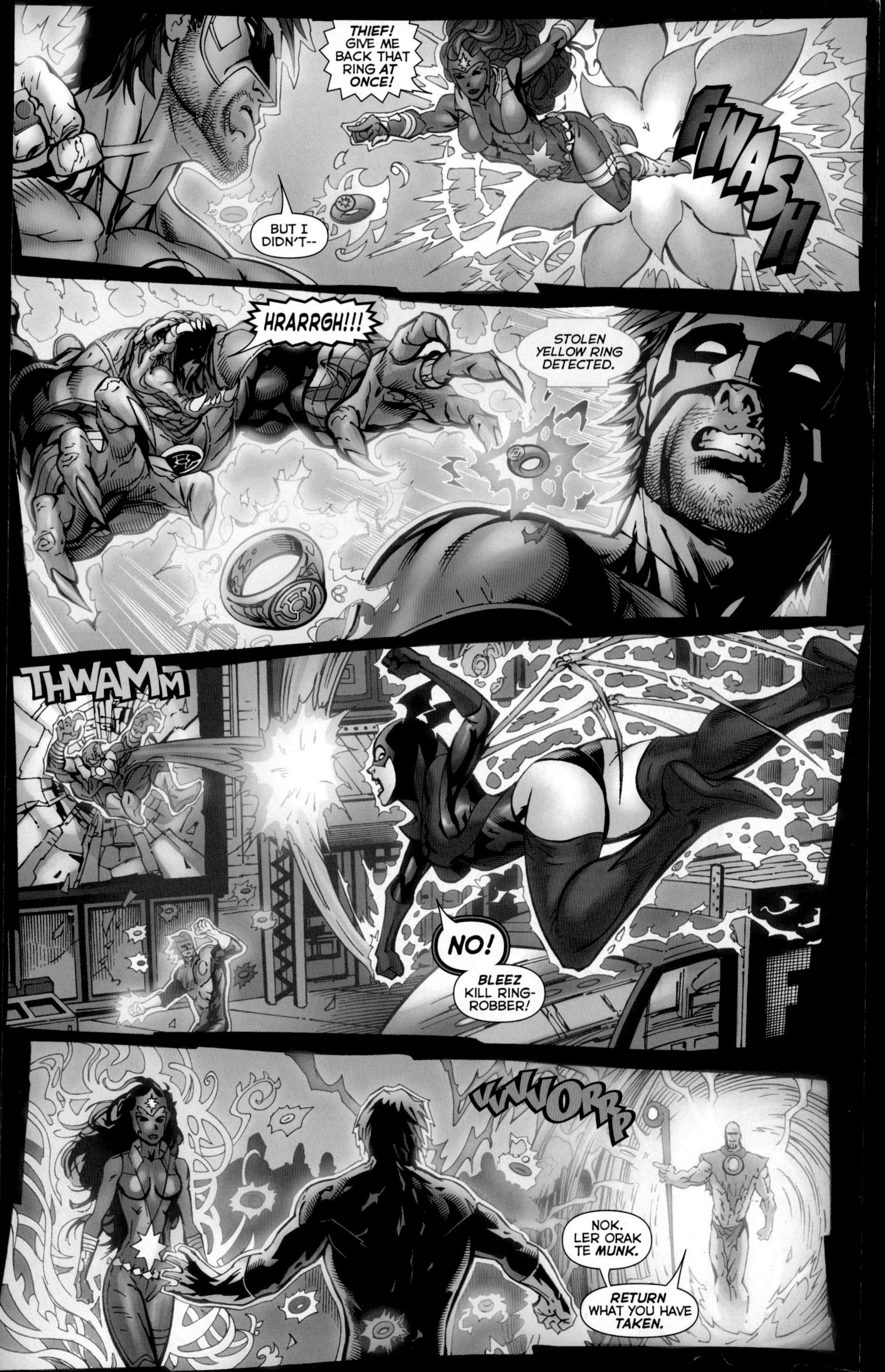
THIEF! GIVE ME BACK THAT RING AT ONCE!
BUT I DIDN'T--
FWASH
HRARRGH!!!
STOLEN YELLOW RING DETECTED.
THWAMM
NO!
BLEEZ KILL RING-ROBBER!
VVVWORRP
NOK. LER ORAK TE MUNK.
RETURN WHAT YOU HAVE TAKEN.

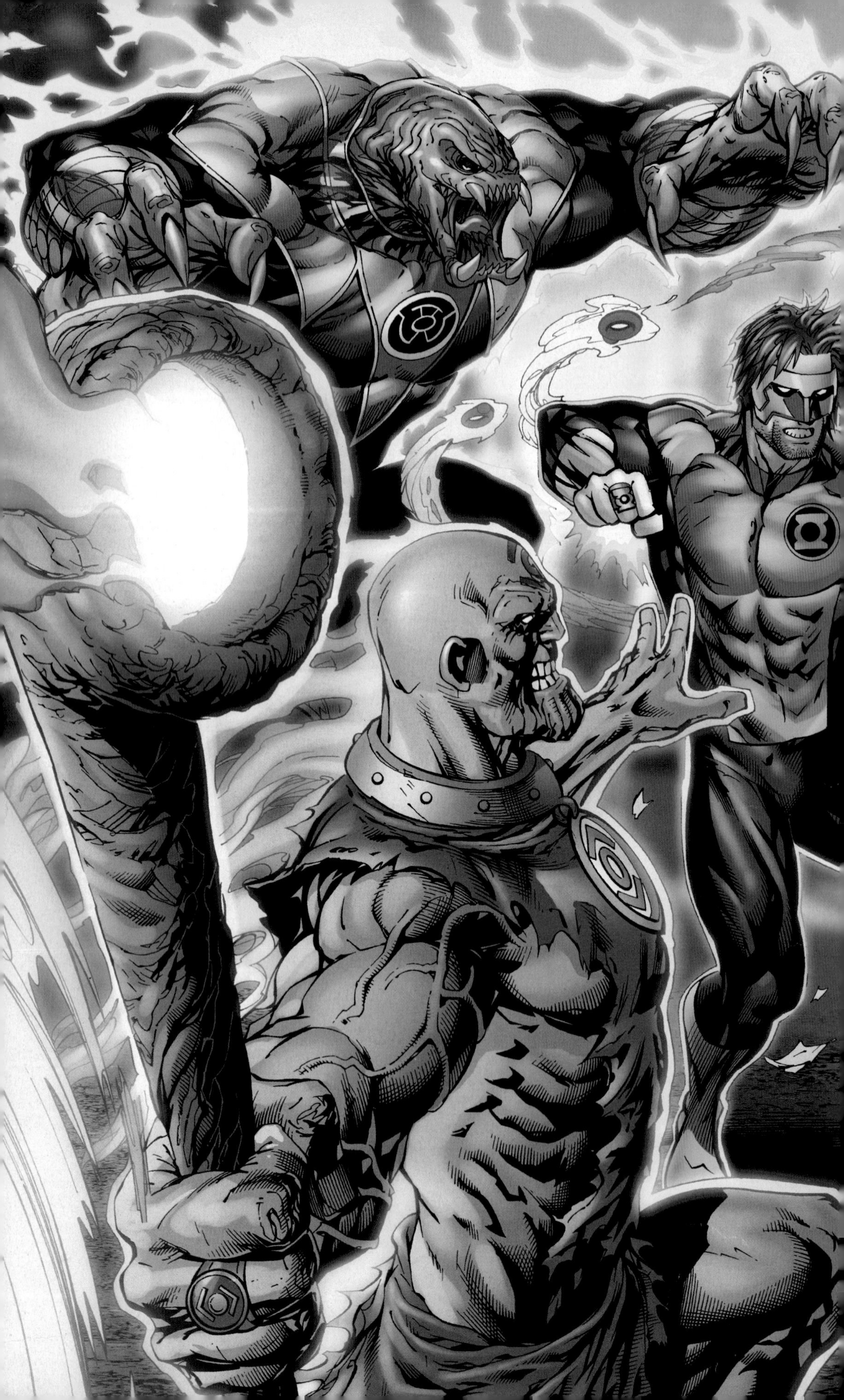

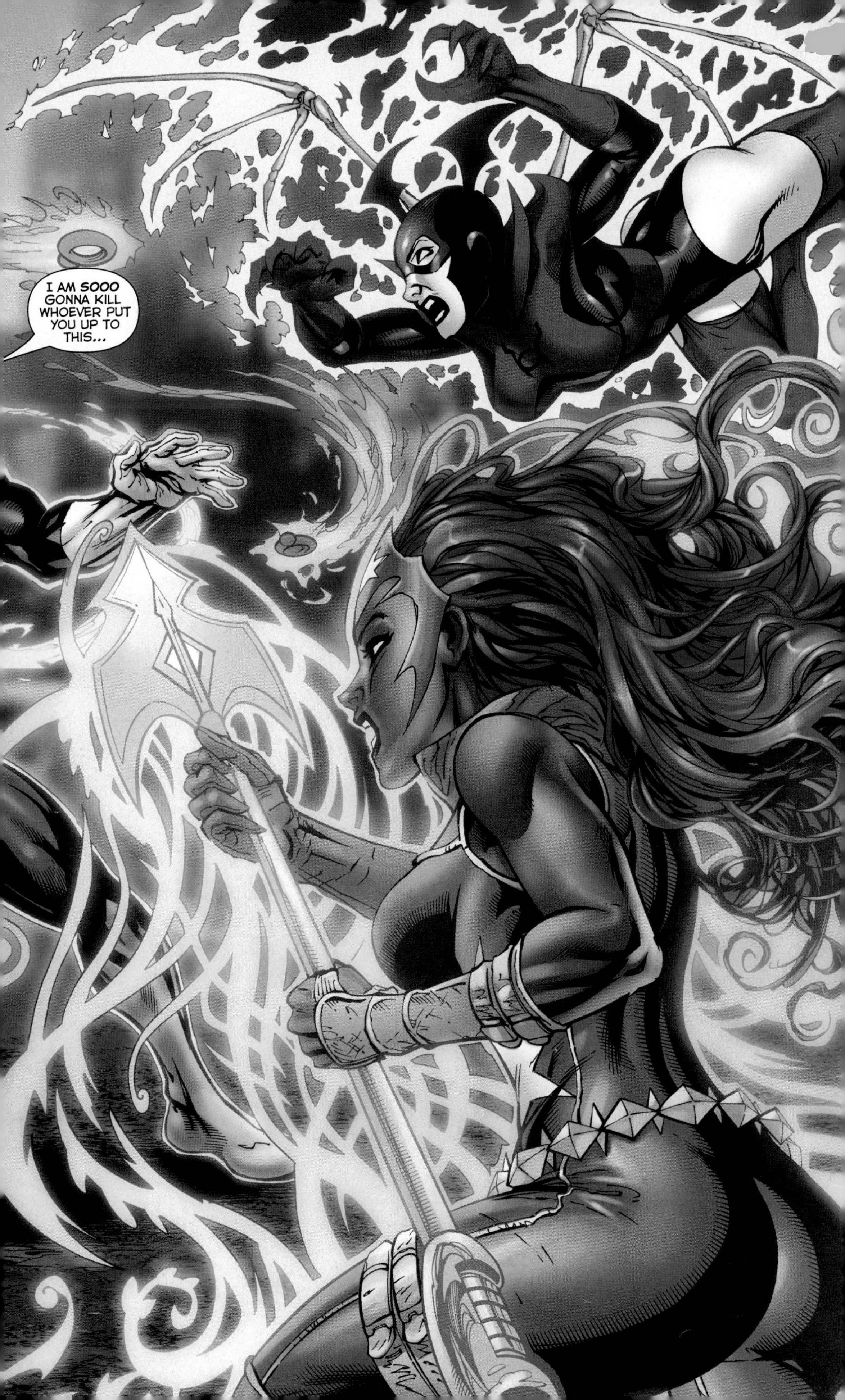
I AM SOOO GONNA KILL WHOEVER PUT YOU UP TO THIS...

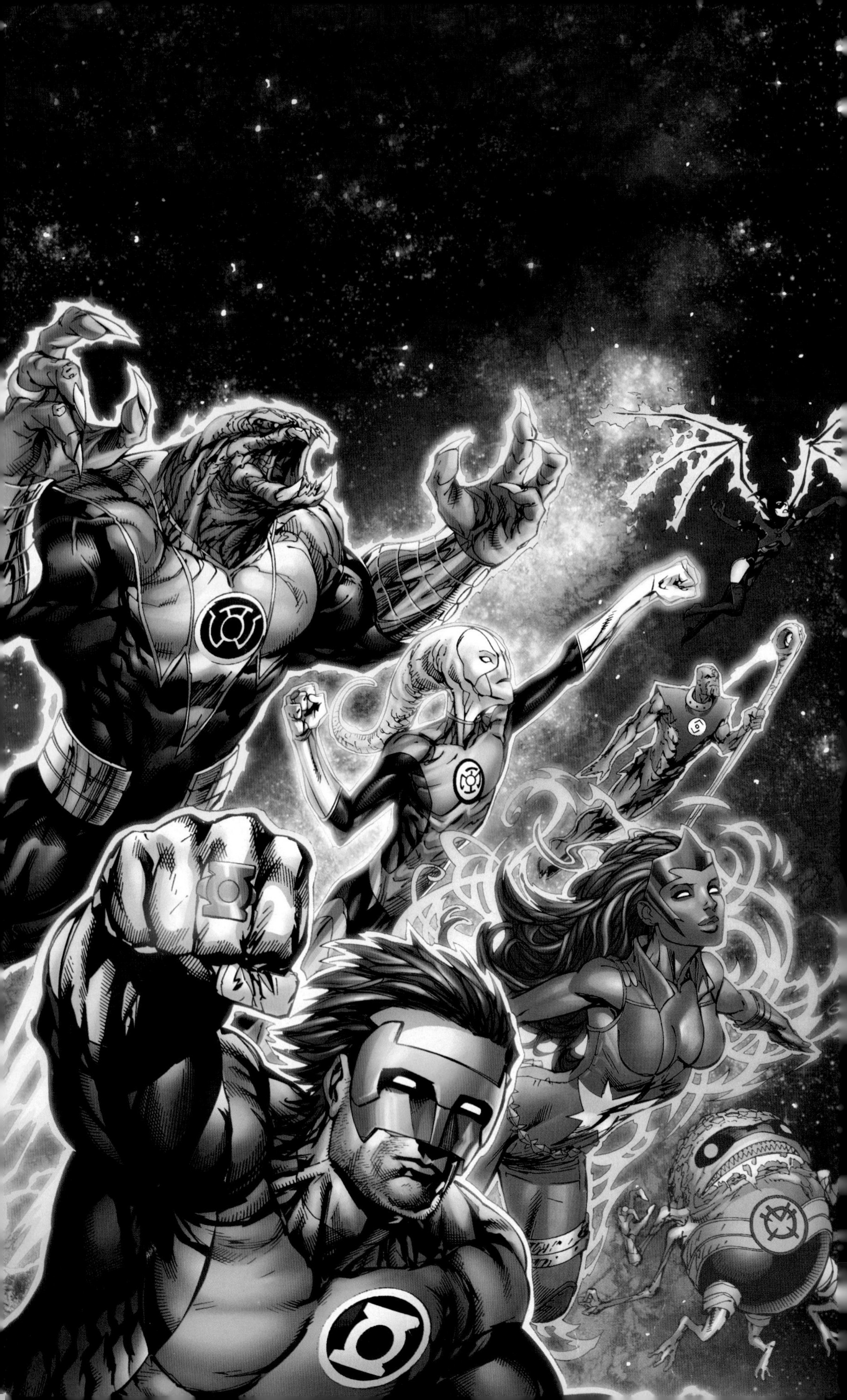

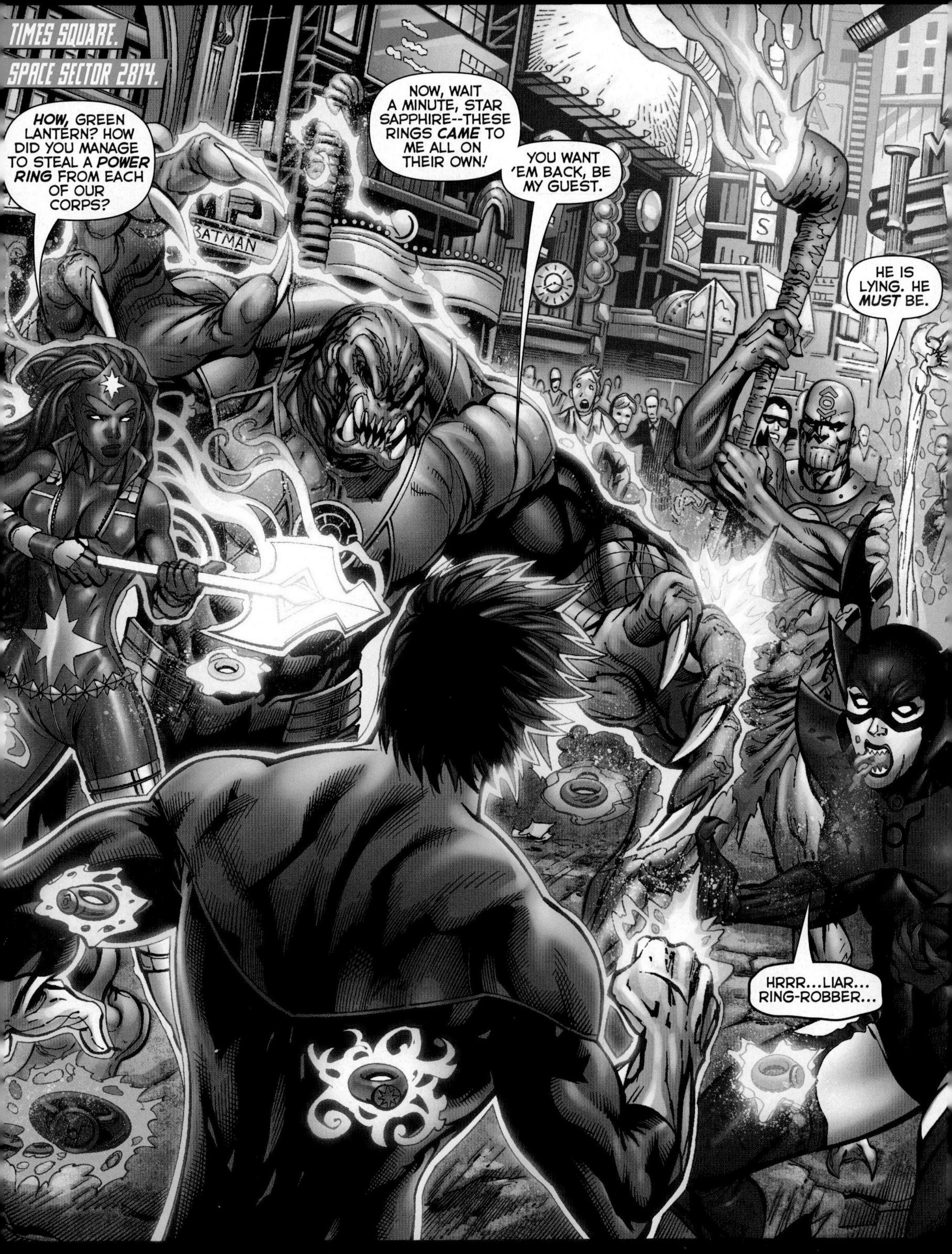
TIMES SQUARE.
SPACE SECTOR 2814.
HOW, GREEN LANTERN? HOW DID YOU MANAGE TO STEAL A POWER RING FROM EACH OF OUR CORPS?
NOW, WAIT A MINUTE, STAR SAPPHIRE--THESE RINGS CAME TO ME ALL ON THEIR OWN!
YOU WANT 'EM BACK, BE MY GUEST.
BATMAN
HE IS LYING. HE MUST BE.
HRRR...LIAR... RING-ROBBER...

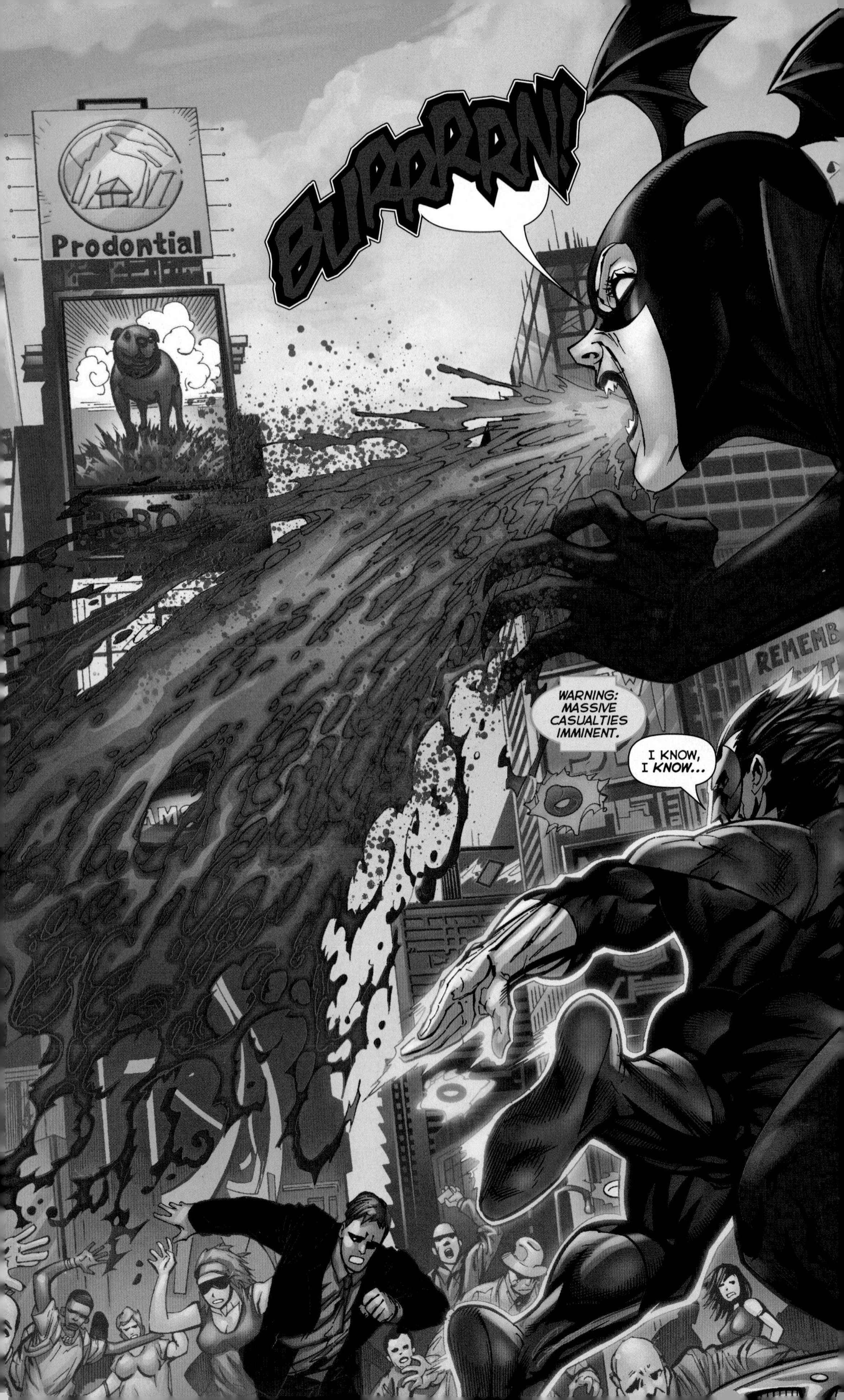
Prodontial
BURRRRN!
REMEMB
WARNING: MASSIVE CASUALTIES IMMINENT.
I KNOW, I KNOW...

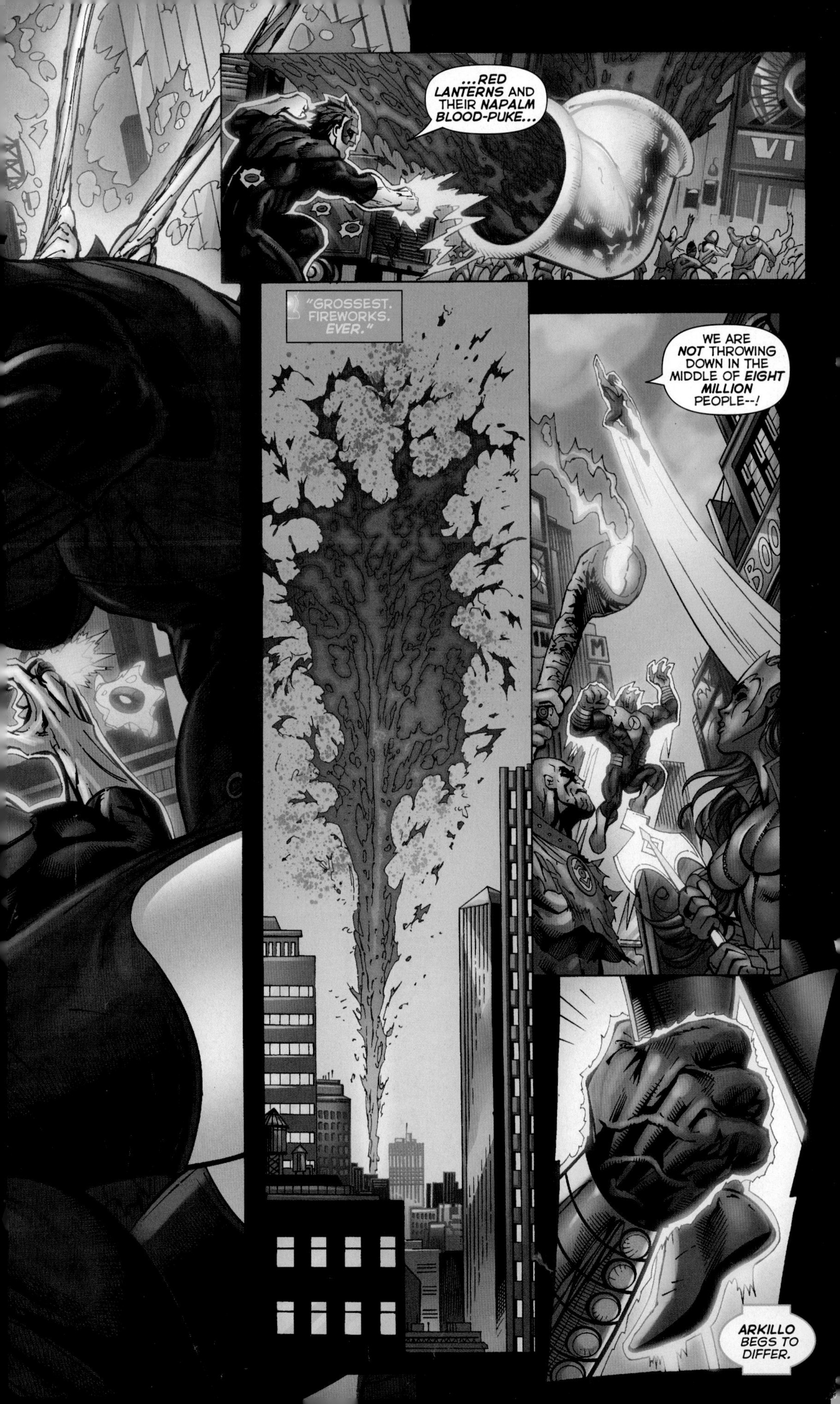
...RED LANTERNS AND THEIR NAPALM BLOOD-PUKE...
"GROSSEST. FIREWORKS. EVER."
WE ARE NOT THROWING DOWN IN THE MIDDLE OF EIGHT MILLION PEOPLE--!
ARKILLO BEGS TO DIFFER.

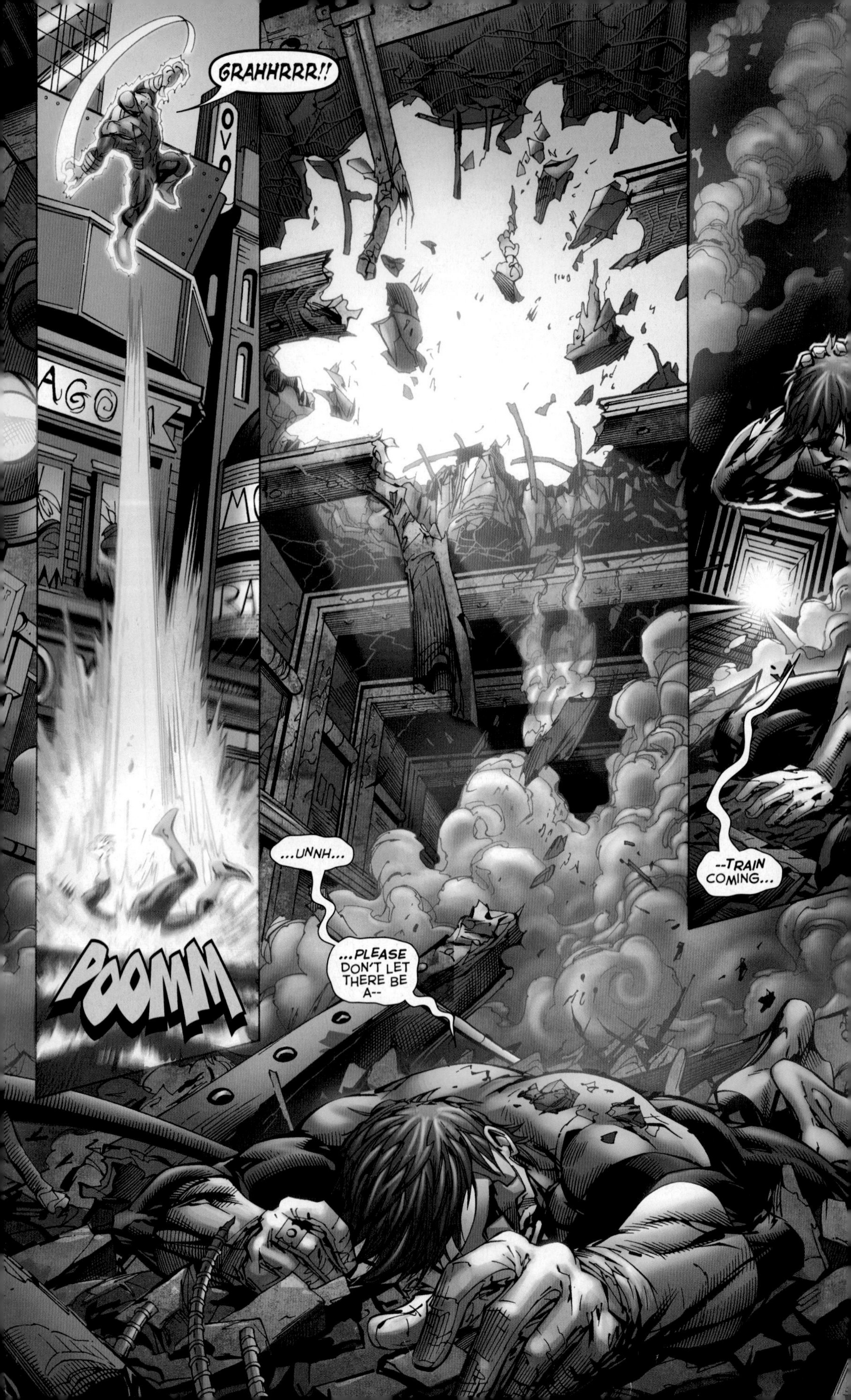
GRAHHRRR!!
POOMM
...UNNH...
...PLEASE DON'T LET THERE BE A--
--TRAIN COMING...

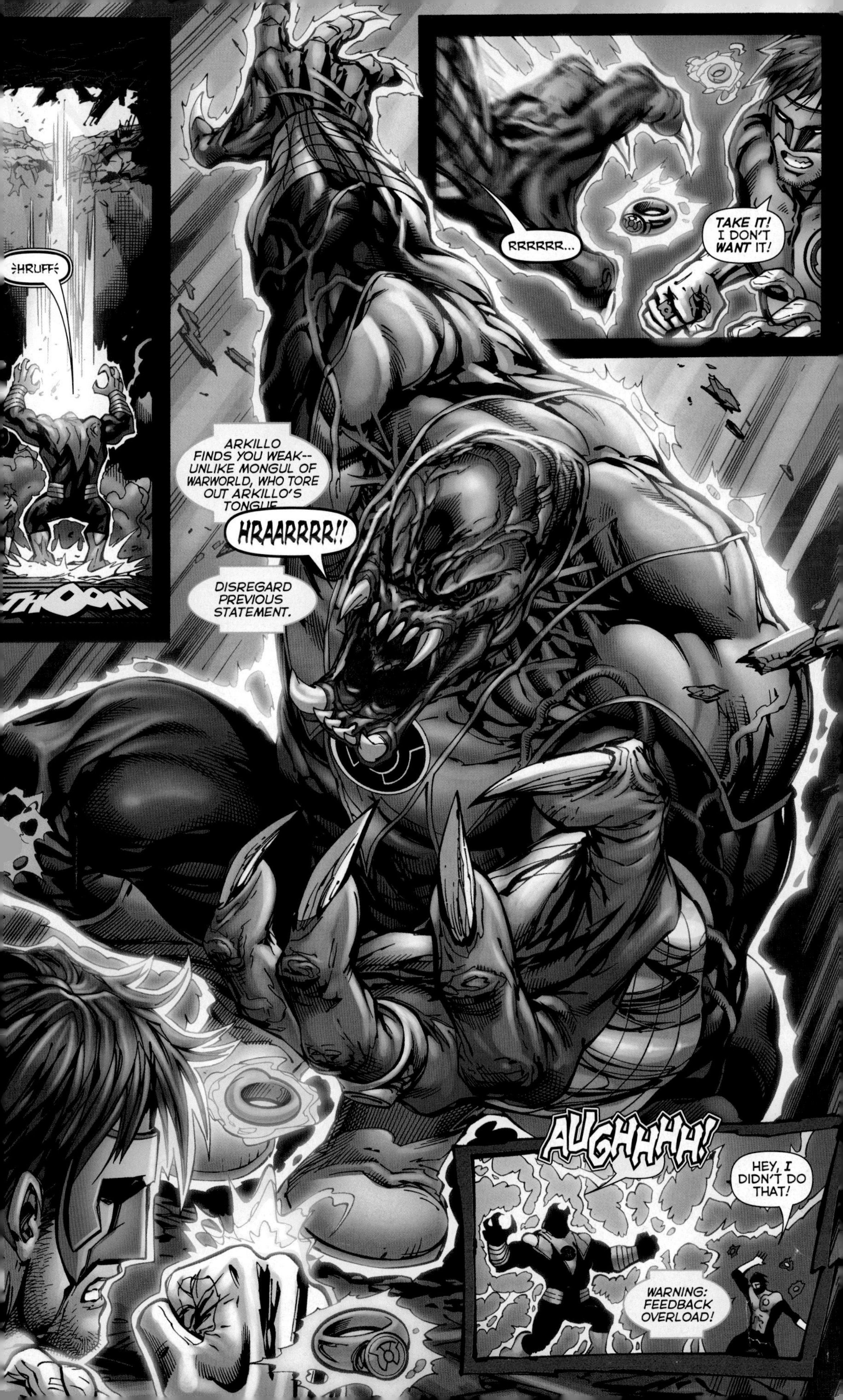
HRUFF
THOOM
RRRRRR...
TAKE IT! I DON'T WANT IT!
ARKILLO FINDS YOU WEAK-- UNLIKE MONGUL OF WARWORLD, WHO TORE OUT ARKILLO'S TONGUE
HRAARRRR!!
DISREGARD PREVIOUS STATEMENT.
AUGHHHH!
HEY, I DIDN'T DO THAT!
WARNING: FEEDBACK OVERLOAD!

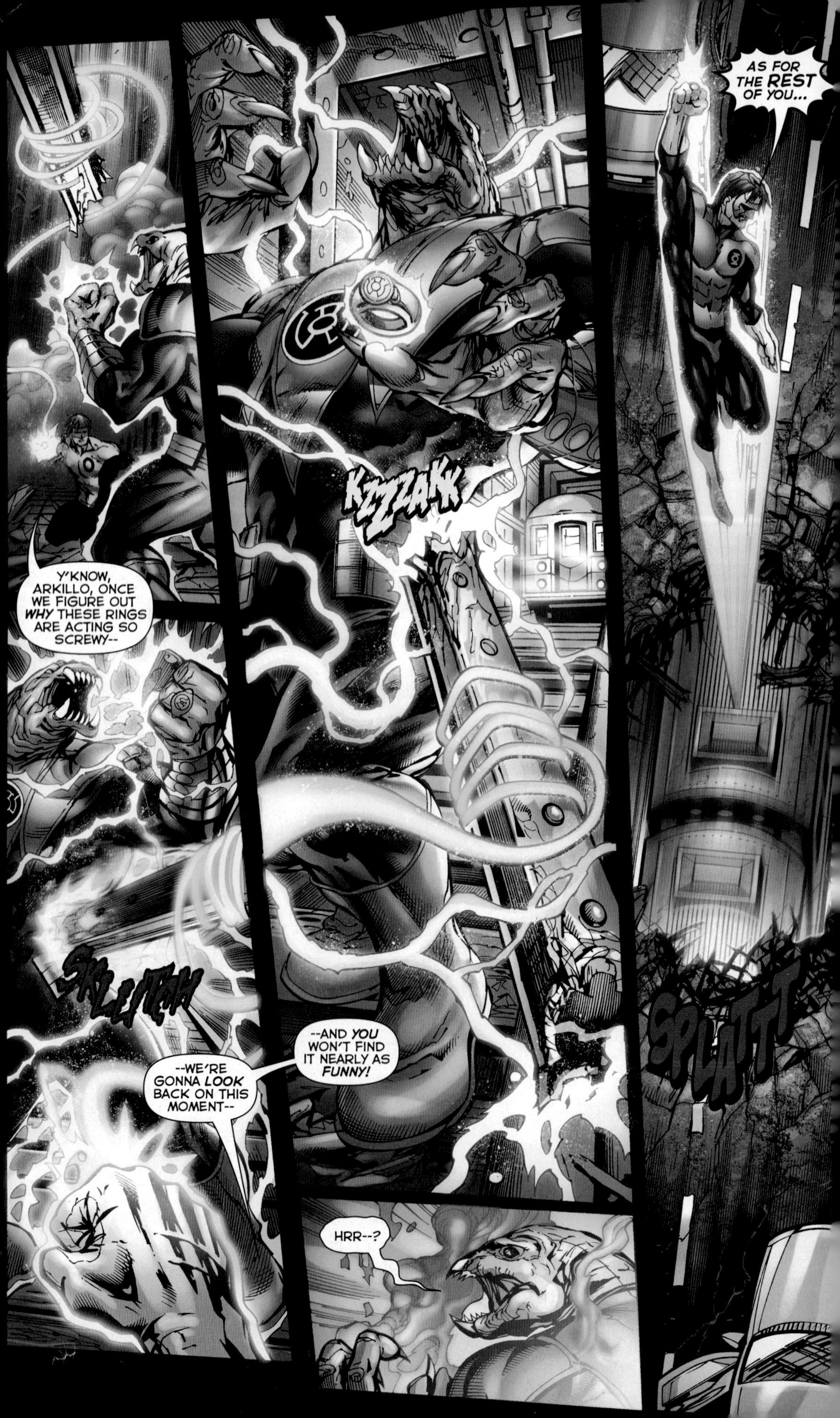
Y'KNOW, ARKILLO, ONCE WE FIGURE OUT WHY THESE RINGS ARE ACTING SO SCREWY--
SKLLITCH
--WE'RE GONNA LOOK BACK ON THIS MOMENT--
KZZZAKK
--AND YOU WON'T FIND IT NEARLY AS FUNNY!
HRR--?
AS FOR THE REST OF YOU...
SPLATT

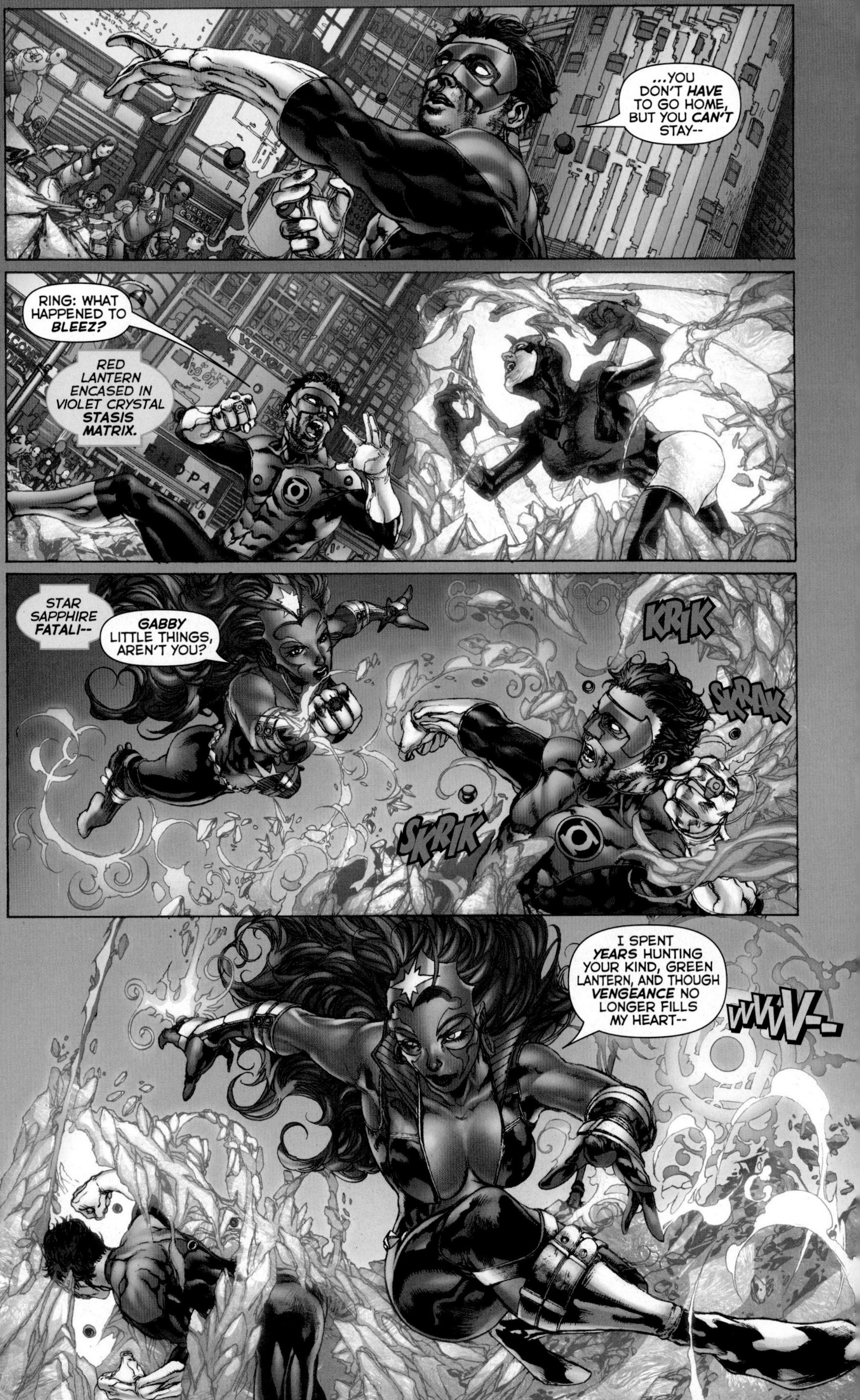
...YOU DON'T HAVE TO GO HOME, BUT YOU CAN'T STAY--
RING: WHAT HAPPENED TO BLEEZ?
RED LANTERN ENCASED IN VIOLET CRYSTAL STASIS MATRIX.
STAR SAPPHIRE FATALI--
GABBY LITTLE THINGS, AREN'T YOU?
KRIK
SKRAK
SKRIK
I SPENT YEARS HUNTING YOUR KIND, GREEN LANTERN, AND THOUGH VENGEANCE NO LONGER FILLS MY HEART--
WVVN--

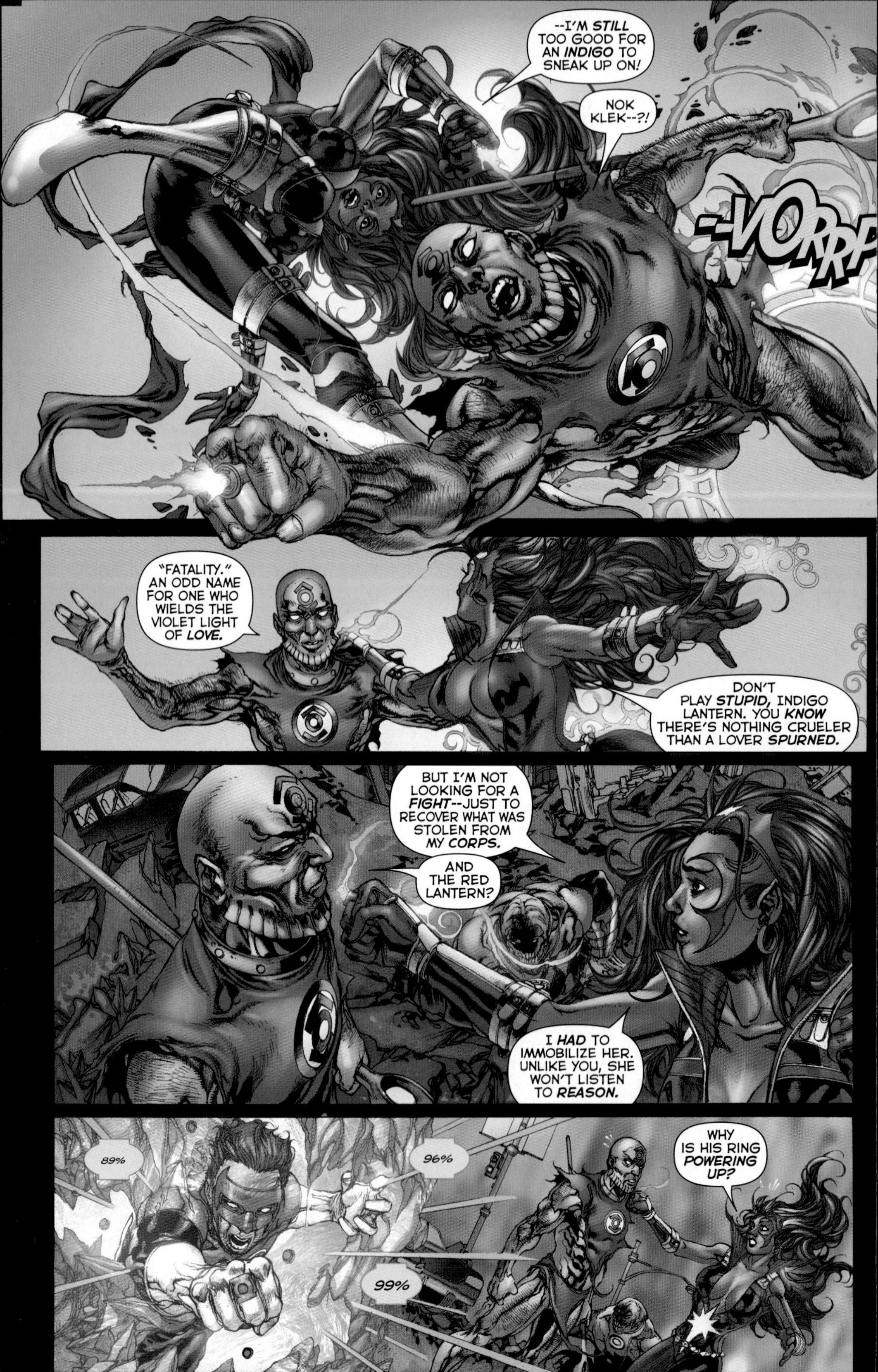

--I'M STILL TOO GOOD FOR AN INDIGO TO SNEAK UP ON!
NOK KLEK--?!
--VORRP
"FATALITY." AN ODD NAME FOR ONE WHO WIELDS THE VIOLET LIGHT OF LOVE.
DON'T PLAY STUPID, INDIGO LANTERN. YOU KNOW THERE'S NOTHING CRUELER THAN A LOVER SPURNED.
BUT I'M NOT LOOKING FOR A FIGHT--JUST TO RECOVER WHAT WAS STOLEN FROM MY CORPS.
AND THE RED LANTERN?
I HAD TO IMMOBILIZE HER. UNLIKE YOU, SHE WON'T LISTEN TO REASON.
89%
96%
99%
WHY IS HIS RING POWERING UP?

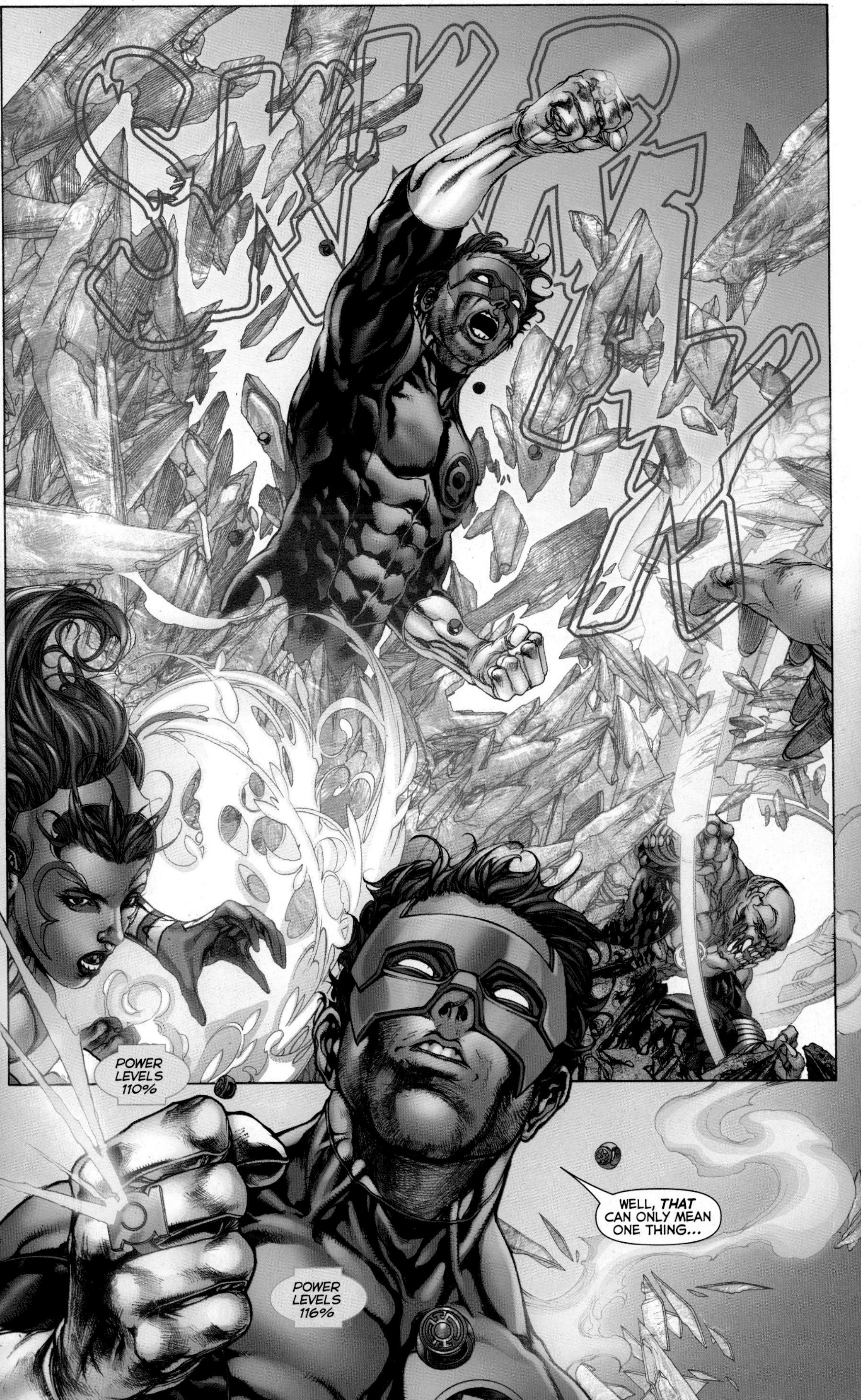
POWER LEVELS 110%
WELL, *THAT* CAN ONLY MEAN ONE THING...
POWER LEVELS 116%

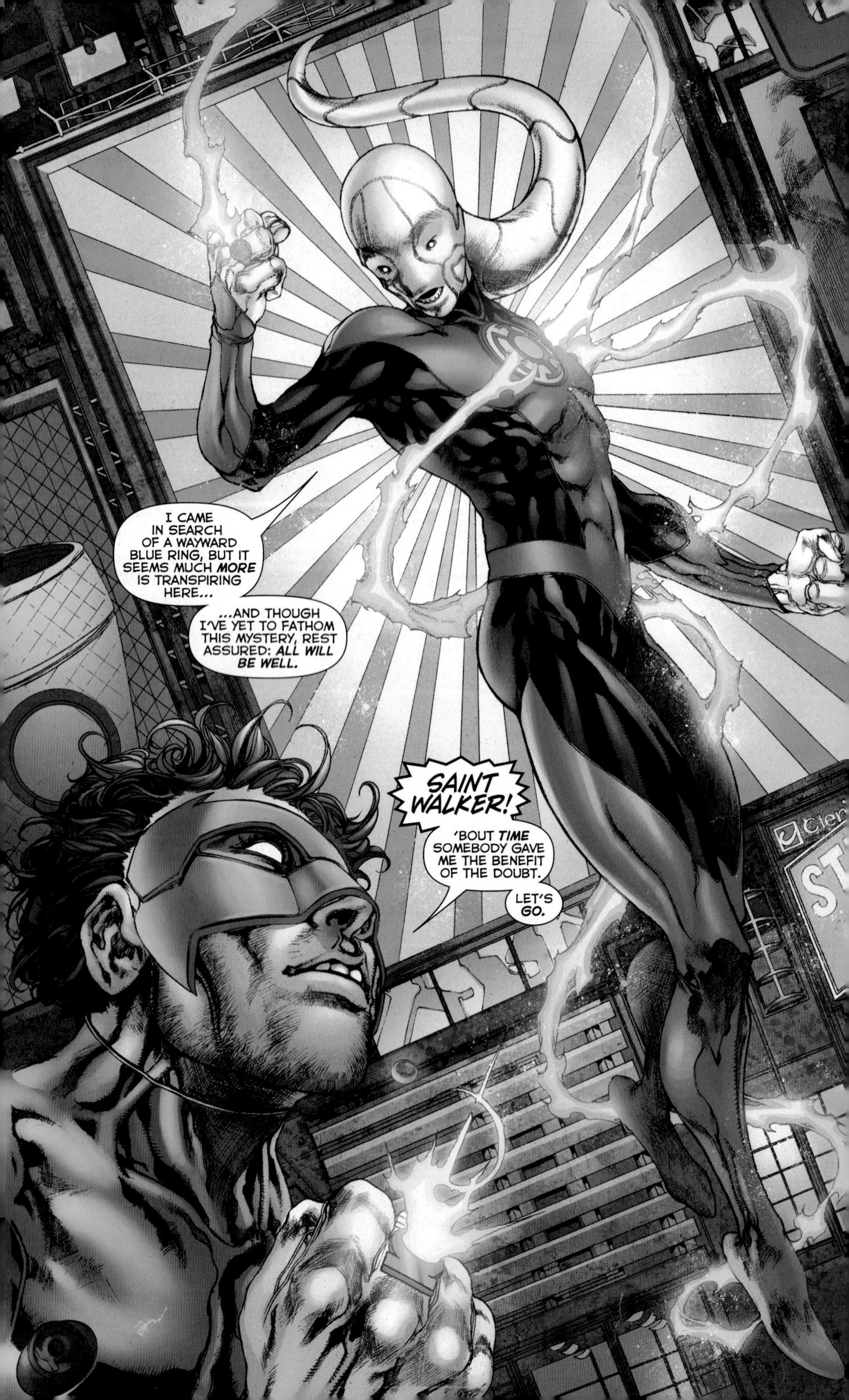
I CAME IN SEARCH OF A WAYWARD BLUE RING, BUT IT SEEMS MUCH MORE IS TRANSPIRING HERE...
...AND THOUGH I'VE YET TO FATHOM THIS MYSTERY, REST ASSURED: ALL WILL BE WELL.
SAINT WALKER!
'BOUT TIME SOMEBODY GAVE ME THE BENEFIT OF THE DOUBT.
LET'S GO.

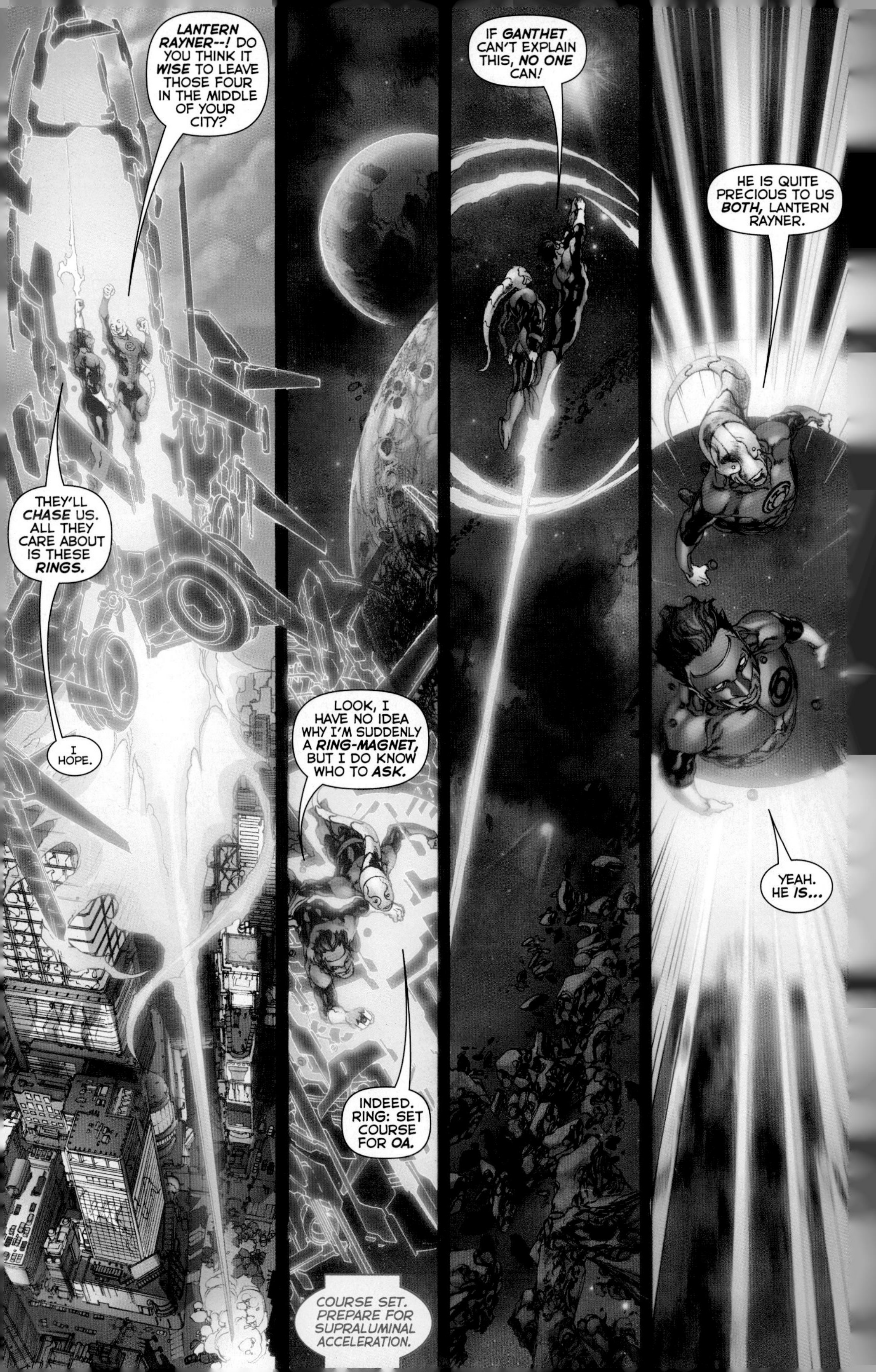
LANTERN RAYNER--! DO YOU THINK IT WISE TO LEAVE THOSE FOUR IN THE MIDDLE OF YOUR CITY?
THEY'LL CHASE US. ALL THEY CARE ABOUT IS THESE RINGS.
I HOPE.
LOOK, I HAVE NO IDEA WHY I'M SUDDENLY A RING-MAGNET, BUT I DO KNOW WHO TO ASK.
INDEED. RING: SET COURSE FOR OA.
COURSE SET. PREPARE FOR SUPRALUMINAL ACCELERATION.
IF GANTHET CAN'T EXPLAIN THIS, NO ONE CAN!
HE IS QUITE PRECIOUS TO US BOTH, LANTERN RAYNER.
YEAH. HE IS...

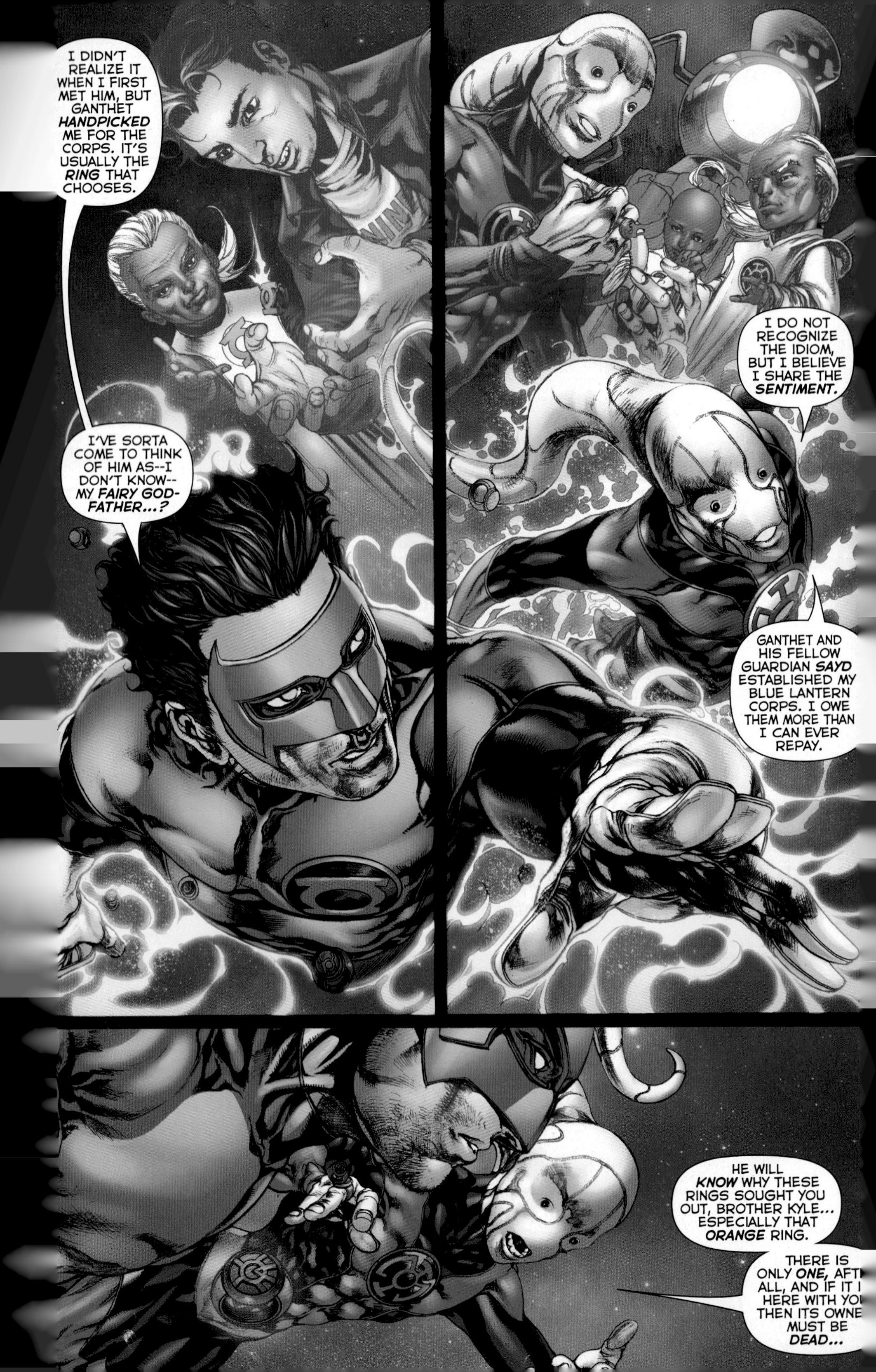
I DIDN'T REALIZE IT WHEN I FIRST MET HIM, BUT GANTHET HANDPICKED ME FOR THE CORPS. IT'S USUALLY THE RING THAT CHOOSES.
I'VE SORTA COME TO THINK OF HIM AS--I DON'T KNOW--MY FAIRY GOD-FATHER...?
I DO NOT RECOGNIZE THE IDIOM, BUT I BELIEVE I SHARE THE SENTIMENT.
GANTHET AND HIS FELLOW GUARDIAN SAYD ESTABLISHED MY BLUE LANTERN CORPS. I OWE THEM MORE THAN I CAN EVER REPAY.
HE WILL KNOW WHY THESE RINGS SOUGHT YOU OUT, BROTHER KYLE... ESPECIALLY THAT ORANGE RING.
THERE IS ONLY ONE, AFT ALL, AND IF IT I HERE WITH YO THEN ITS OWNE MUST BE DEAD...

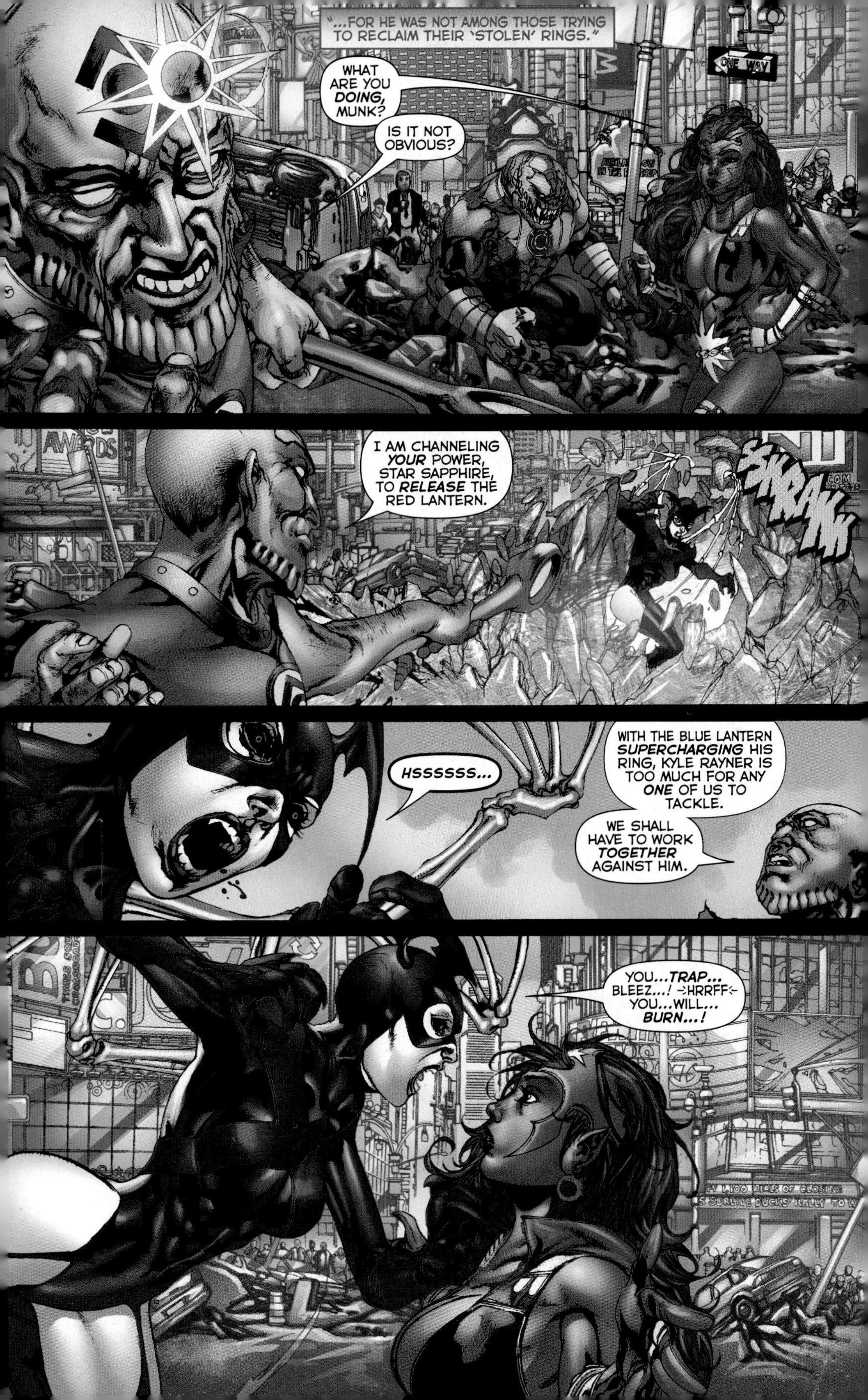
"...FOR HE WAS NOT AMONG THOSE TRYING TO RECLAIM THEIR 'STOLEN' RINGS."
WHAT ARE YOU DOING, MUNK?
IS IT NOT OBVIOUS?
I AM CHANNELING YOUR POWER, STAR SAPPHIRE, TO RELEASE THE RED LANTERN.
SHRAKK
HSSSSSS...
WITH THE BLUE LANTERN SUPERCHARGING HIS RING, KYLE RAYNER IS TOO MUCH FOR ANY ONE OF US TO TACKLE.
WE SHALL HAVE TO WORK TOGETHER AGAINST HIM.
YOU...TRAP... BLEEZ...! HRRFF YOU...WILL... BURN...!

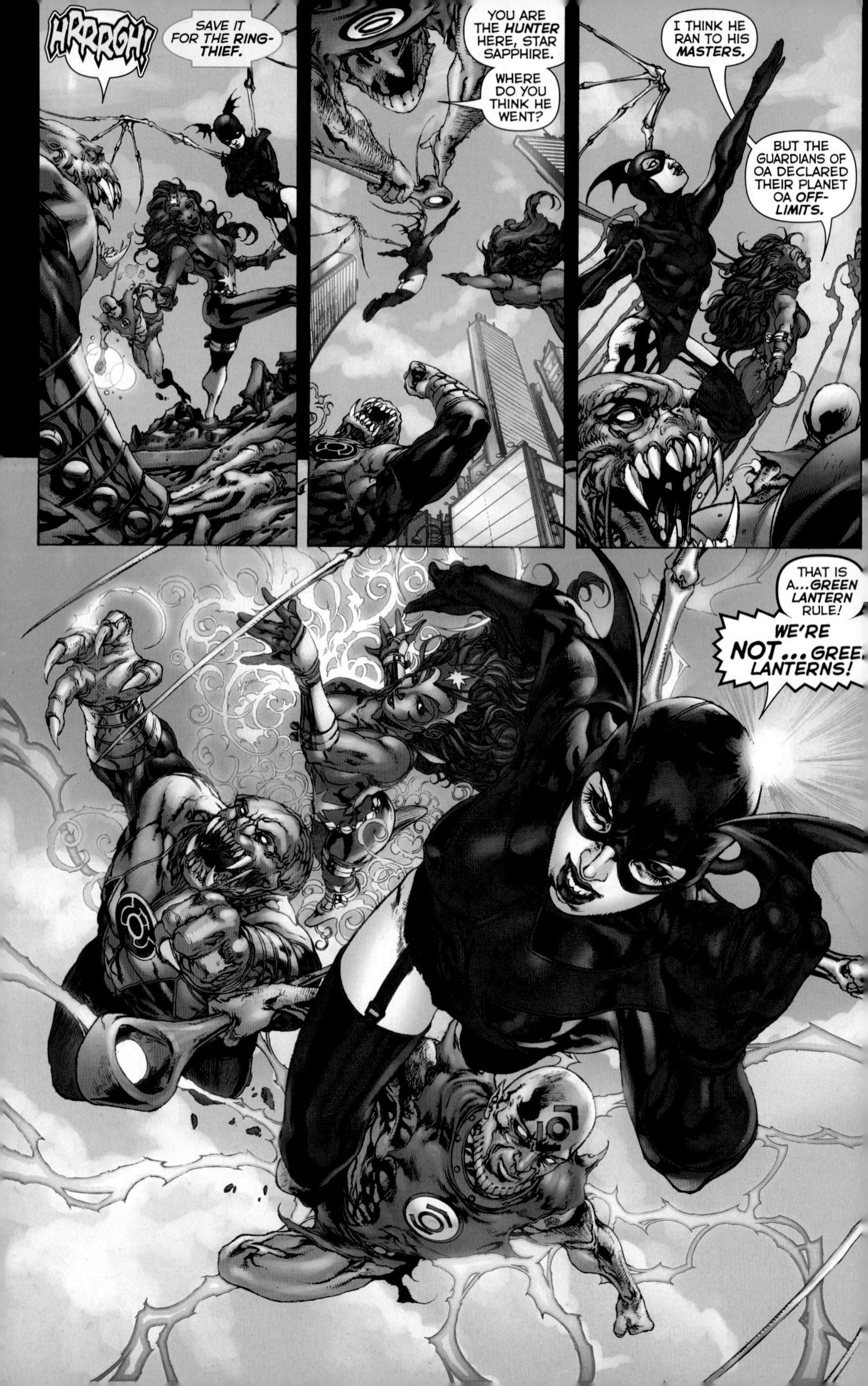
HRRRGH!
SAVE IT FOR THE RING-THIEF.
YOU ARE THE HUNTER HERE, STAR SAPPHIRE.
WHERE DO YOU THINK HE WENT?
I THINK HE RAN TO HIS MASTERS.
BUT THE GUARDIANS OF OA DECLARED THEIR PLANET OA OFF-LIMITS.
THAT IS A...GREEN LANTERN RULE!
WE'RE NOT...GREE. LANTERNS!

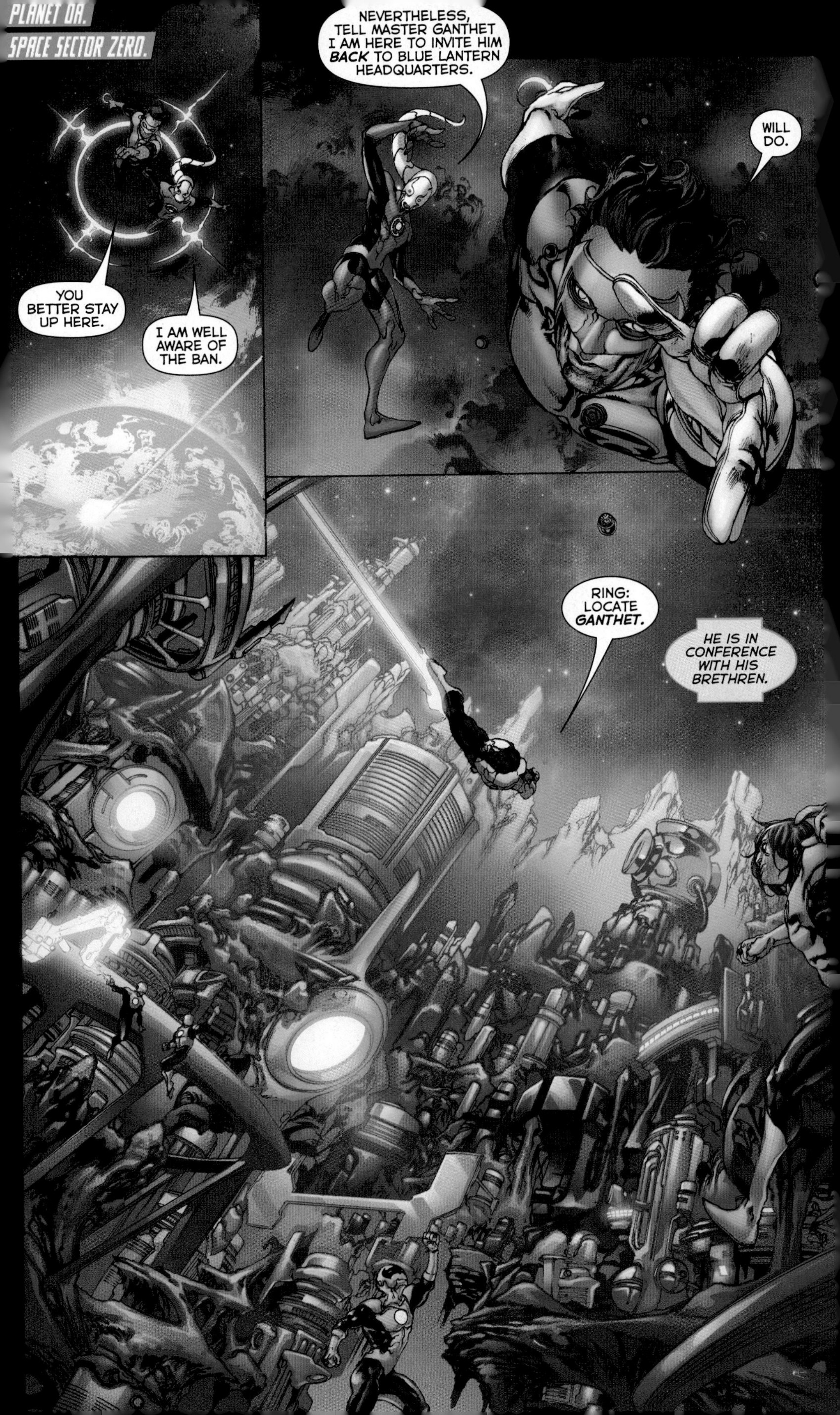
PLANET OA.
SPACE SECTOR ZERO.
YOU BETTER STAY UP HERE.
I AM WELL AWARE OF THE BAN.
NEVERTHELESS, TELL MASTER GANTHET I AM HERE TO INVITE HIM BACK TO BLUE LANTERN HEADQUARTERS.
WILL DO.
RING: LOCATE GANTHET.
HE IS IN CONFERENCE WITH HIS BRETHREN.

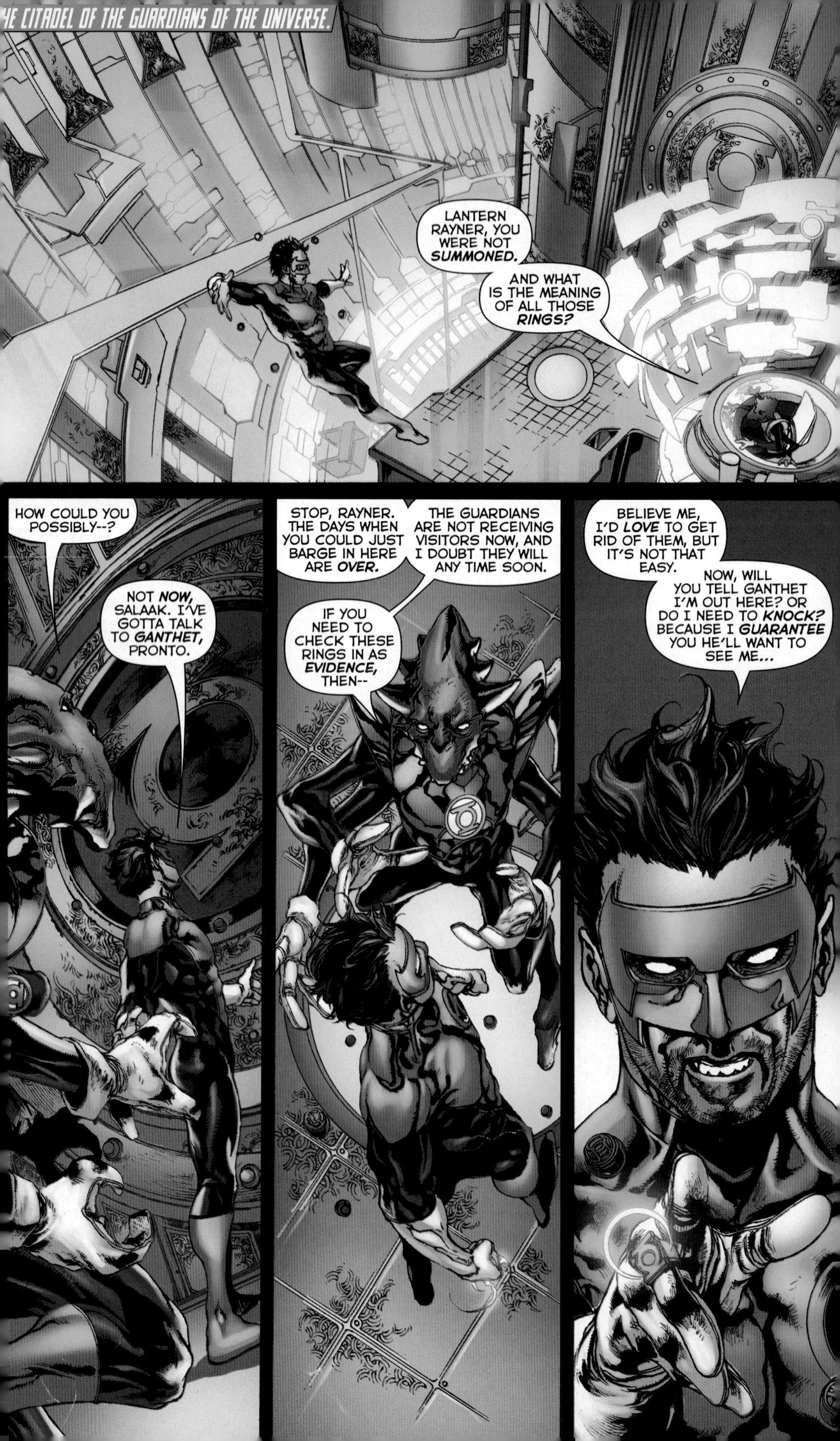
HE CITADEL OF THE GUARDIANS OF THE UNIVERSE.
LANTERN RAYNER, YOU WERE NOT SUMMONED.
AND WHAT IS THE MEANING OF ALL THOSE RINGS?
HOW COULD YOU POSSIBLY--?
NOT NOW, SALAAK. I'VE GOTTA TALK TO GANTHET, PRONTO.
STOP, RAYNER. THE DAYS WHEN YOU COULD JUST BARGE IN HERE ARE OVER.
THE GUARDIANS ARE NOT RECEIVING VISITORS NOW, AND I DOUBT THEY WILL ANY TIME SOON.
IF YOU NEED TO CHECK THESE RINGS IN AS EVIDENCE, THEN--
BELIEVE ME, I'D LOVE TO GET RID OF THEM, BUT IT'S NOT THAT EASY.
NOW, WILL YOU TELL GANTHET I'M OUT HERE? OR DO I NEED TO KNOCK? BECAUSE I GUARANTEE YOU HE'LL WANT TO SEE ME...

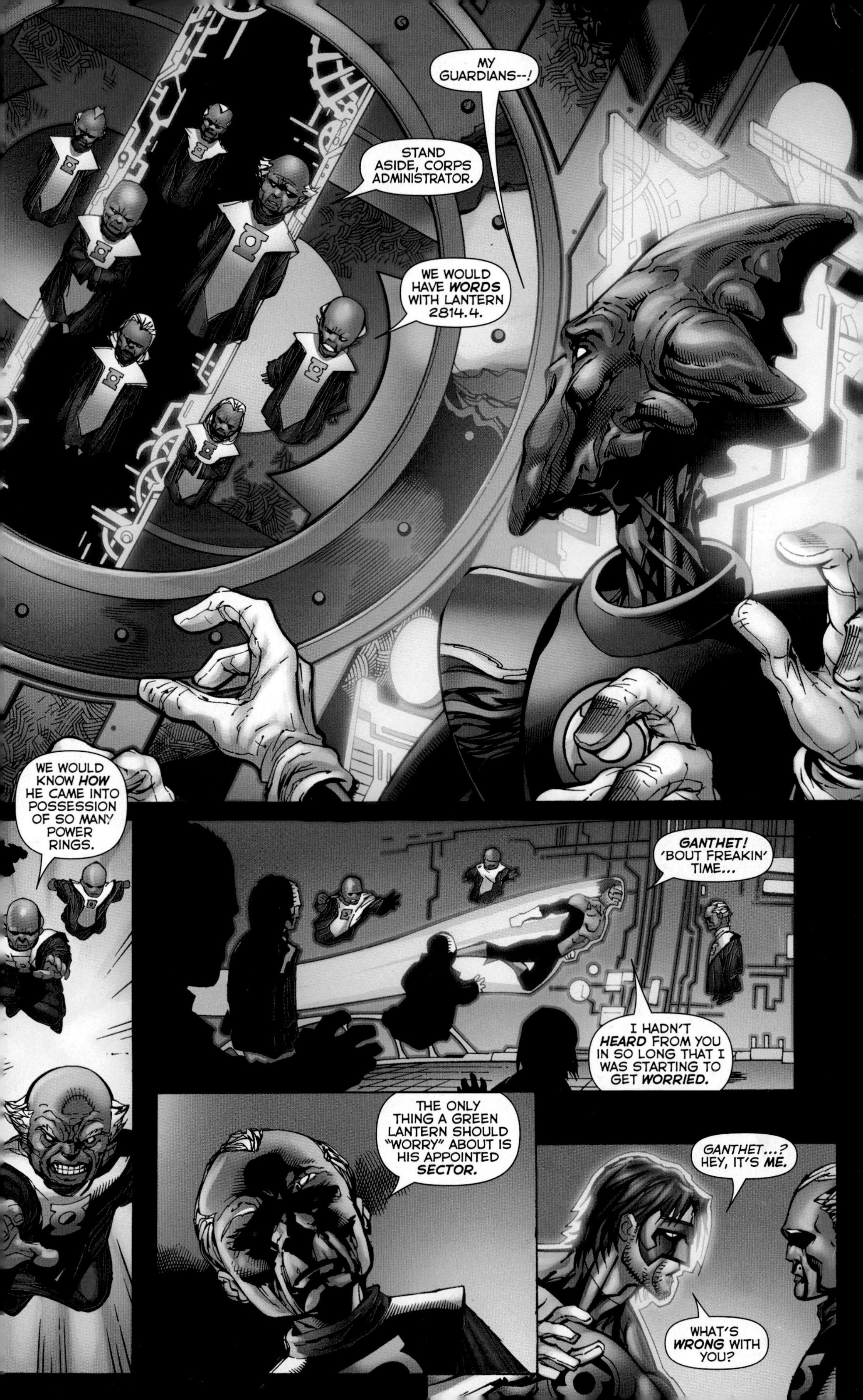
MY GUARDIANS--!
STAND ASIDE, CORPS ADMINISTRATOR.
WE WOULD HAVE **WORDS** WITH LANTERN 2814.4.
WE WOULD KNOW **HOW** HE CAME INTO POSSESSION OF SO MANY POWER RINGS.
GANTHET! 'BOUT FREAKIN' TIME...
I HADN'T **HEARD** FROM YOU IN SO LONG THAT I WAS STARTING TO GET **WORRIED.**
THE ONLY THING A GREEN LANTERN SHOULD "WORRY" ABOUT IS HIS APPOINTED **SECTOR.**
GANTHET...? HEY, IT'S **ME.**
WHAT'S **WRONG** WITH YOU?

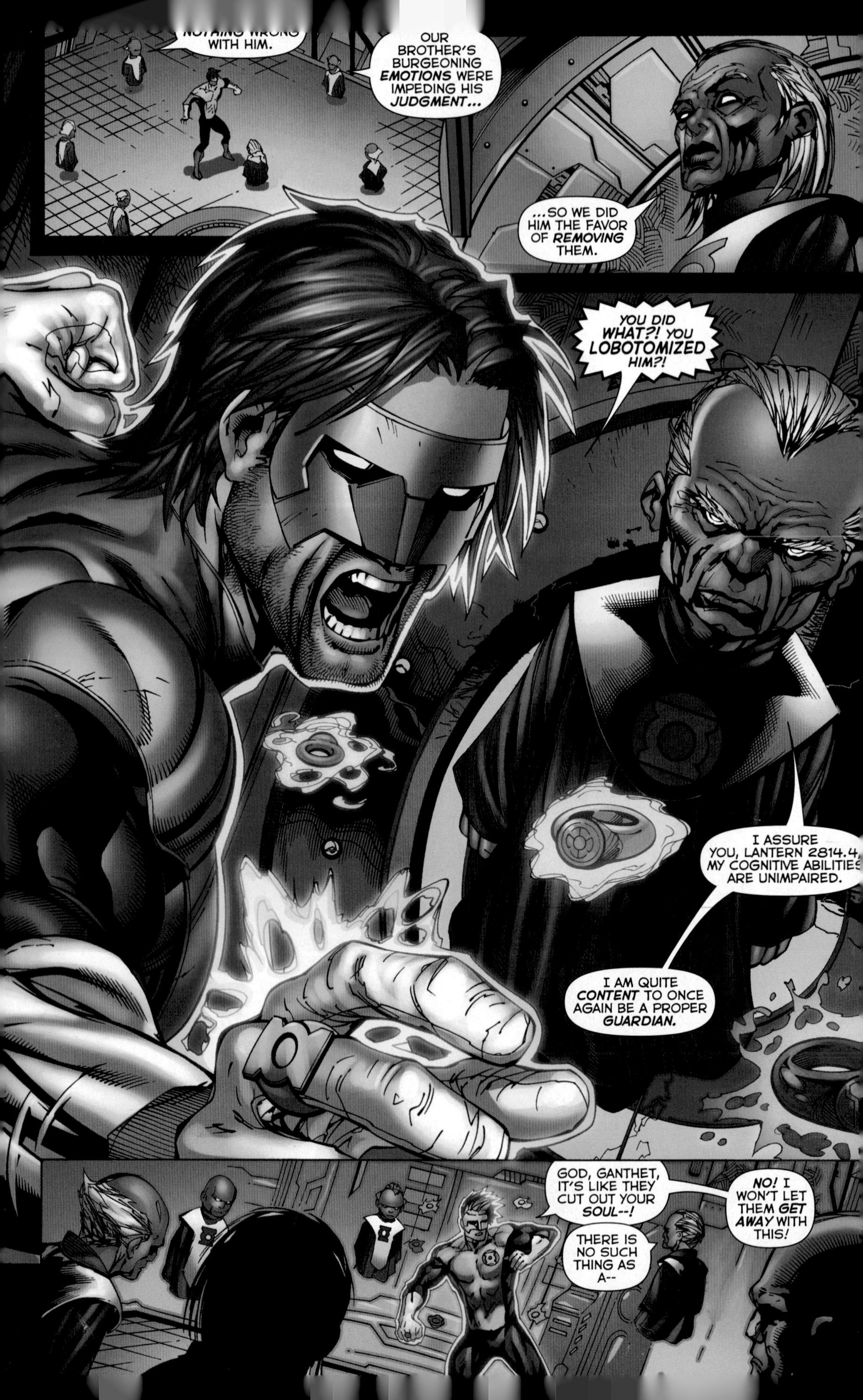
NOTHING WRONG WITH HIM.
OUR BROTHER'S BURGEONING EMOTIONS WERE IMPEDING HIS JUDGMENT...
...SO WE DID HIM THE FAVOR OF REMOVING THEM.
YOU DID WHAT?! YOU LOBOTOMIZED HIM?!
I ASSURE YOU, LANTERN 2814.4, MY COGNITIVE ABILITIES ARE UNIMPAIRED.
I AM QUITE CONTENT TO ONCE AGAIN BE A PROPER GUARDIAN.
GOD, GANTHET, IT'S LIKE THEY CUT OUT YOUR SOUL--!
THERE IS NO SUCH THING AS A--
NO! I WON'T LET THEM GET AWAY WITH THIS!

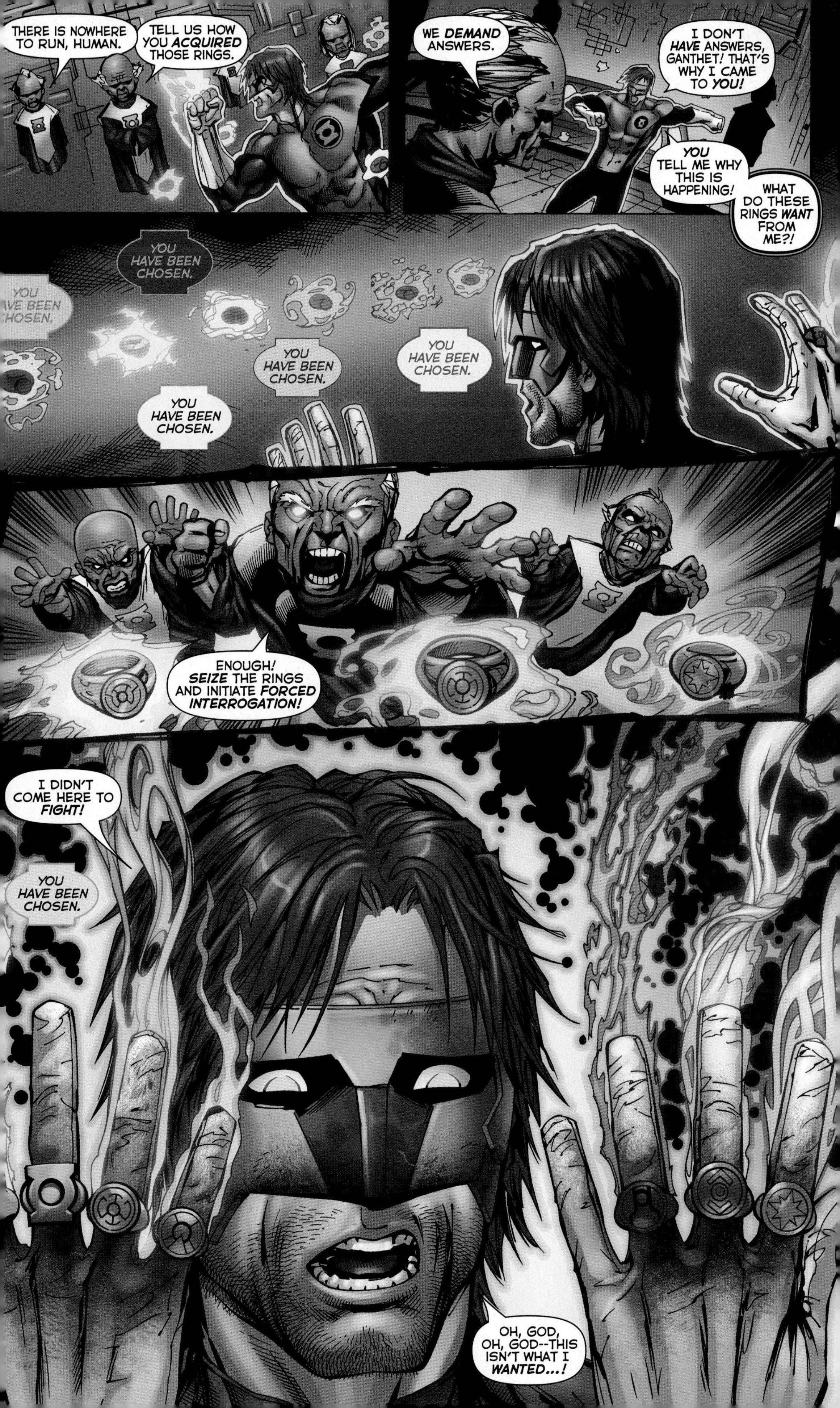

THERE IS NOWHERE TO RUN, HUMAN.
TELL US HOW YOU ACQUIRED THOSE RINGS.
WE DEMAND ANSWERS.
I DON'T HAVE ANSWERS, GANTHET! THAT'S WHY I CAME TO YOU!
YOU TELL ME WHY THIS IS HAPPENING!
WHAT DO THESE RINGS WANT FROM ME?!
YOU HAVE BEEN CHOSEN.
YOU HAVE BEEN CHOSEN.
YOU HAVE BEEN CHOSEN.
YOU HAVE BEEN CHOSEN.
YOU HAVE BEEN CHOSEN.
ENOUGH! SEIZE THE RINGS AND INITIATE FORCED INTERROGATION!
I DIDN'T COME HERE TO FIGHT!
YOU HAVE BEEN CHOSEN.
OH, GOD, OH, GOD--THIS ISN'T WHAT I WANTED...!

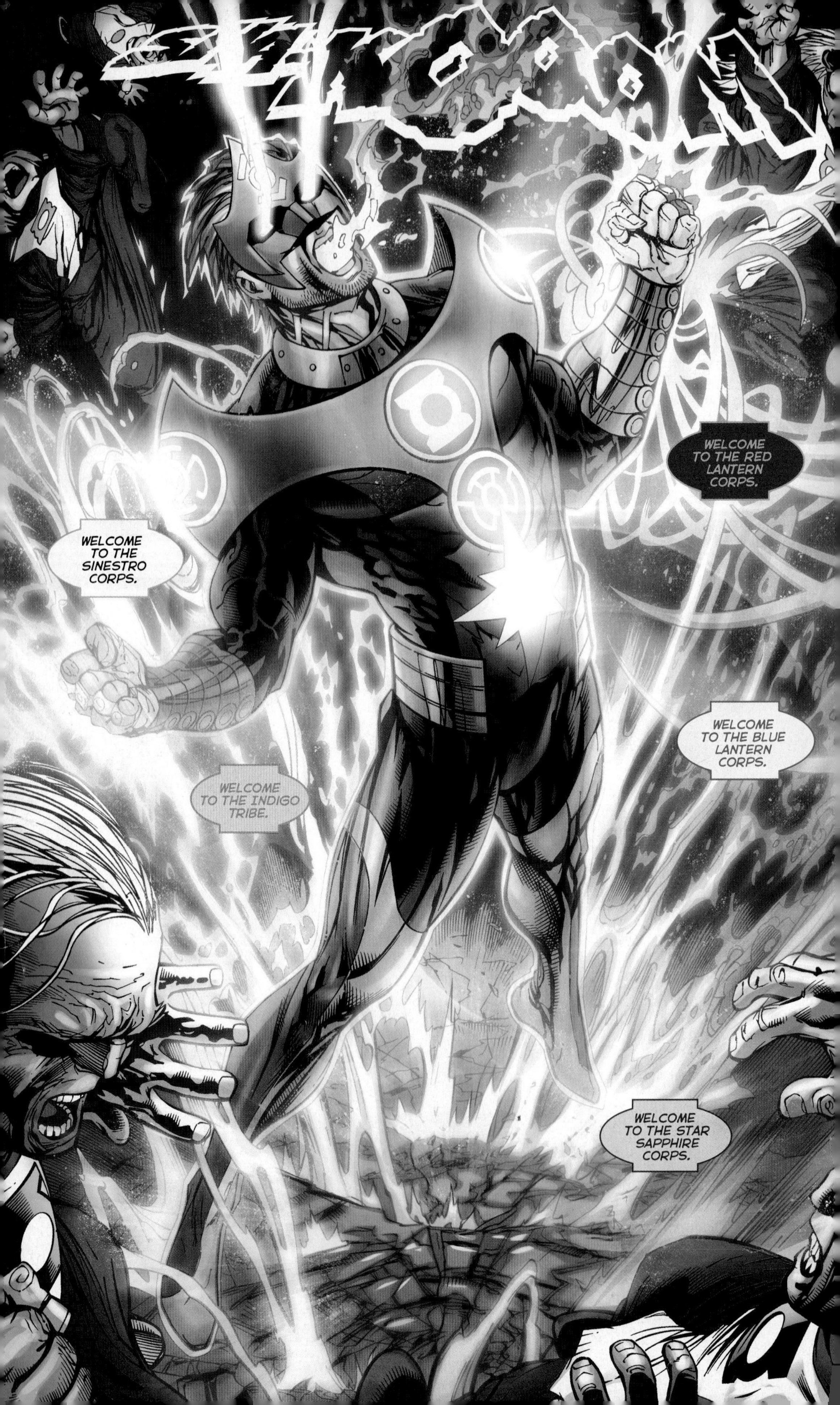
WELCOME TO THE RED LANTERN CORPS.
WELCOME TO THE SINESTRO CORPS.
WELCOME TO THE BLUE LANTERN CORPS.
WELCOME TO THE INDIGO TRIBE.
WELCOME TO THE STAR SAPPHIRE CORPS.

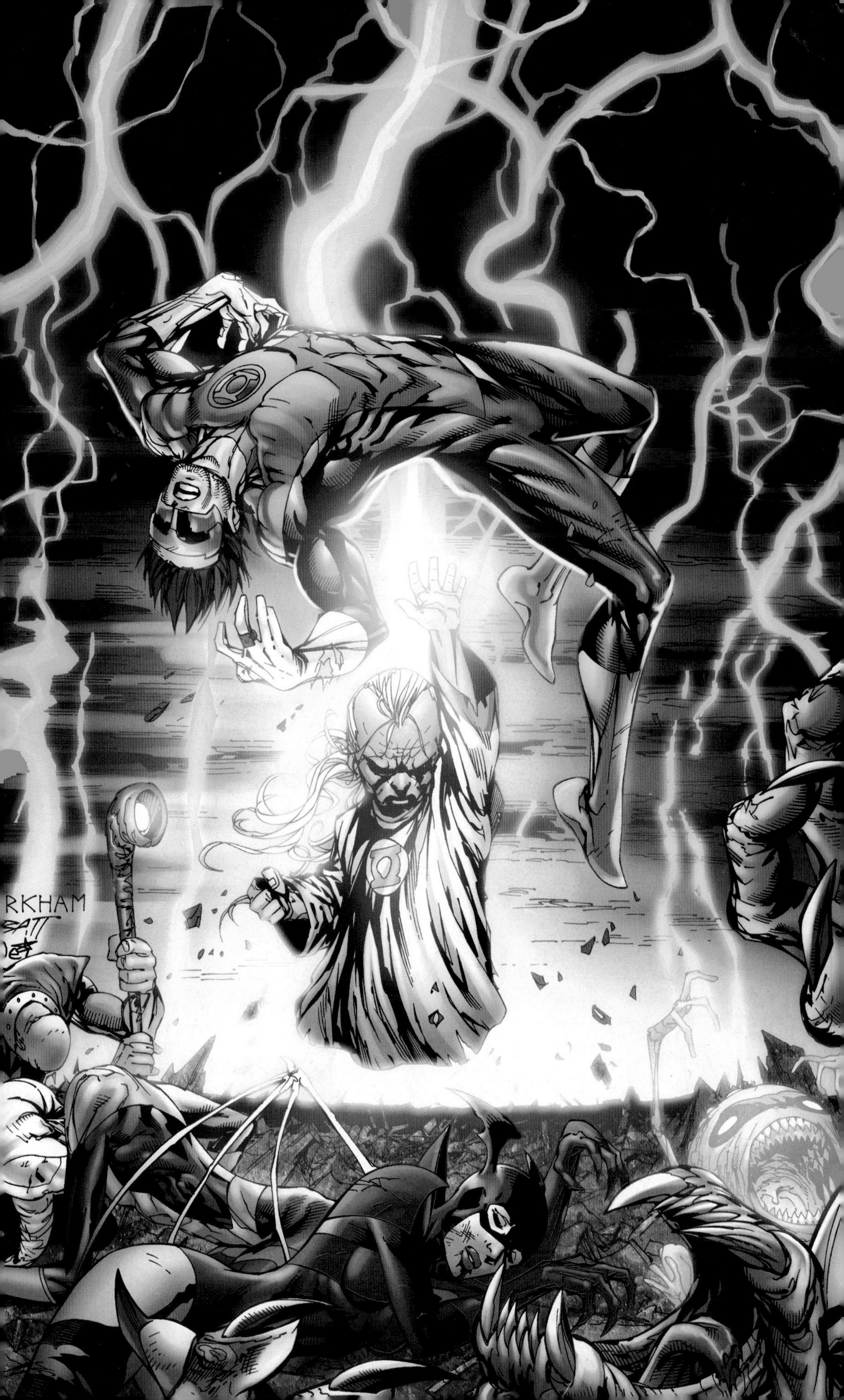
RKHAM

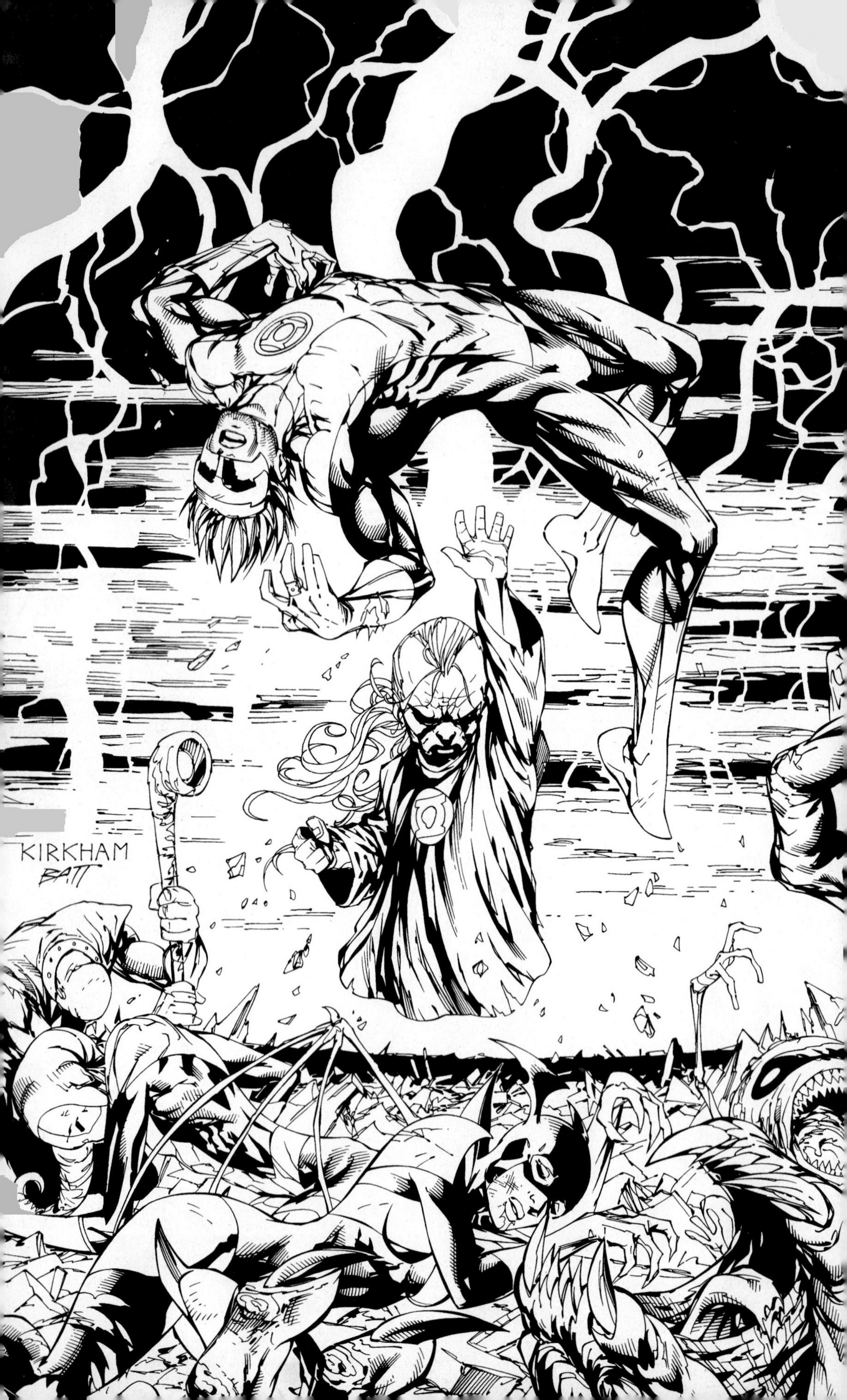
KIRKHAM
BATT

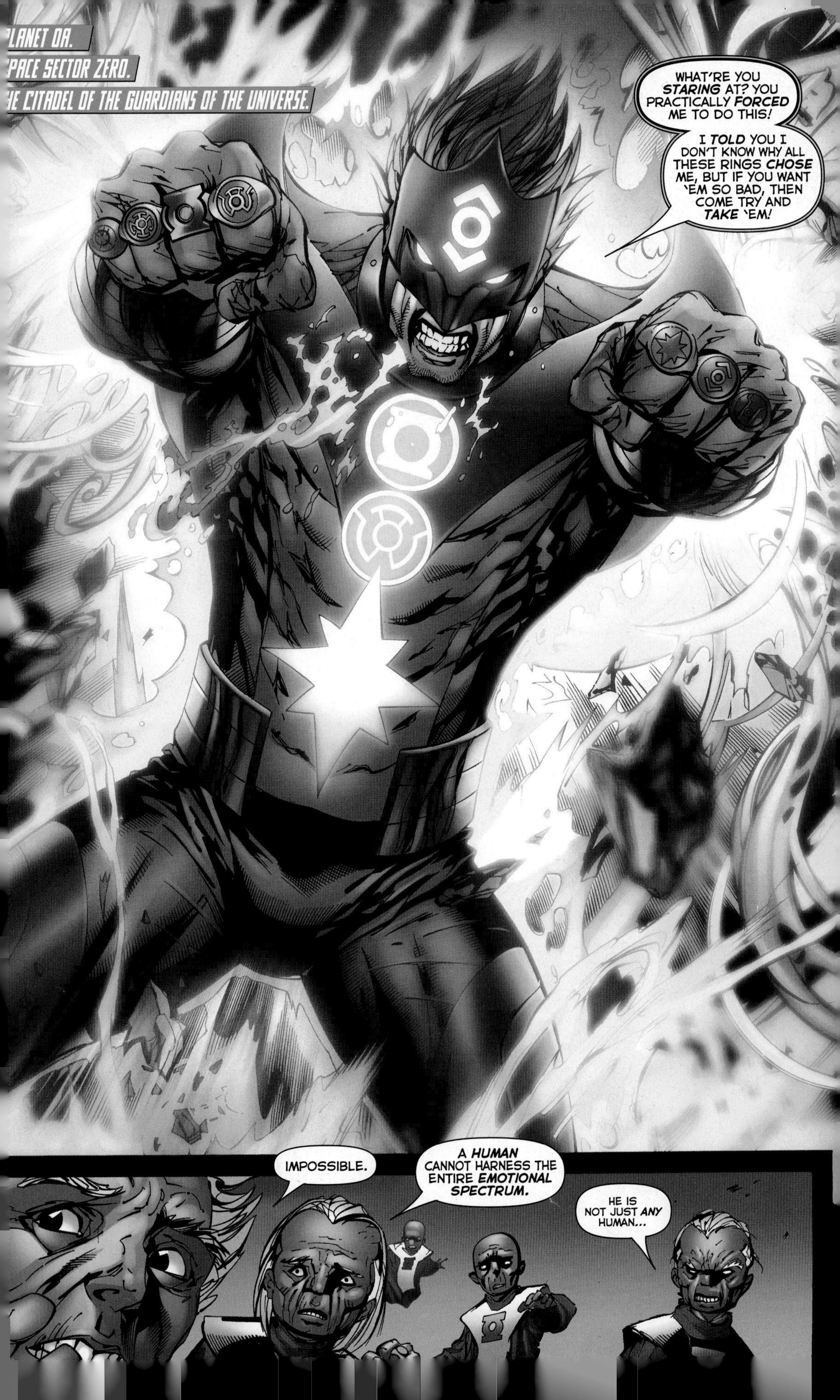

PLANET OA.
SPACE SECTOR ZERO.
THE CITADEL OF THE GUARDIANS OF THE UNIVERSE.
WHAT'RE YOU STARING AT? YOU PRACTICALLY FORCED ME TO DO THIS!
I TOLD YOU I DON'T KNOW WHY ALL THESE RINGS CHOSE ME, BUT IF YOU WANT 'EM SO BAD, THEN COME TRY AND TAKE 'EM!
IMPOSSIBLE.
A HUMAN CANNOT HARNESS THE ENTIRE EMOTIONAL SPECTRUM.
HE IS NOT JUST ANY HUMAN...

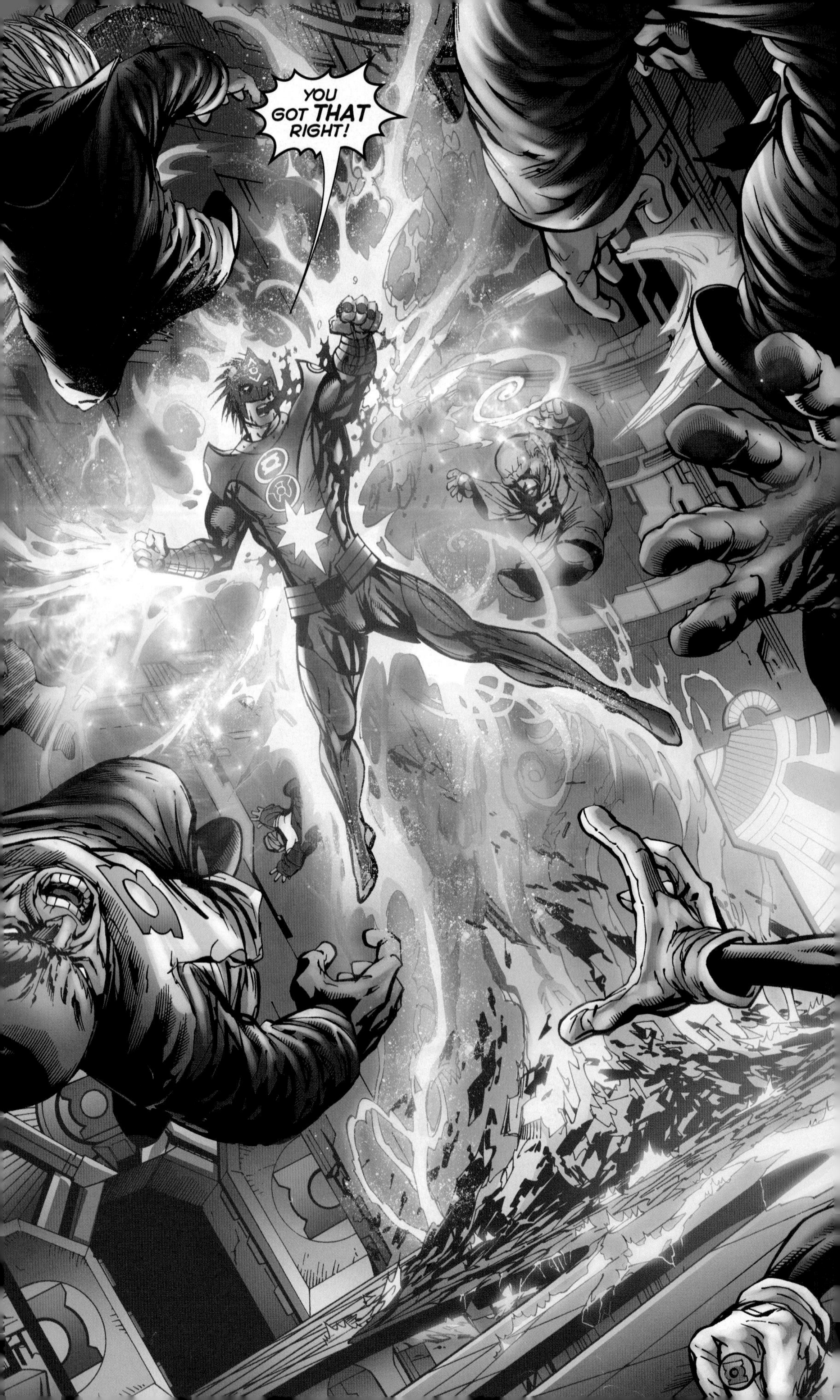
YOU GOT THAT RIGHT!

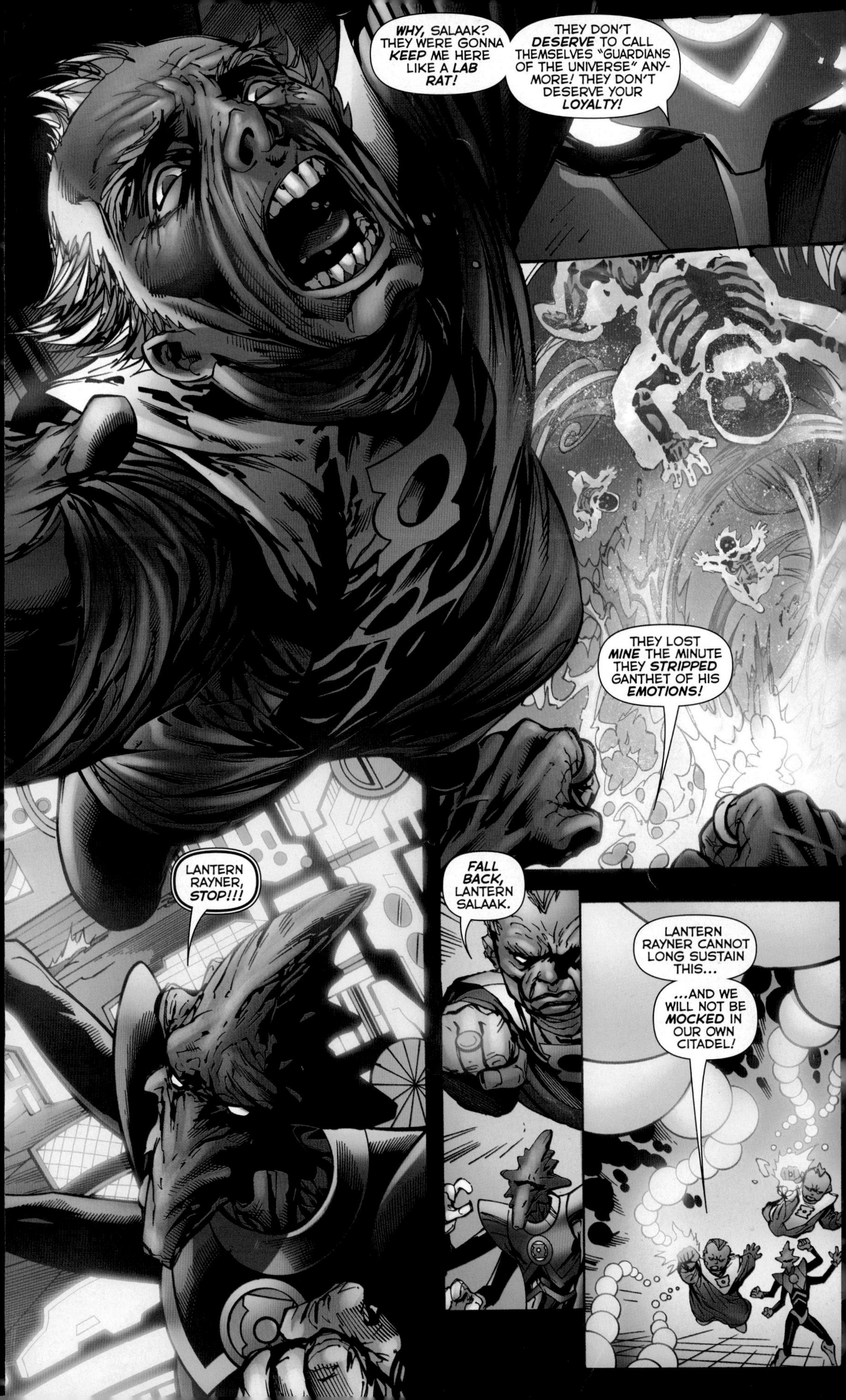
WHY, SALAAK? THEY WERE GONNA KEEP ME HERE LIKE A LAB RAT!
THEY DON'T DESERVE TO CALL THEMSELVES "GUARDIANS OF THE UNIVERSE" ANY-MORE! THEY DON'T DESERVE YOUR LOYALTY!
THEY LOST MINE THE MINUTE THEY STRIPPED GANTHET OF HIS EMOTIONS!
LANTERN RAYNER, STOP!!!
FALL BACK, LANTERN SALAAK.
LANTERN RAYNER CANNOT LONG SUSTAIN THIS...
...AND WE WILL NOT BE MOCKED IN OUR OWN CITADEL!

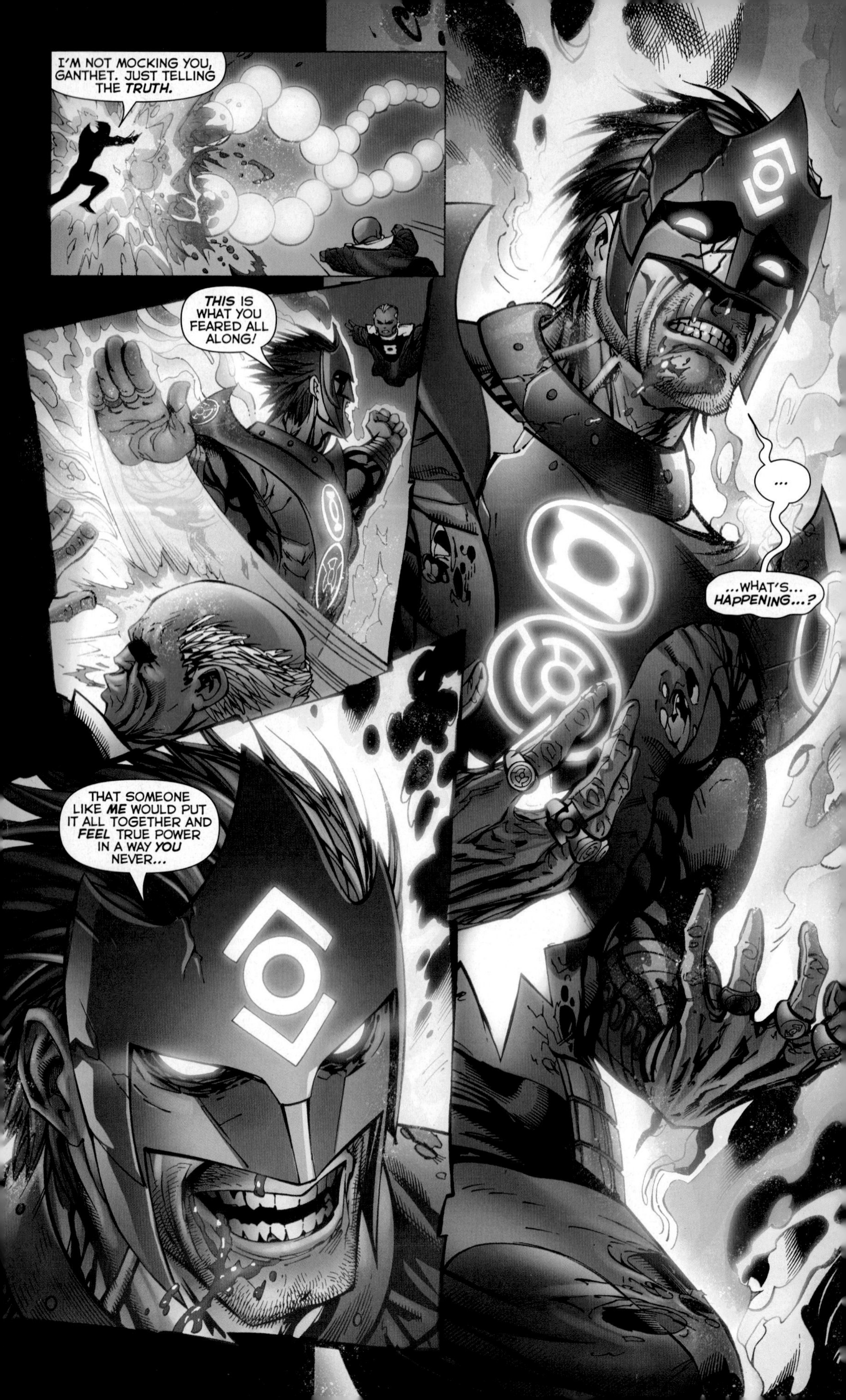
I'M NOT MOCKING YOU, GANTHET. JUST TELLING THE *TRUTH.*
THIS IS WHAT YOU FEARED ALL ALONG!
THAT SOMEONE LIKE *ME* WOULD PUT IT ALL TOGETHER AND *FEEL* TRUE POWER IN A WAY *YOU* NEVER...
...
...WHAT'S... *HAPPENING*...?

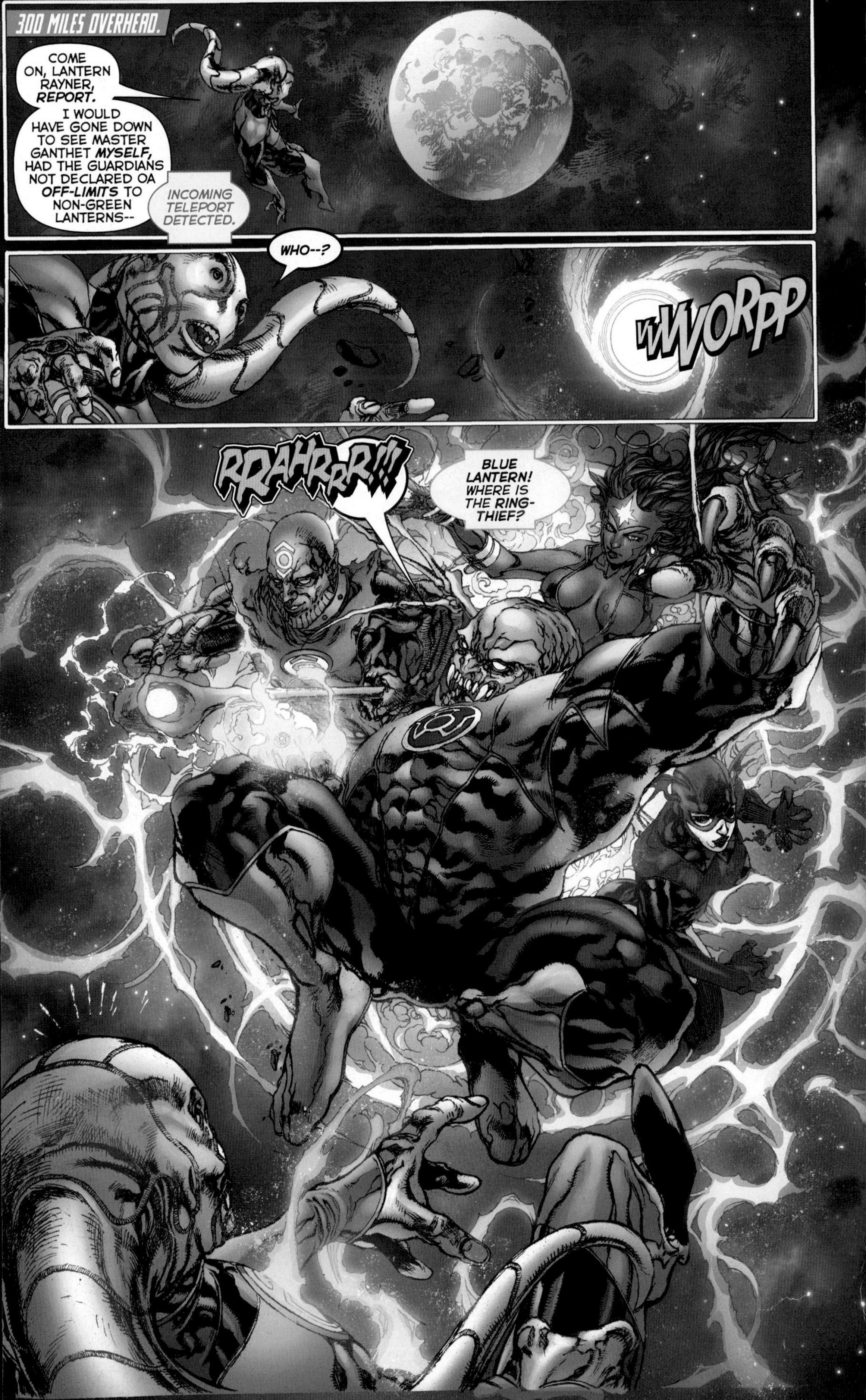

300 MILES OVERHEAD.
COME ON, LANTERN RAYNER, REPORT.
I WOULD HAVE GONE DOWN TO SEE MASTER GANTHET MYSELF, HAD THE GUARDIANS NOT DECLARED OA OFF-LIMITS TO NON-GREEN LANTERNS--
INCOMING TELEPORT DETECTED.
WHO--?
VVVVORPP
RRAHRRR!!!
BLUE LANTERN! WHERE IS THE RING-THIEF?

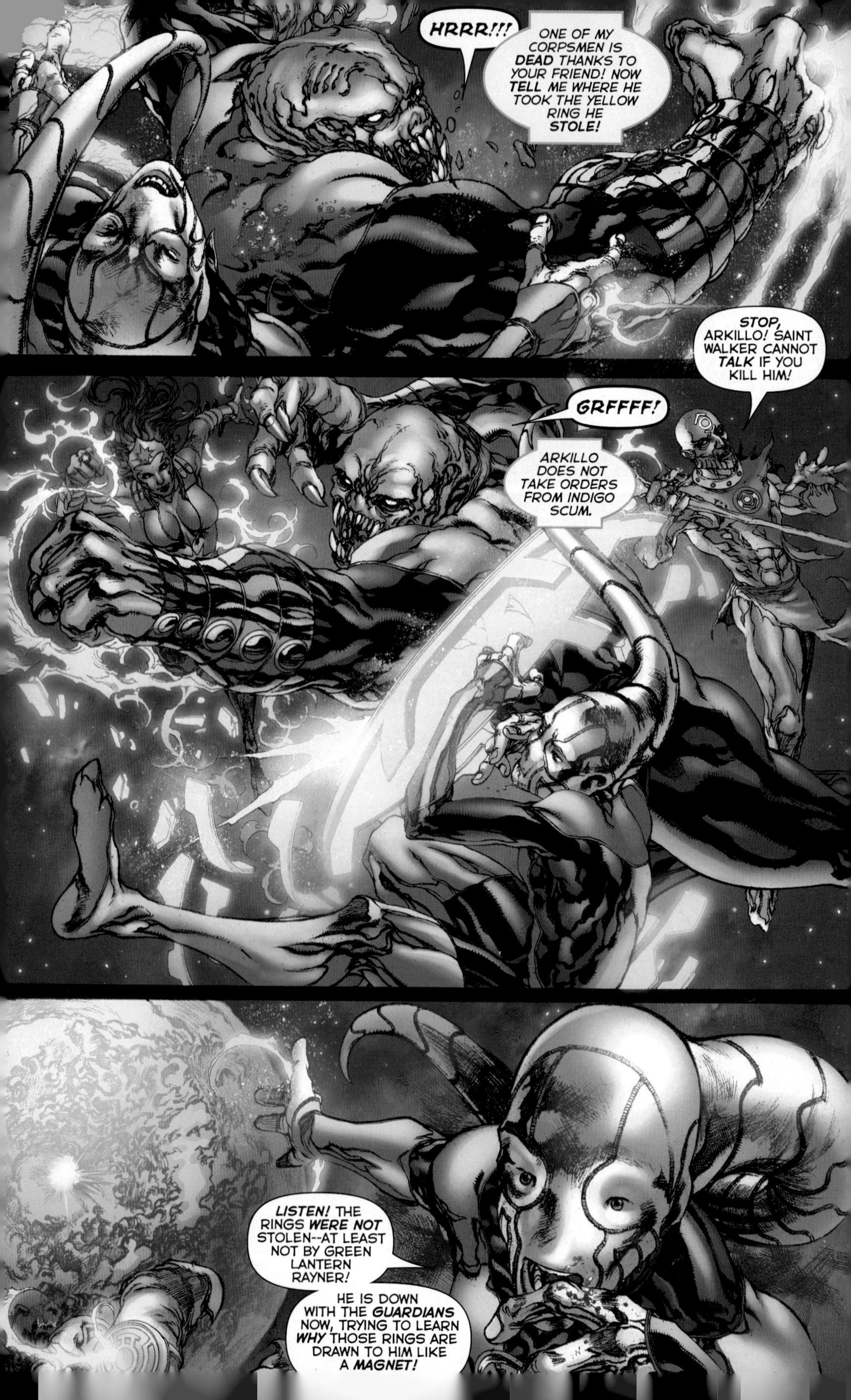
HRRR!!!
ONE OF MY CORPSMEN IS DEAD THANKS TO YOUR FRIEND! NOW TELL ME WHERE HE TOOK THE YELLOW RING HE STOLE!
STOP, ARKILLO! SAINT WALKER CANNOT TALK IF YOU KILL HIM!
GRFFFF!
ARKILLO DOES NOT TAKE ORDERS FROM INDIGO SCUM.
LISTEN! THE RINGS WERE NOT STOLEN--AT LEAST NOT BY GREEN LANTERN RAYNER!
HE IS DOWN WITH THE GUARDIANS NOW, TRYING TO LEARN WHY THOSE RINGS ARE DRAWN TO HIM LIKE A MAGNET!

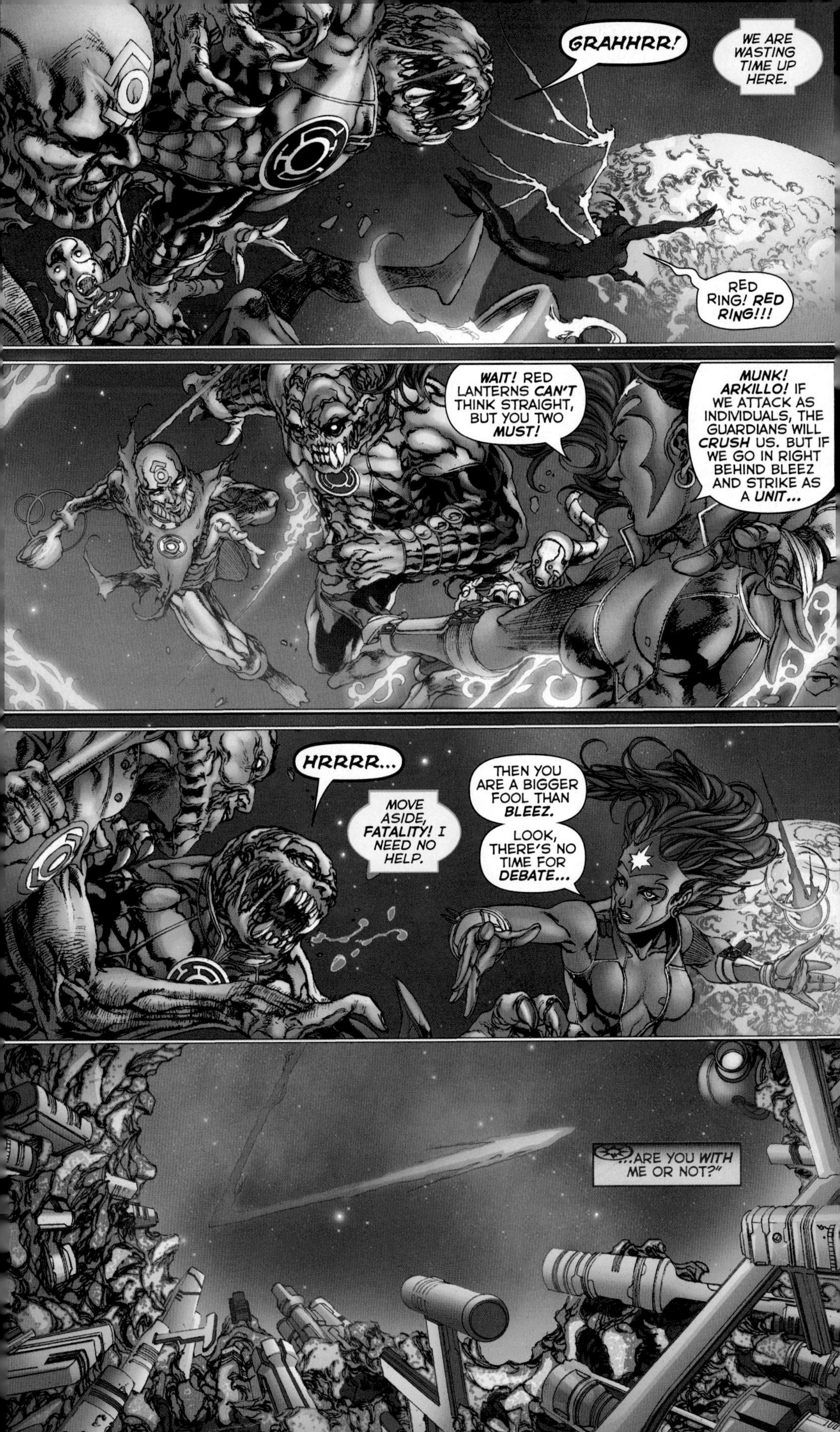
GRAHHRR!
WE ARE WASTING TIME UP HERE.
RED RING! RED RING!!!
WAIT! RED LANTERNS CAN'T THINK STRAIGHT, BUT YOU TWO MUST!
MUNK! ARKILLO! IF WE ATTACK AS INDIVIDUALS, THE GUARDIANS WILL CRUSH US. BUT IF WE GO IN RIGHT BEHIND BLEEZ AND STRIKE AS A UNIT...
HRRRR...
MOVE ASIDE, FATALITY! I NEED NO HELP.
THEN YOU ARE A BIGGER FOOL THAN BLEEZ.
LOOK, THERE'S NO TIME FOR DEBATE...
"...ARE YOU WITH ME OR NOT?"

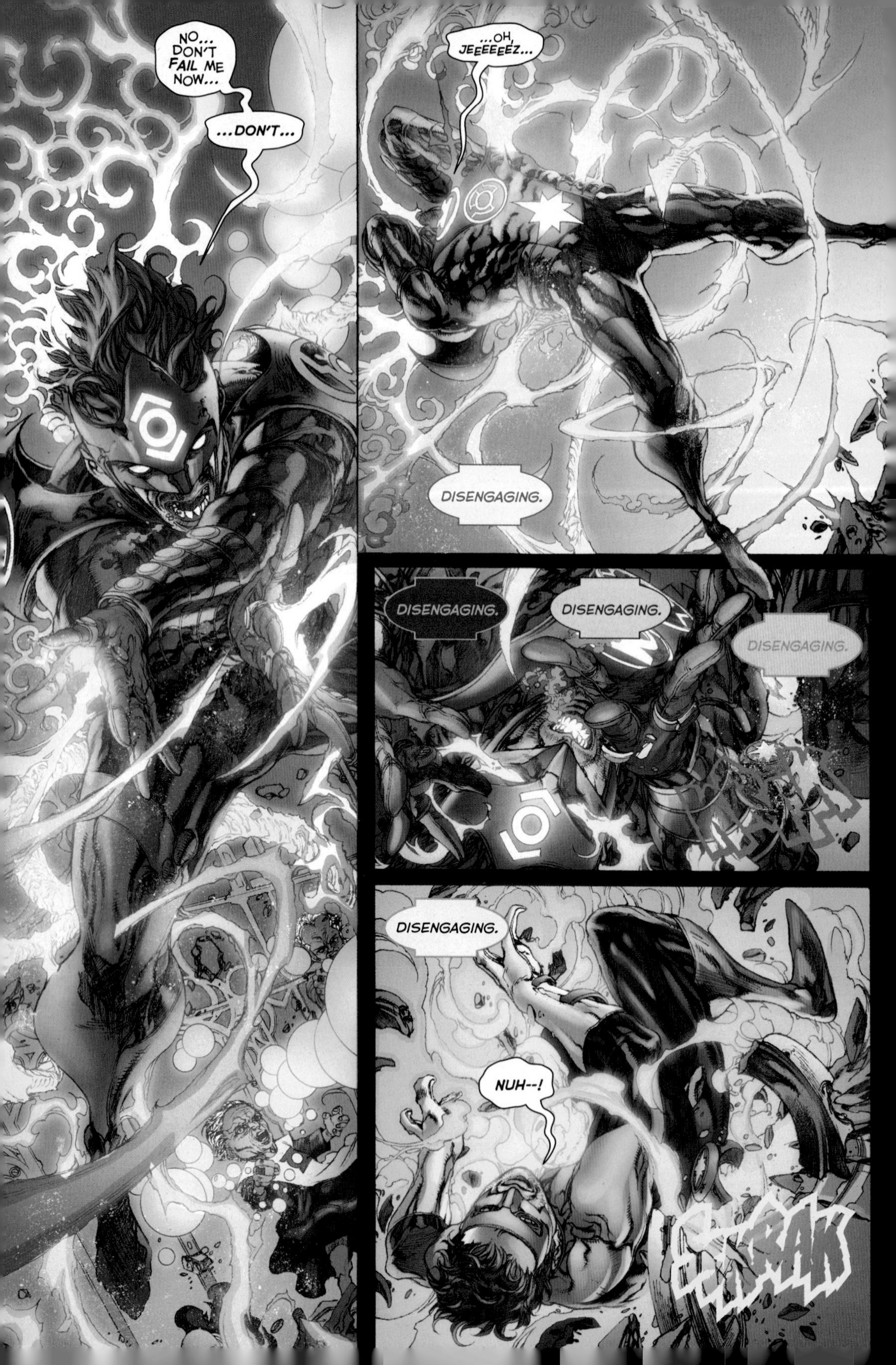
NO... DON'T FAIL ME NOW...
...DON'T...
...OH, JEEEEEEZ...
DISENGAGING.
DISENGAGING.
DISENGAGING.
DISENGAGING.
DISENGAGING.
NUH--!

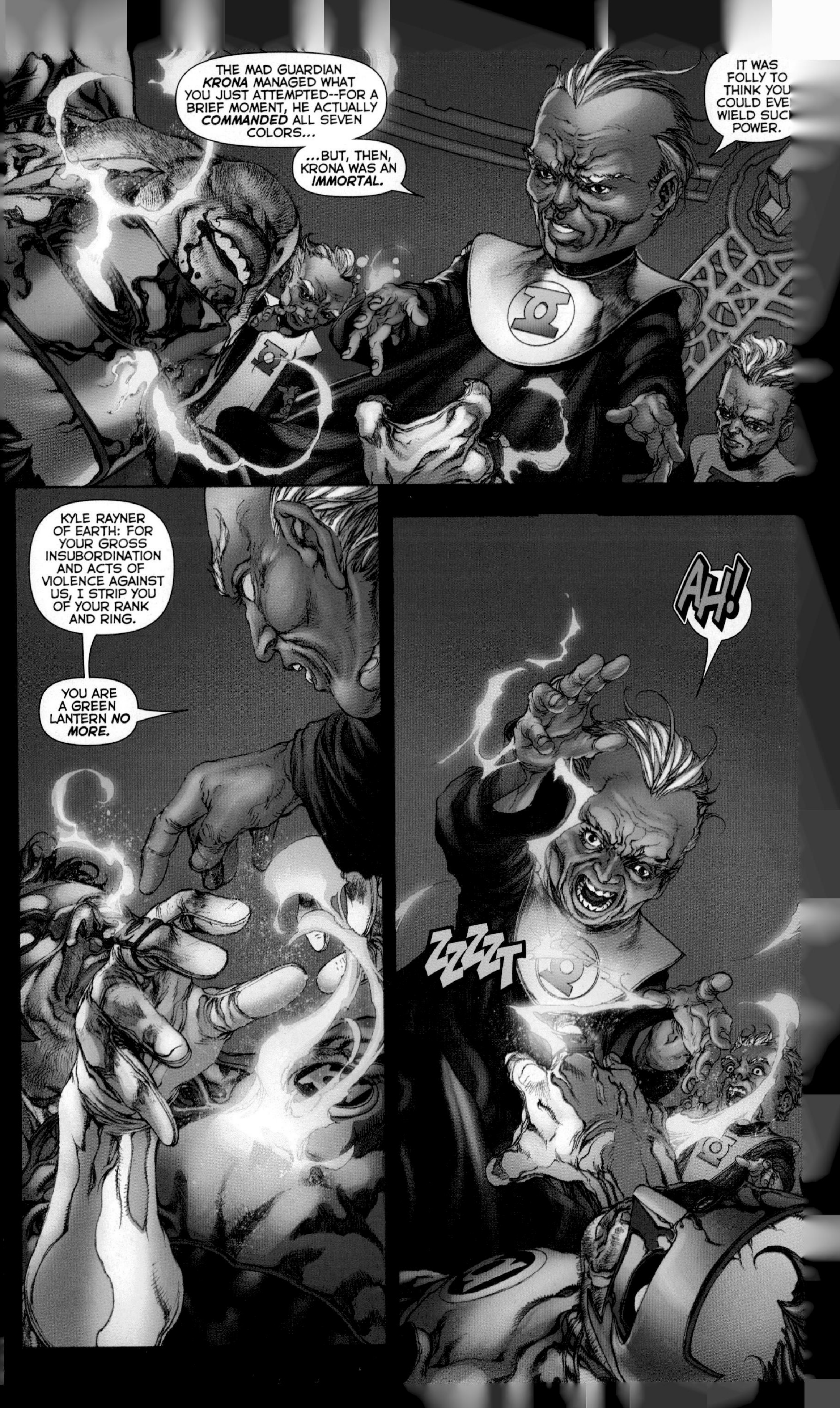
THE MAD GUARDIAN KRONA MANAGED WHAT YOU JUST ATTEMPTED--FOR A BRIEF MOMENT, HE ACTUALLY COMMANDED ALL SEVEN COLORS...
...BUT, THEN, KRONA WAS AN IMMORTAL.
IT WAS FOLLY TO THINK YOU COULD EVE WIELD SUC POWER.
KYLE RAYNER OF EARTH: FOR YOUR GROSS INSUBORDINATION AND ACTS OF VIOLENCE AGAINST US, I STRIP YOU OF YOUR RANK AND RING.
YOU ARE A GREEN LANTERN NO MORE.
AH!
ZZZZZT

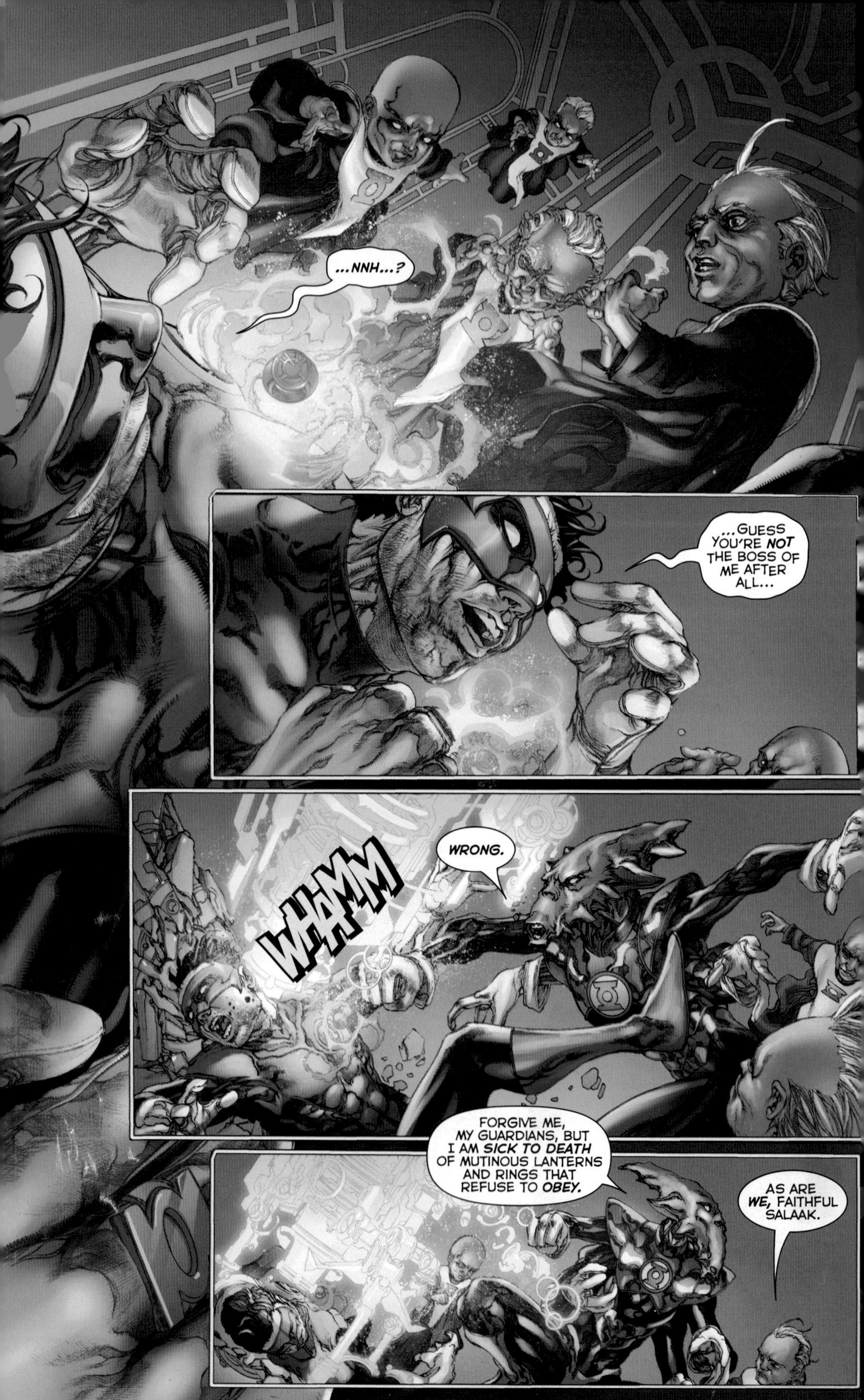
...NNH...?
...GUESS YOU'RE NOT THE BOSS OF ME AFTER ALL...
WRONG.
WHAMM
FORGIVE ME, MY GUARDIANS, BUT I AM SICK TO DEATH OF MUTINOUS LANTERNS AND RINGS THAT REFUSE TO OBEY.
AS ARE WE, FAITHFUL SALAAK.

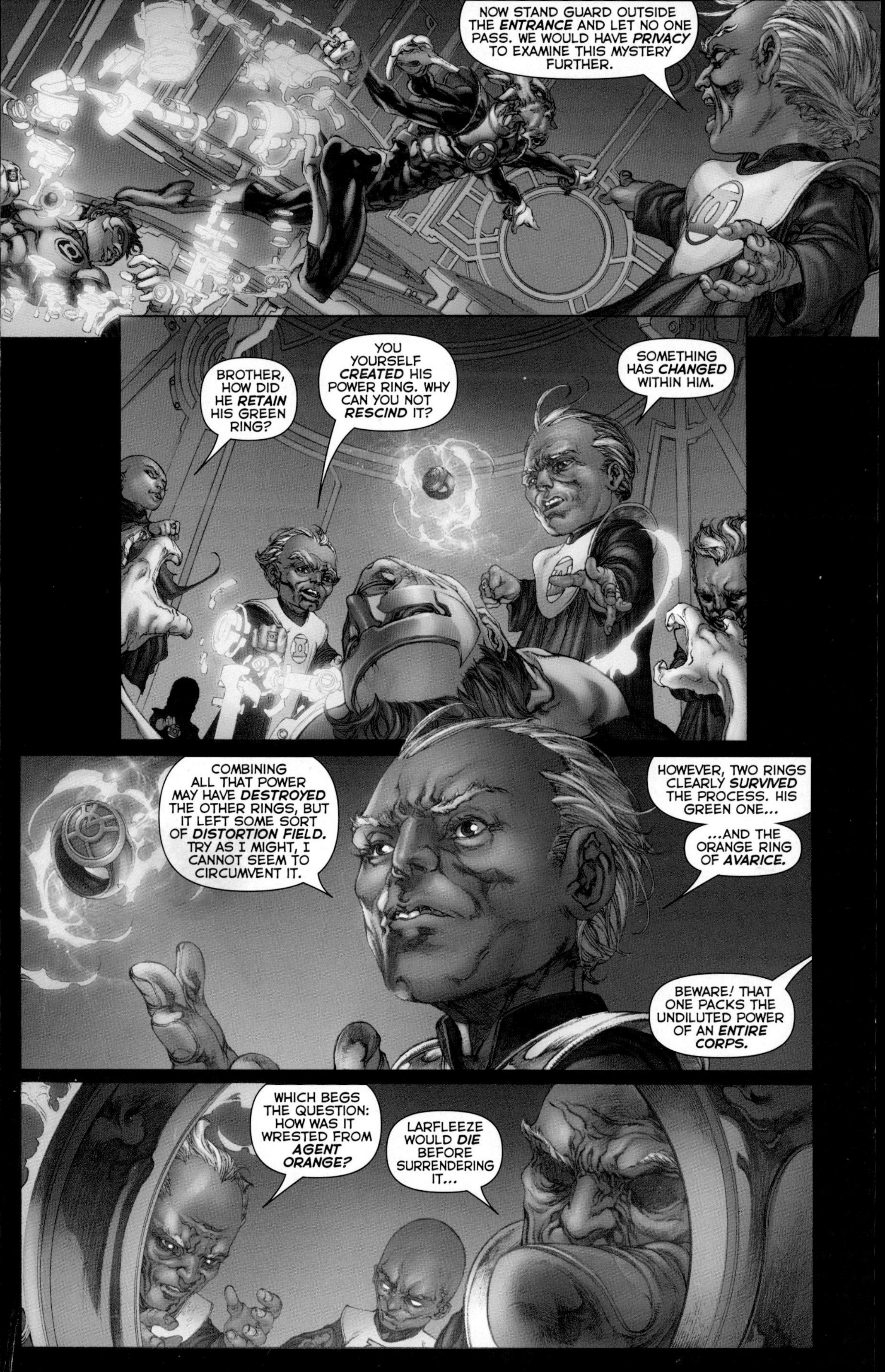
NOW STAND GUARD OUTSIDE THE ENTRANCE AND LET NO ONE PASS. WE WOULD HAVE PRIVACY TO EXAMINE THIS MYSTERY FURTHER.
BROTHER, HOW DID HE RETAIN HIS GREEN RING?
YOU YOURSELF CREATED HIS POWER RING. WHY CAN YOU NOT RESCIND IT?
SOMETHING HAS CHANGED WITHIN HIM.
COMBINING ALL THAT POWER MAY HAVE DESTROYED THE OTHER RINGS, BUT IT LEFT SOME SORT OF DISTORTION FIELD. TRY AS I MIGHT, I CANNOT SEEM TO CIRCUMVENT IT.
HOWEVER, TWO RINGS CLEARLY SURVIVED THE PROCESS. HIS GREEN ONE...
...AND THE ORANGE RING OF AVARICE.
BEWARE! THAT ONE PACKS THE UNDILUTED POWER OF AN ENTIRE CORPS.
WHICH BEGS THE QUESTION: HOW WAS IT WRESTED FROM AGENT ORANGE?
LARFLEEZE WOULD DIE BEFORE SURRENDERING IT...

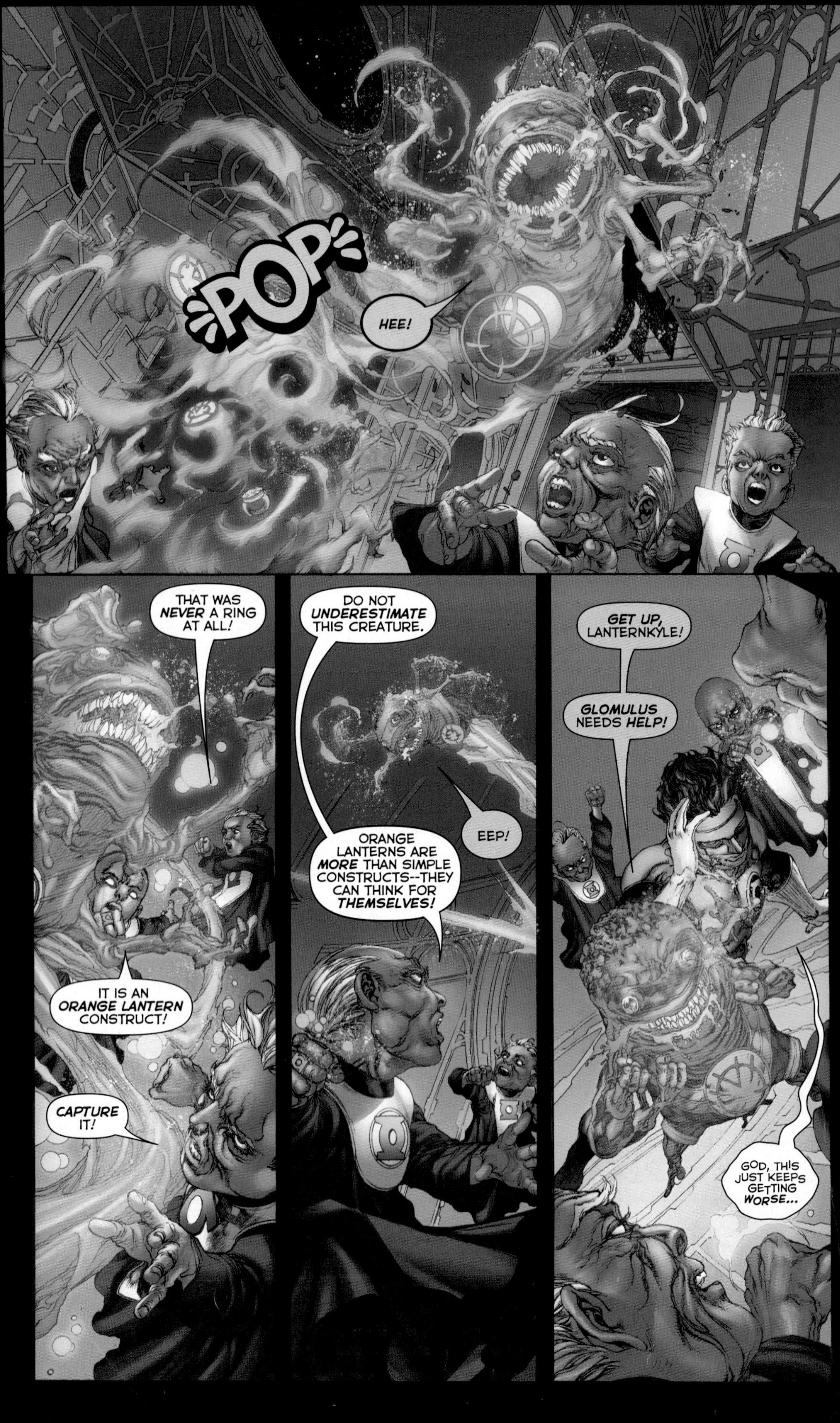
POP
HEE!
THAT WAS NEVER A RING AT ALL!
IT IS AN ORANGE LANTERN CONSTRUCT!
CAPTURE IT!
DO NOT UNDERESTIMATE THIS CREATURE.
EEP!
ORANGE LANTERNS ARE MORE THAN SIMPLE CONSTRUCTS--THEY CAN THINK FOR THEMSELVES!
GET UP, LANTERNKYLE!
GLOMULUS NEEDS HELP!
GOD, THIS JUST KEEPS GETTING WORSE...

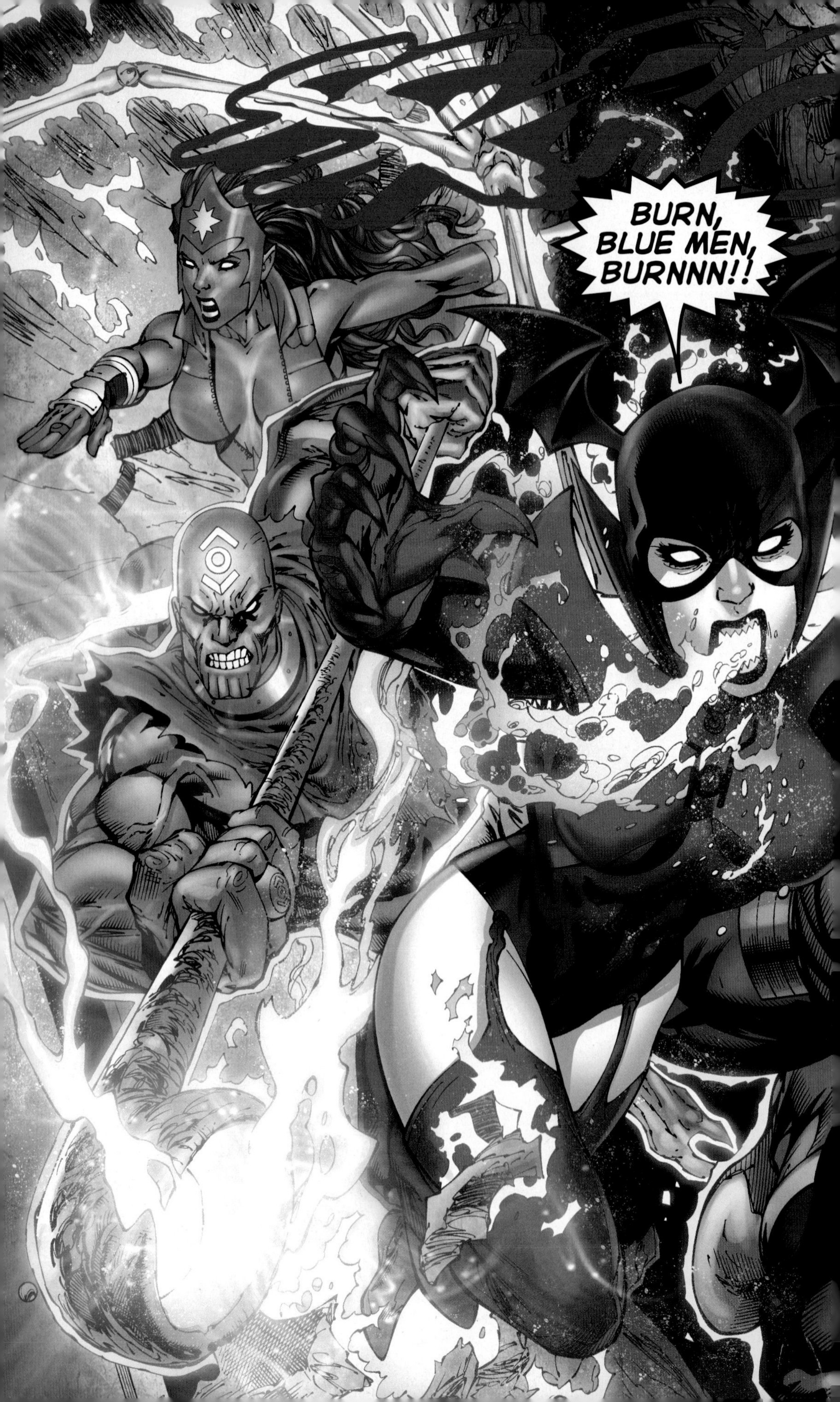
BURN, BLUE MEN, BURNNN!!

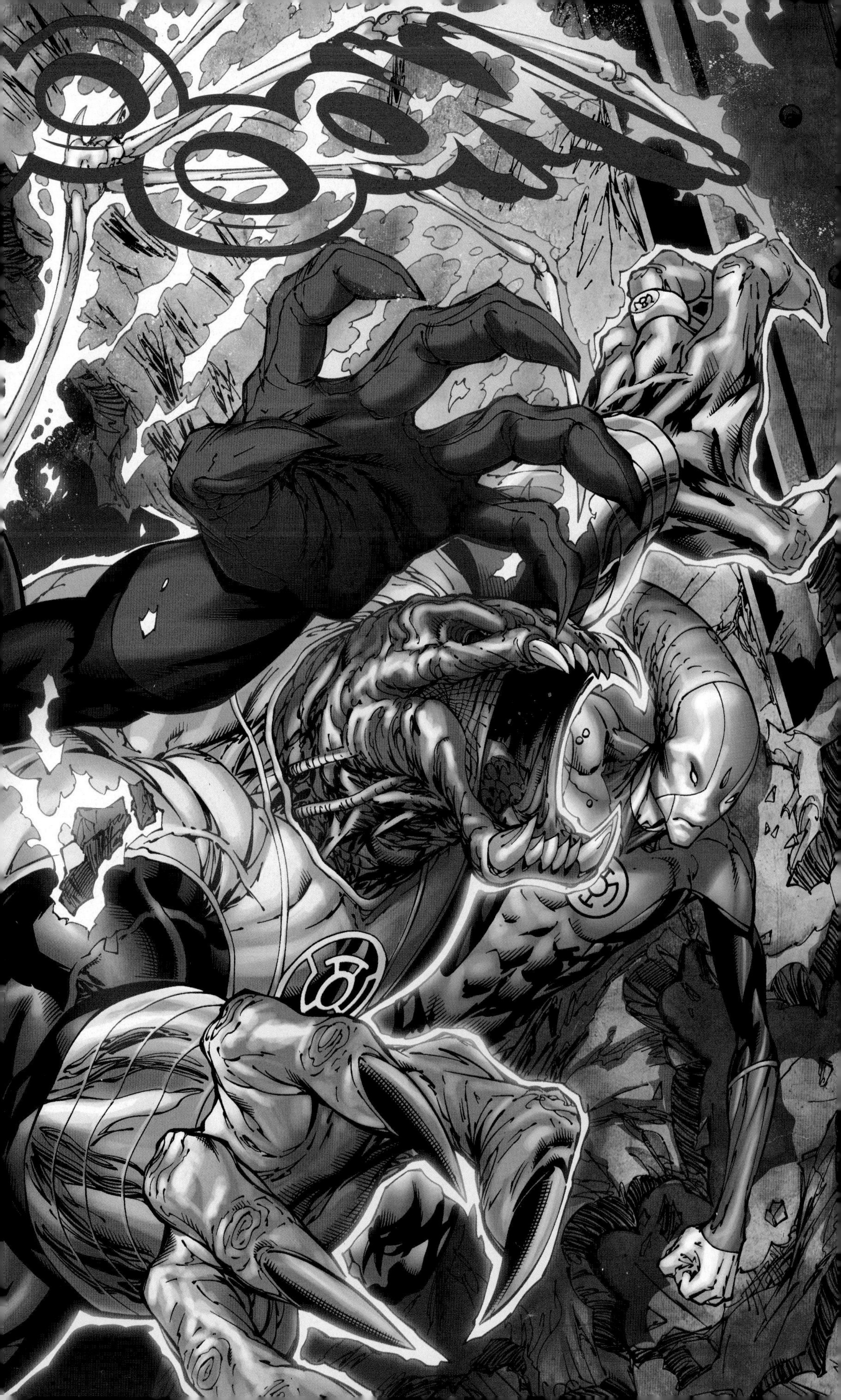

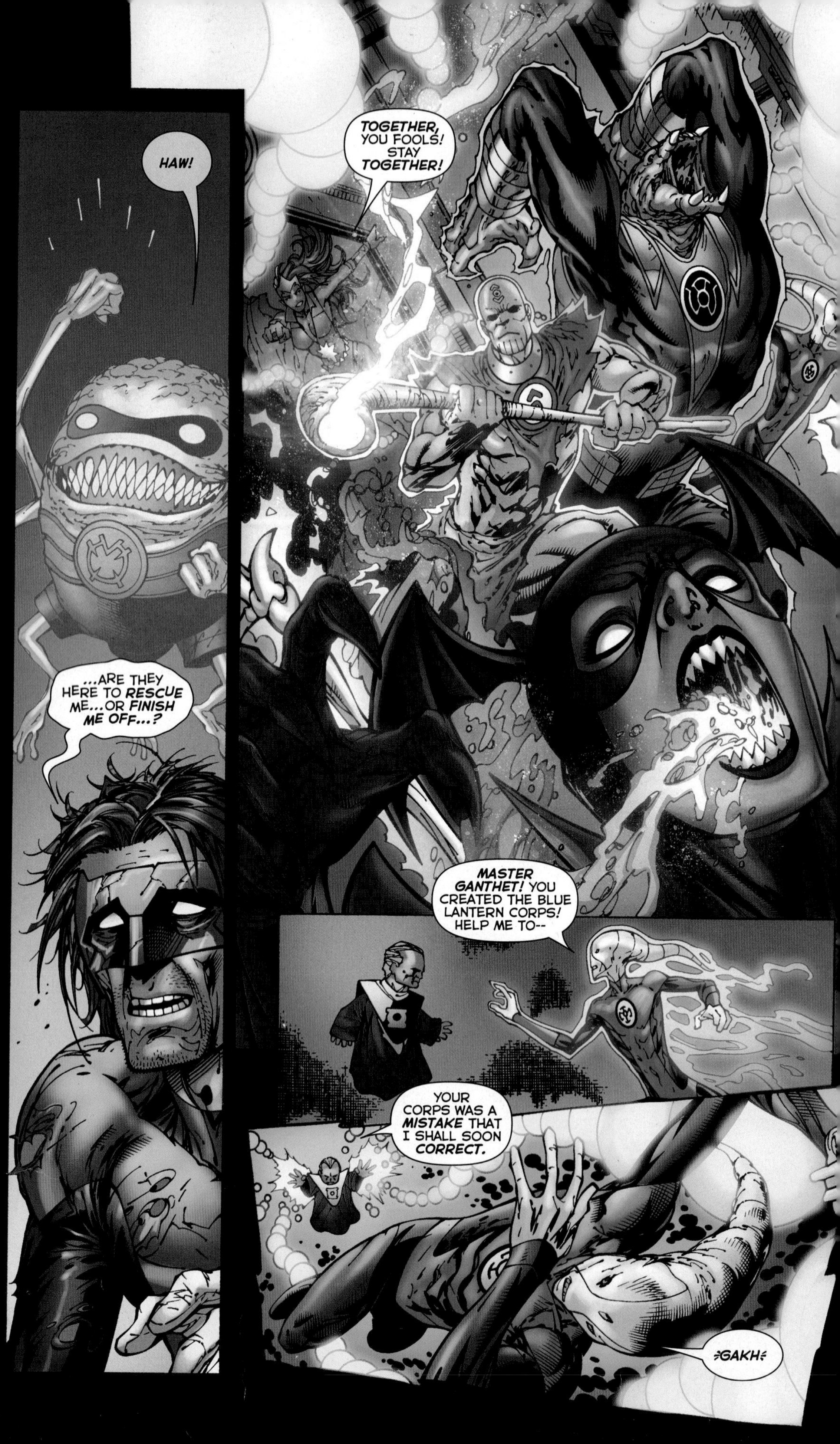
HAW!
TOGETHER, YOU FOOLS! STAY TOGETHER!
...ARE THEY HERE TO RESCUE ME...OR FINISH ME OFF...?
MASTER GANTHET! YOU CREATED THE BLUE LANTERN CORPS! HELP ME TO--
YOUR CORPS WAS A MISTAKE THAT I SHALL SOON CORRECT.
GAKH

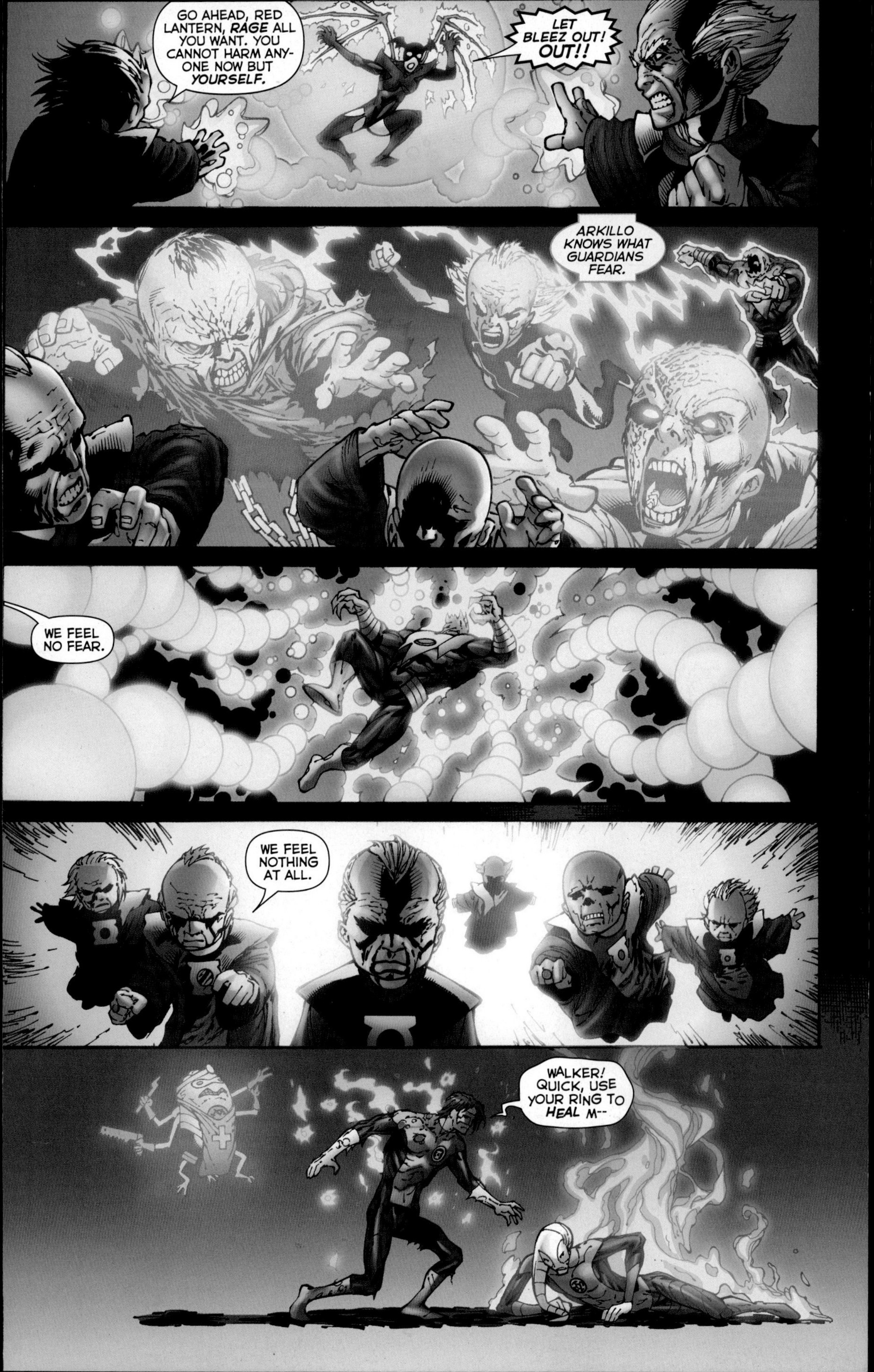
GO AHEAD, RED LANTERN, RAGE ALL YOU WANT. YOU CANNOT HARM ANY-ONE NOW BUT YOURSELF.
LET BLEEZ OUT! OUT!!--
ARKILLO KNOWS WHAT GUARDIANS FEAR.
WE FEEL NO FEAR.
WE FEEL NOTHING AT ALL.
WALKER! QUICK, USE YOUR RING TO HEAL M--

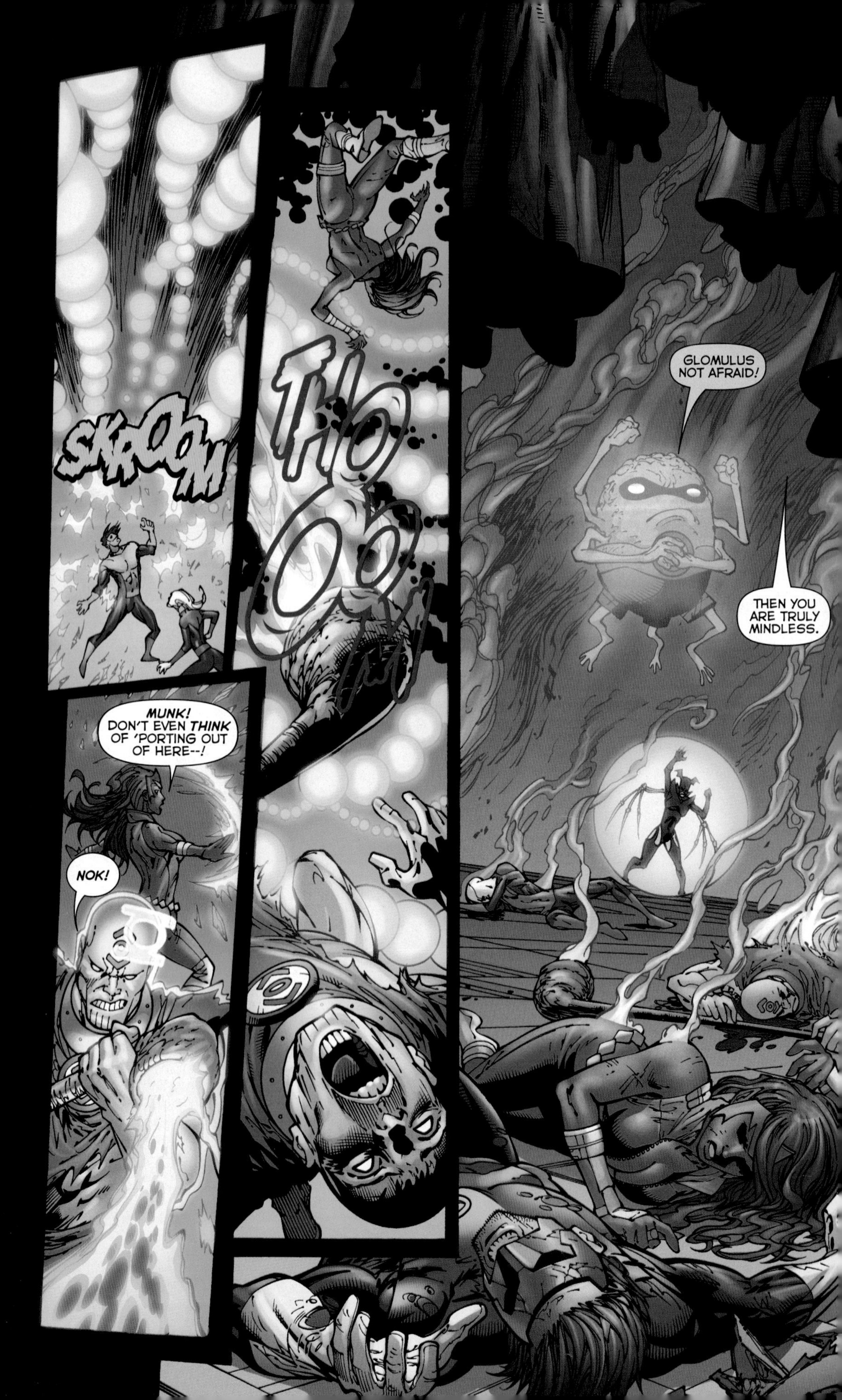
SKROOM
MUNK! DON'T EVEN THINK OF 'PORTING OUT OF HERE--!
NOK!
GLOMULUS NOT AFRAID!
THEN YOU ARE TRULY MINDLESS.

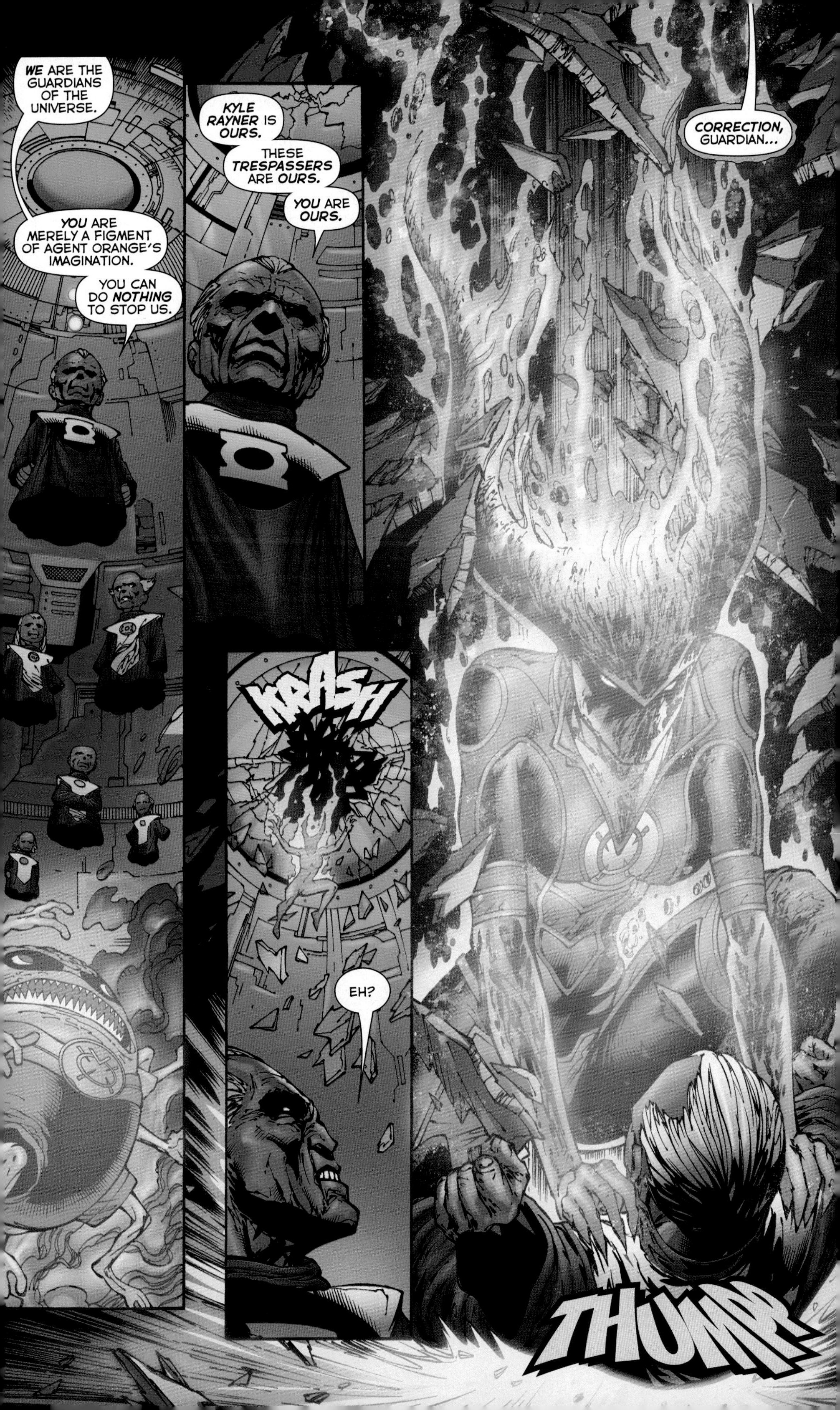

WE ARE THE GUARDIANS OF THE UNIVERSE.
YOU ARE MERELY A FIGMENT OF AGENT ORANGE'S IMAGINATION.
YOU CAN DO NOTHING TO STOP US.
KYLE RAYNER IS OURS.
THESE TRESPASSERS ARE OURS.
YOU ARE OURS.
KRASH
EH?
CORRECTION, GUARDIAN...
THUMP

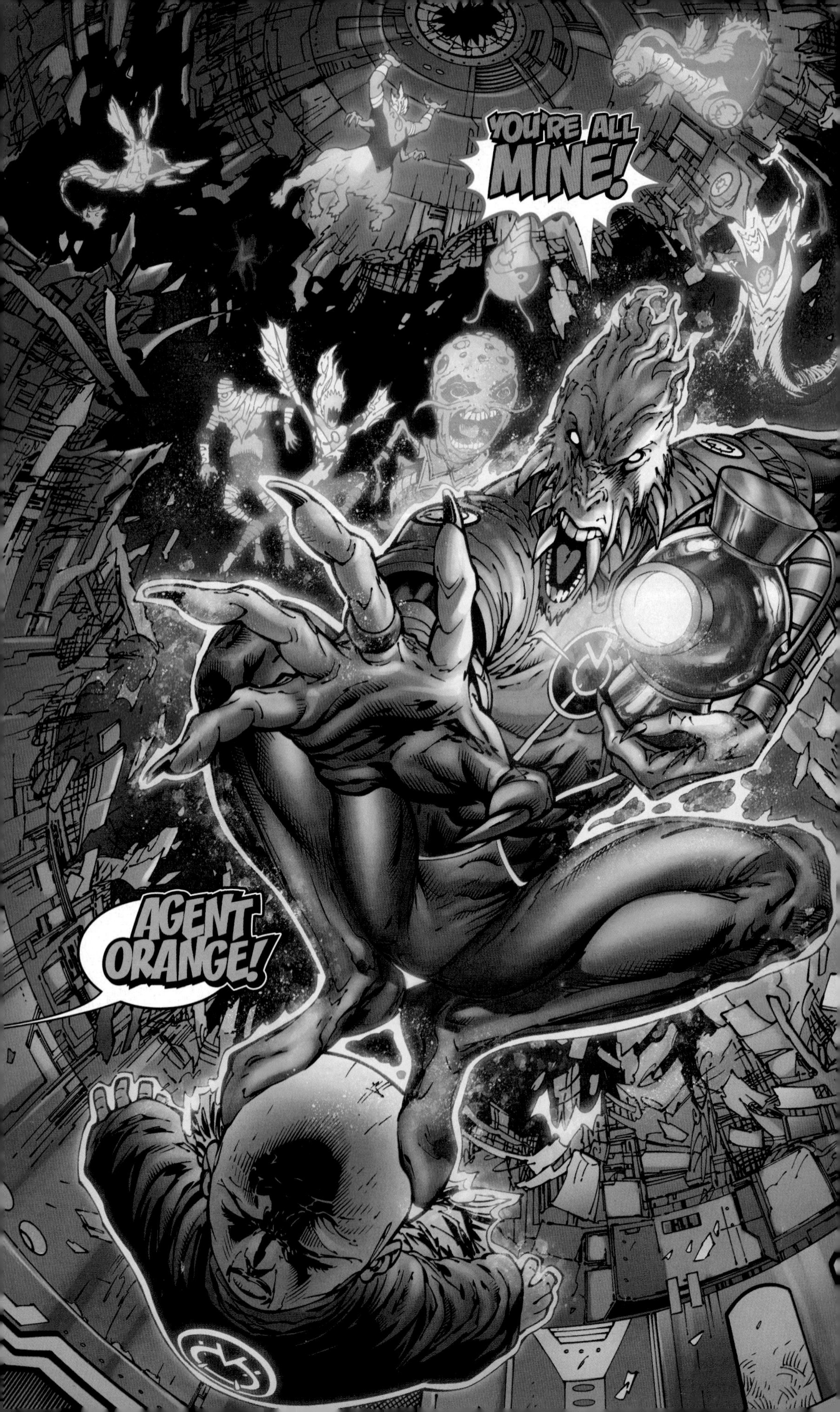
YOU'RE ALL MINE!
AGENT ORANGE!

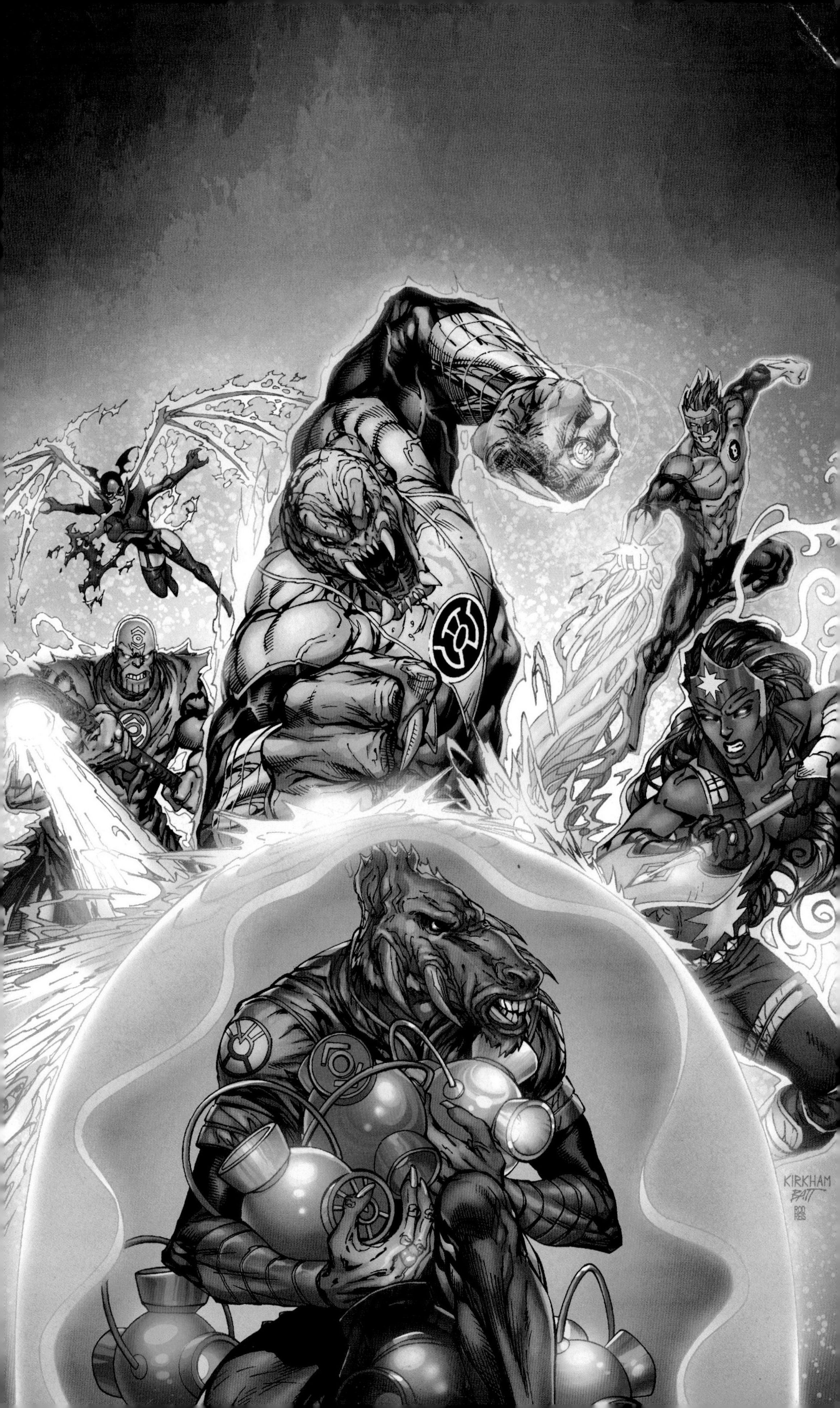
KIRKHAM
BATT
ROD REIS

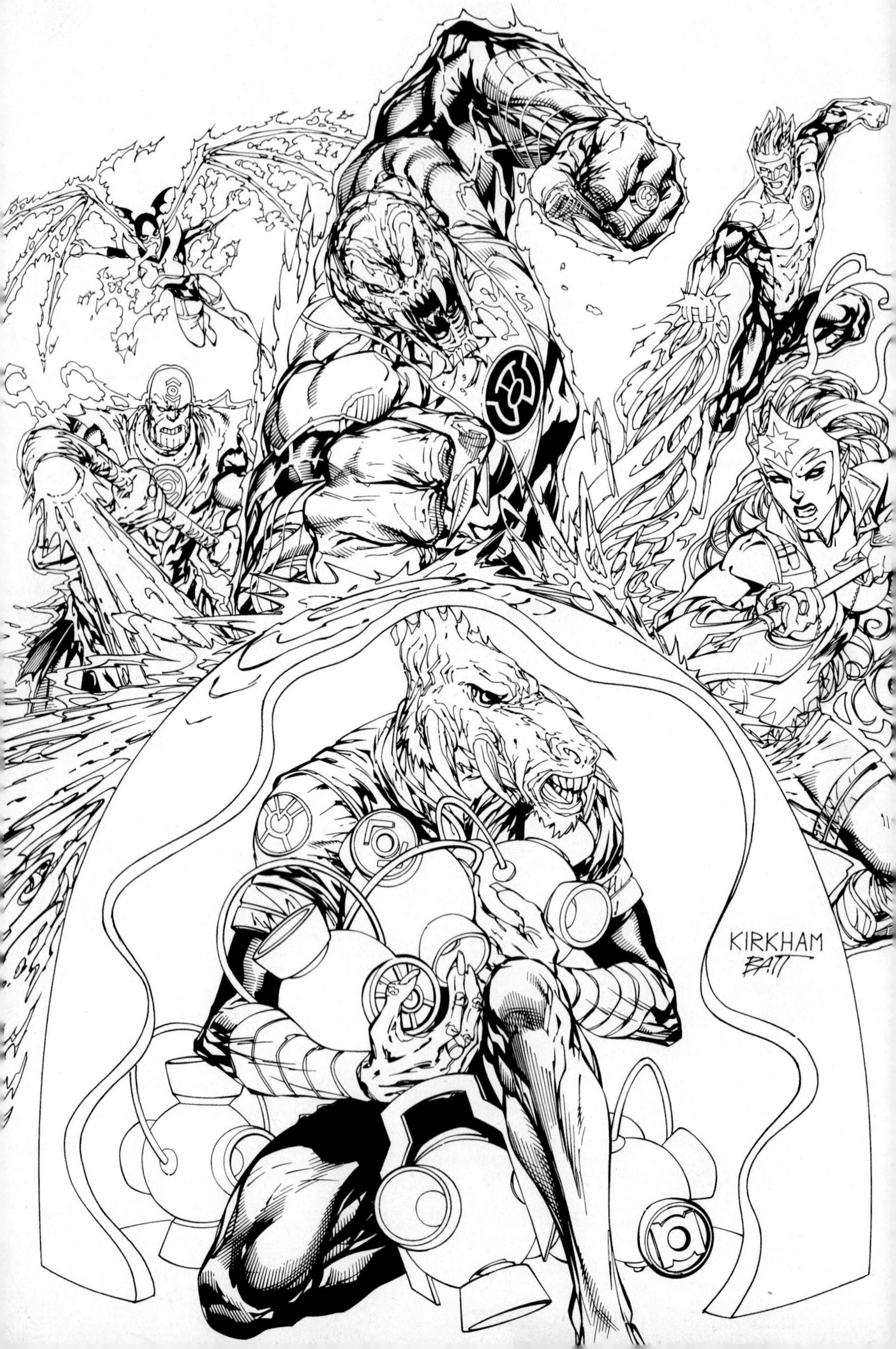
KIRKHAM
BATT

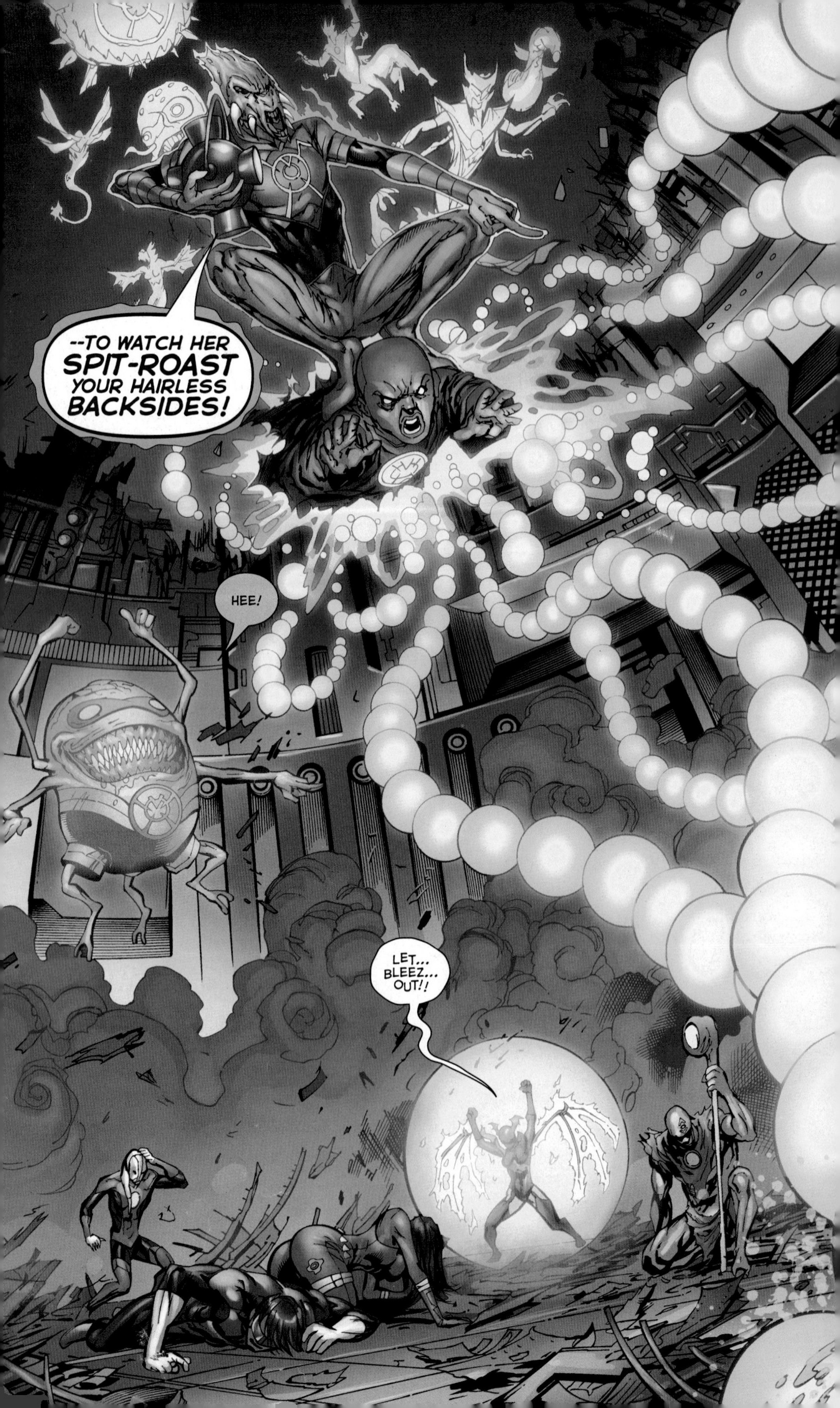
--TO WATCH HER SPIT-ROAST YOUR HAIRLESS BACKSIDES!
HEE!
LET... BLEEZ... OUT!!

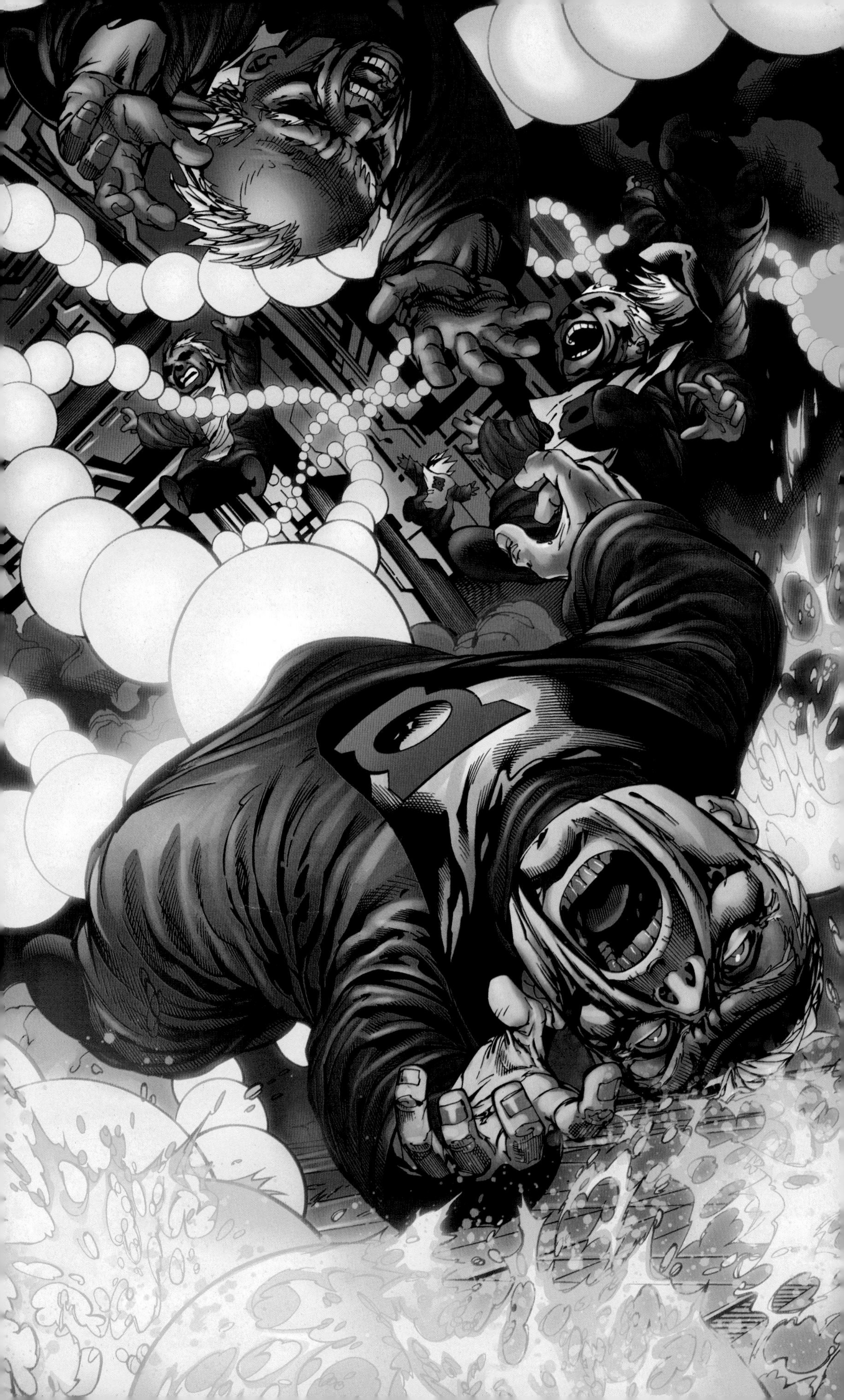

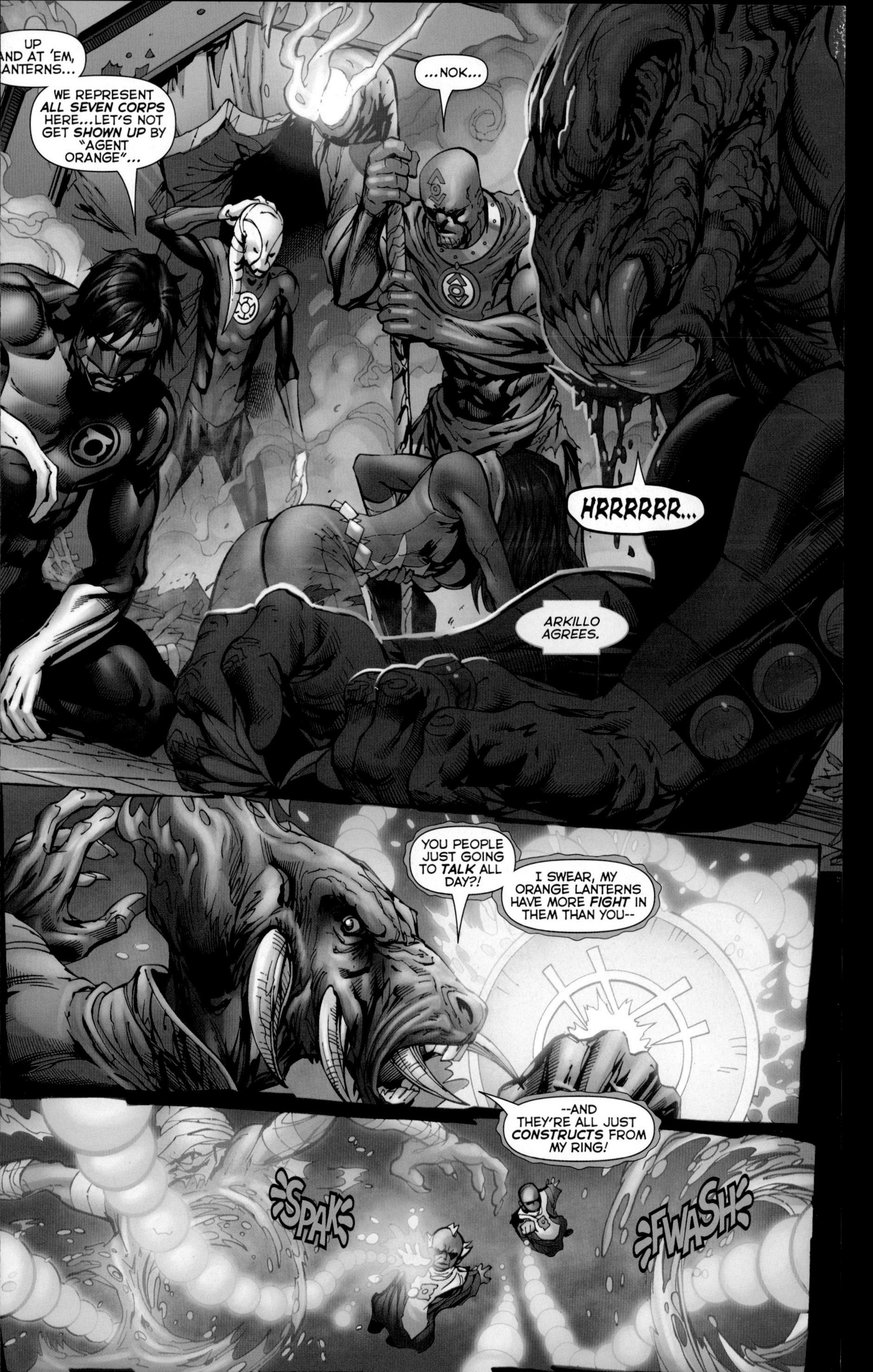
UP AND AT 'EM, LANTERNS...
WE REPRESENT ALL SEVEN CORPS HERE...LET'S NOT GET SHOWN UP BY "AGENT ORANGE"...
...NOK...
HRRRRRR...
ARKILLO AGREES.
YOU PEOPLE JUST GOING TO TALK ALL DAY?!
I SWEAR, MY ORANGE LANTERNS HAVE MORE FIGHT IN THEM THAN YOU--
--AND THEY'RE ALL JUST CONSTRUCTS FROM MY RING!
SPAK
FWASH

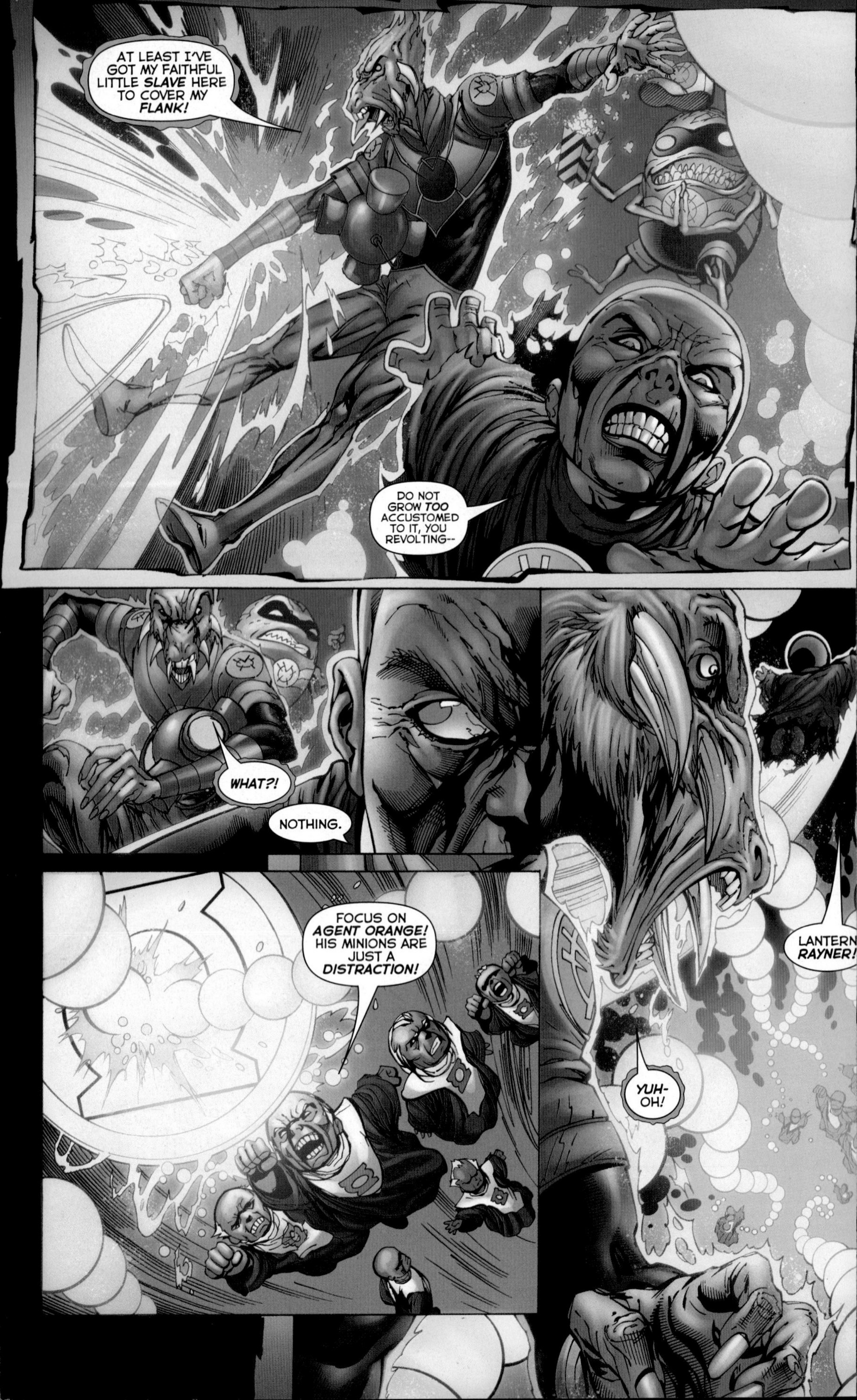
AT LEAST I'VE GOT MY FAITHFUL LITTLE **SLAVE** HERE TO COVER MY ***FLANK!***
DO NOT GROW ***TOO*** ACCUSTOMED TO IT, YOU REVOLTING--
WHAT?!
NOTHING.
LANTERN ***RAYNER!***
FOCUS ON ***AGENT ORANGE!*** HIS MINIONS ARE JUST A ***DISTRACTION!***
YUH-OH!

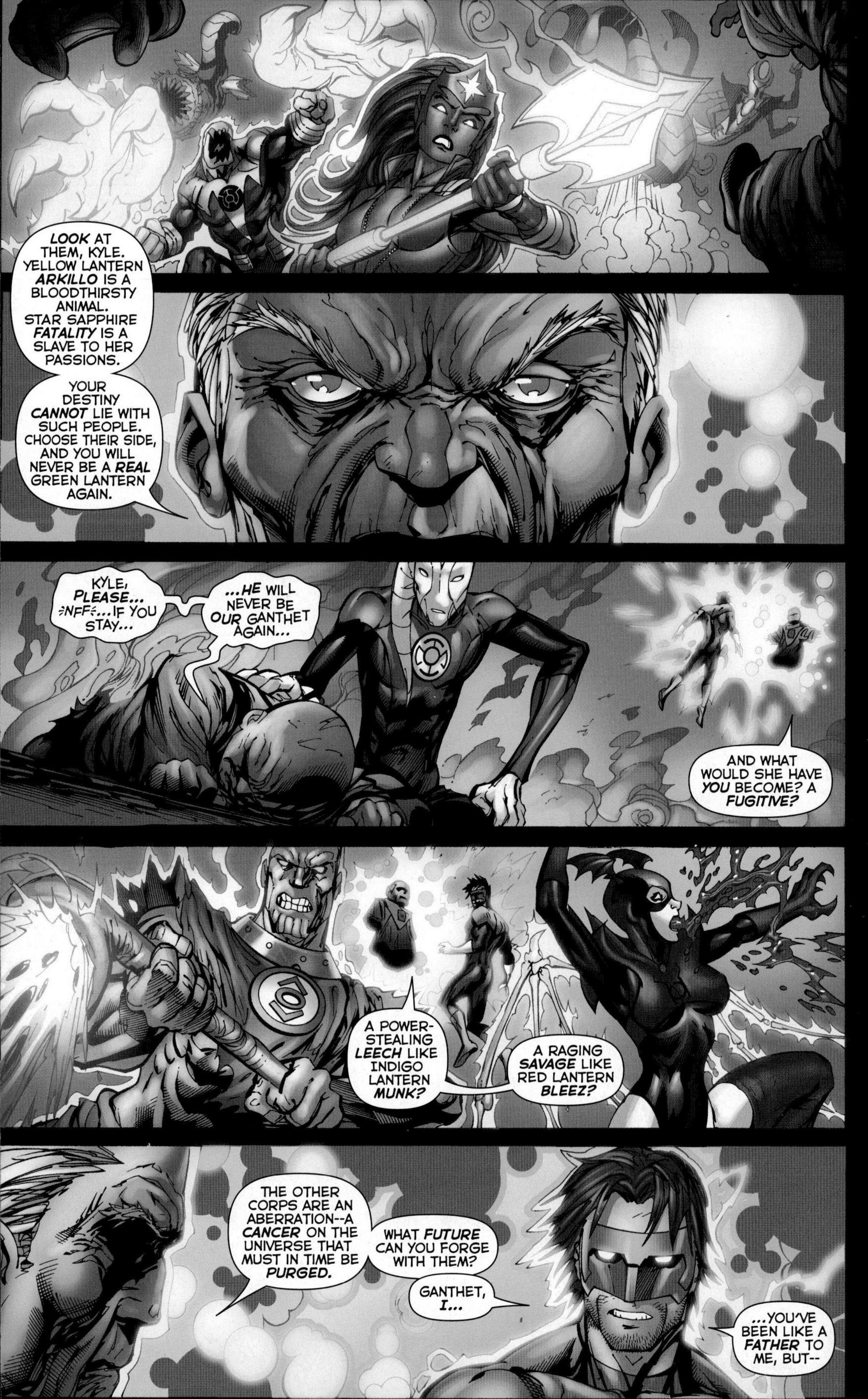
LOOK AT THEM, KYLE. YELLOW LANTERN ARKILLO IS A BLOODTHIRSTY ANIMAL. STAR SAPPHIRE FATALITY IS A SLAVE TO HER PASSIONS.
YOUR DESTINY CANNOT LIE WITH SUCH PEOPLE. CHOOSE THEIR SIDE, AND YOU WILL NEVER BE A REAL GREEN LANTERN AGAIN.
KYLE, PLEASE... NFF...IF YOU STAY...
...HE WILL NEVER BE OUR GANTHET AGAIN...
AND WHAT WOULD SHE HAVE YOU BECOME? A FUGITIVE?
A POWER-STEALING LEECH LIKE INDIGO LANTERN MUNK?
A RAGING SAVAGE LIKE RED LANTERN BLEEZ?
THE OTHER CORPS ARE AN ABERRATION--A CANCER ON THE UNIVERSE THAT MUST IN TIME BE PURGED.
WHAT FUTURE CAN YOU FORGE WITH THEM?
GANTHET, I...
...YOU'VE BEEN LIKE A FATHER TO ME, BUT--

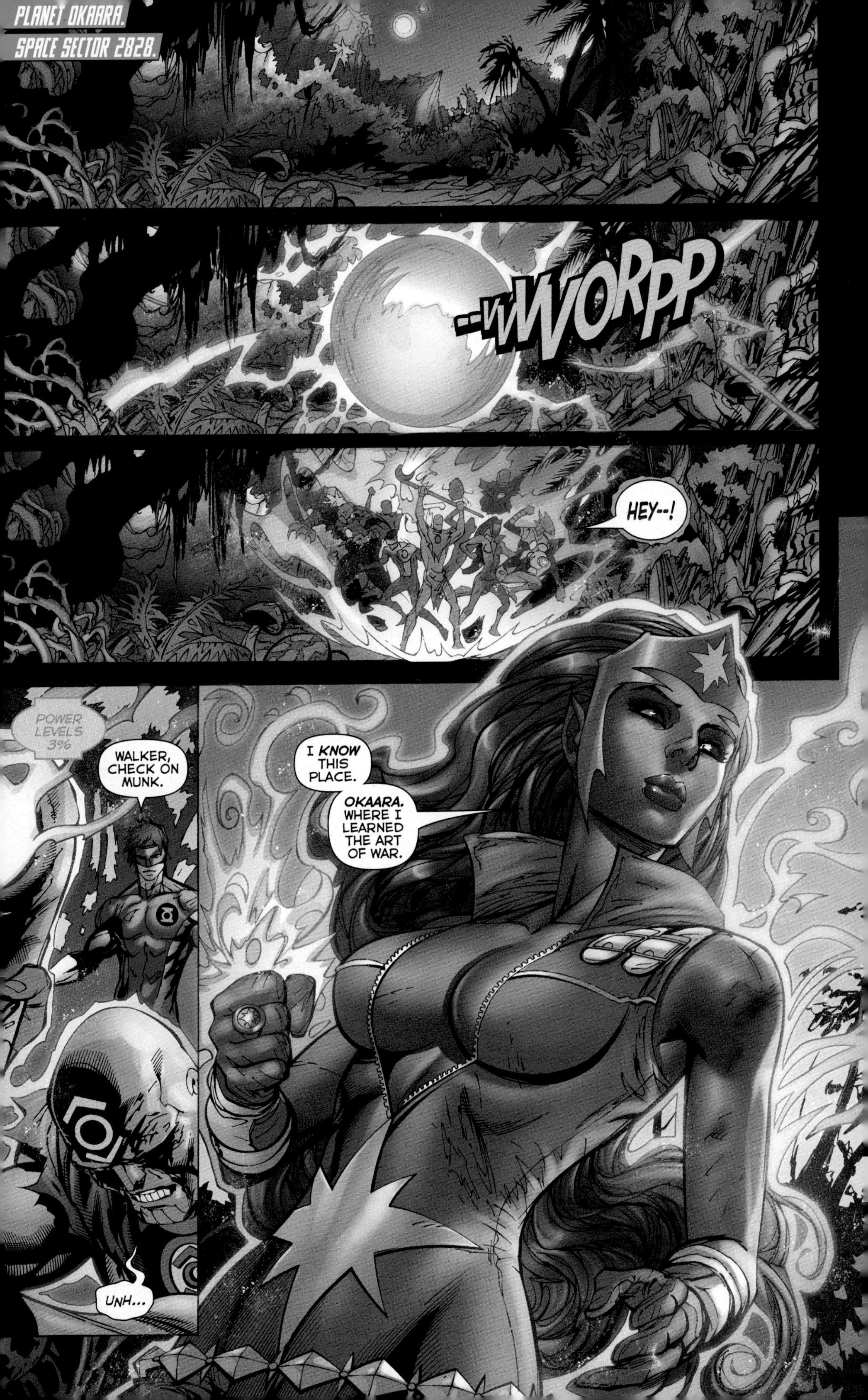
PLANET OKAARA.
SPACE SECTOR 2828.
--VVVWORPP
HEY--!
POWER LEVELS 3%
WALKER, CHECK ON MUNK.
I KNOW THIS PLACE.
OKAARA. WHERE I LEARNED THE ART OF WAR.
UNH...

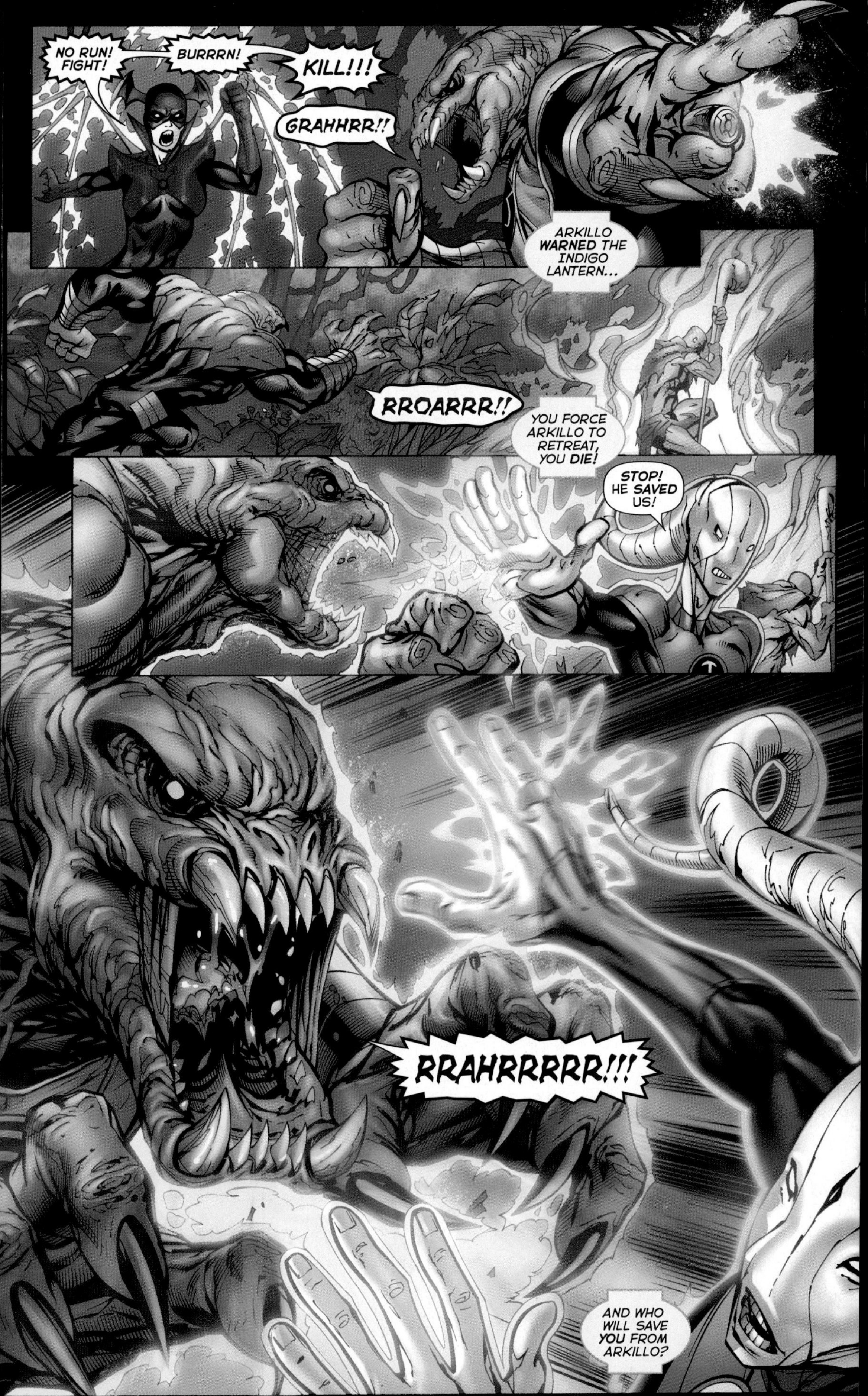
NO RUN! FIGHT!
BURRRN!
KILL!!!
GRAHHRR!!
ARKILLO WARNED THE INDIGO LANTERN...
RROARRR!!
YOU FORCE ARKILLO TO RETREAT, YOU DIE!
STOP! HE SAVED US!
RRAHRRRRR!!!
AND WHO WILL SAVE YOU FROM ARKILLO?

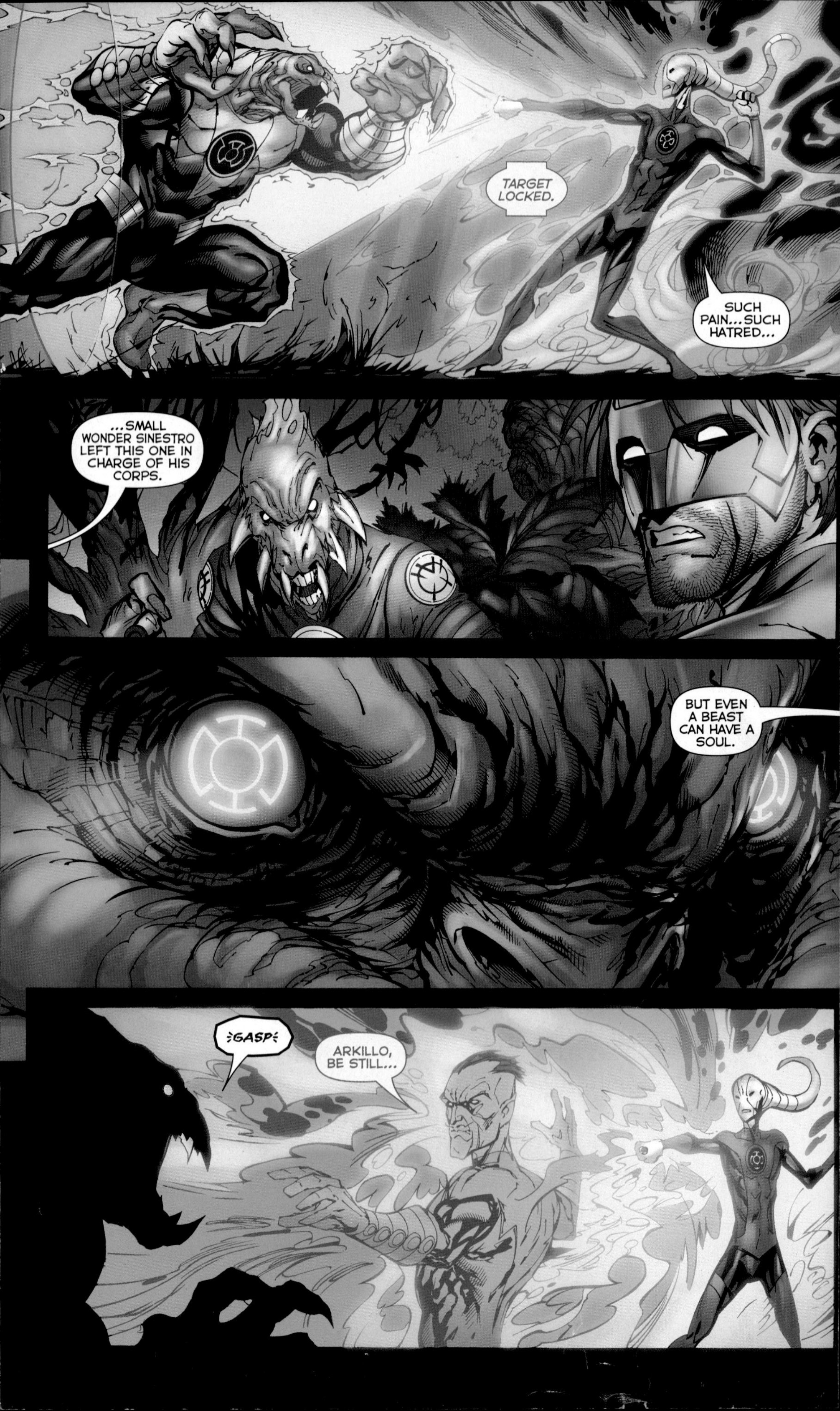
TARGET LOCKED.
SUCH PAIN...SUCH HATRED...
...SMALL WONDER SINESTRO LEFT THIS ONE IN CHARGE OF HIS CORPS.
BUT EVEN A BEAST CAN HAVE A SOUL.
GASP
ARKILLO, BE STILL...

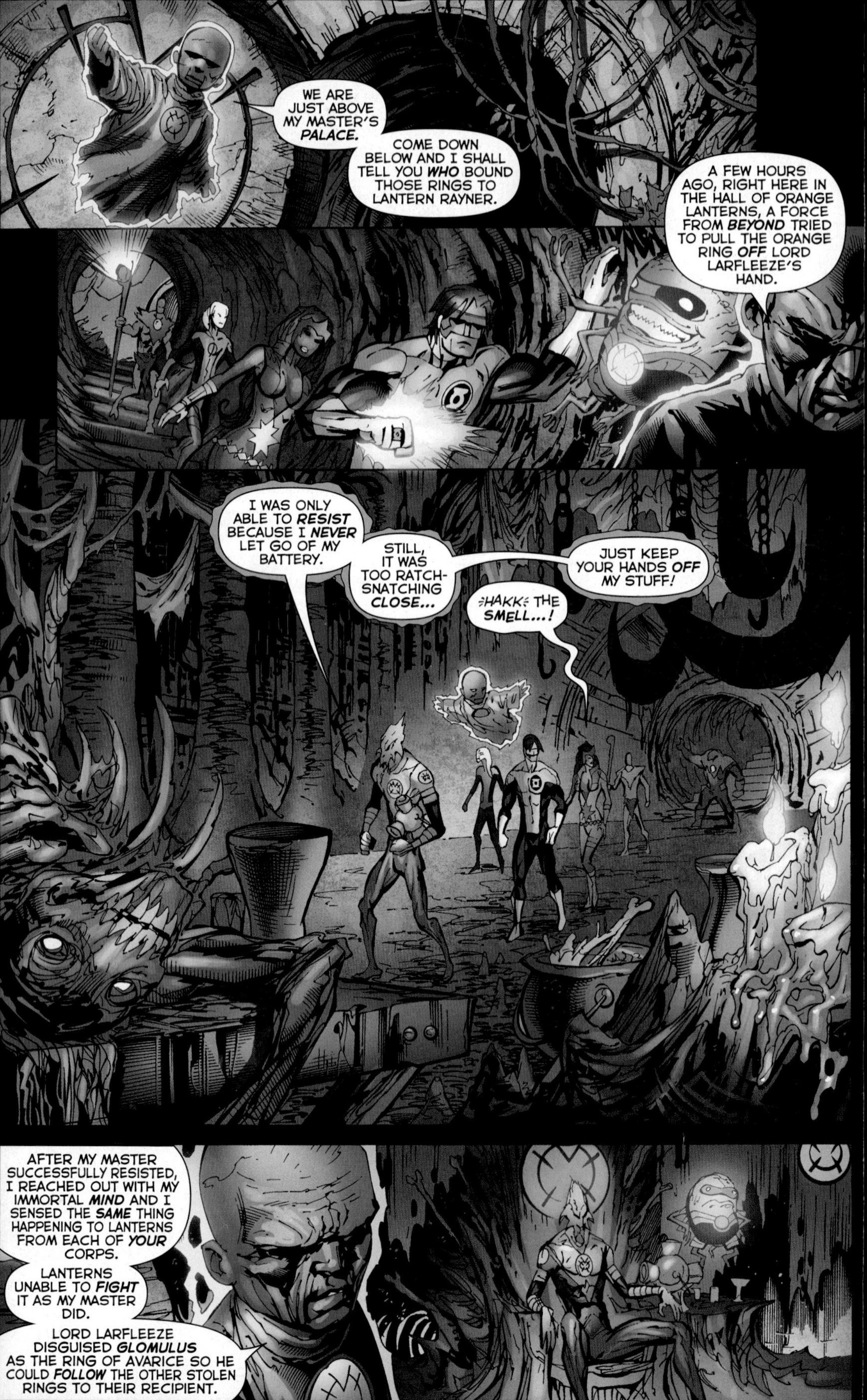
WE ARE JUST ABOVE MY MASTER'S *PALACE.*
COME DOWN BELOW AND I SHALL TELL YOU *WHO* BOUND THOSE RINGS TO LANTERN RAYNER.
A FEW HOURS AGO, RIGHT HERE IN THE HALL OF ORANGE LANTERNS, A FORCE FROM *BEYOND* TRIED TO PULL THE ORANGE RING *OFF* LORD LARFLEEZE'S HAND.
I WAS ONLY ABLE TO *RESIST* BECAUSE I *NEVER* LET GO OF MY BATTERY.
STILL, IT WAS TOO RATCH-SNATCHING *CLOSE...*
JUST KEEP YOUR HANDS *OFF* MY STUFF!
HAKK THE *SMELL...!*
AFTER MY MASTER SUCCESSFULLY RESISTED, I REACHED OUT WITH MY IMMORTAL *MIND* AND I SENSED THE *SAME* THING HAPPENING TO LANTERNS FROM EACH OF *YOUR* CORPS.
LANTERNS UNABLE TO *FIGHT* IT AS MY MASTER DID.
LORD LARFLEEZE DISGUISED *GLOMULUS* AS THE RING OF AVARICE SO HE COULD *FOLLOW* THE OTHER STOLEN RINGS TO THEIR RECIPIENT.

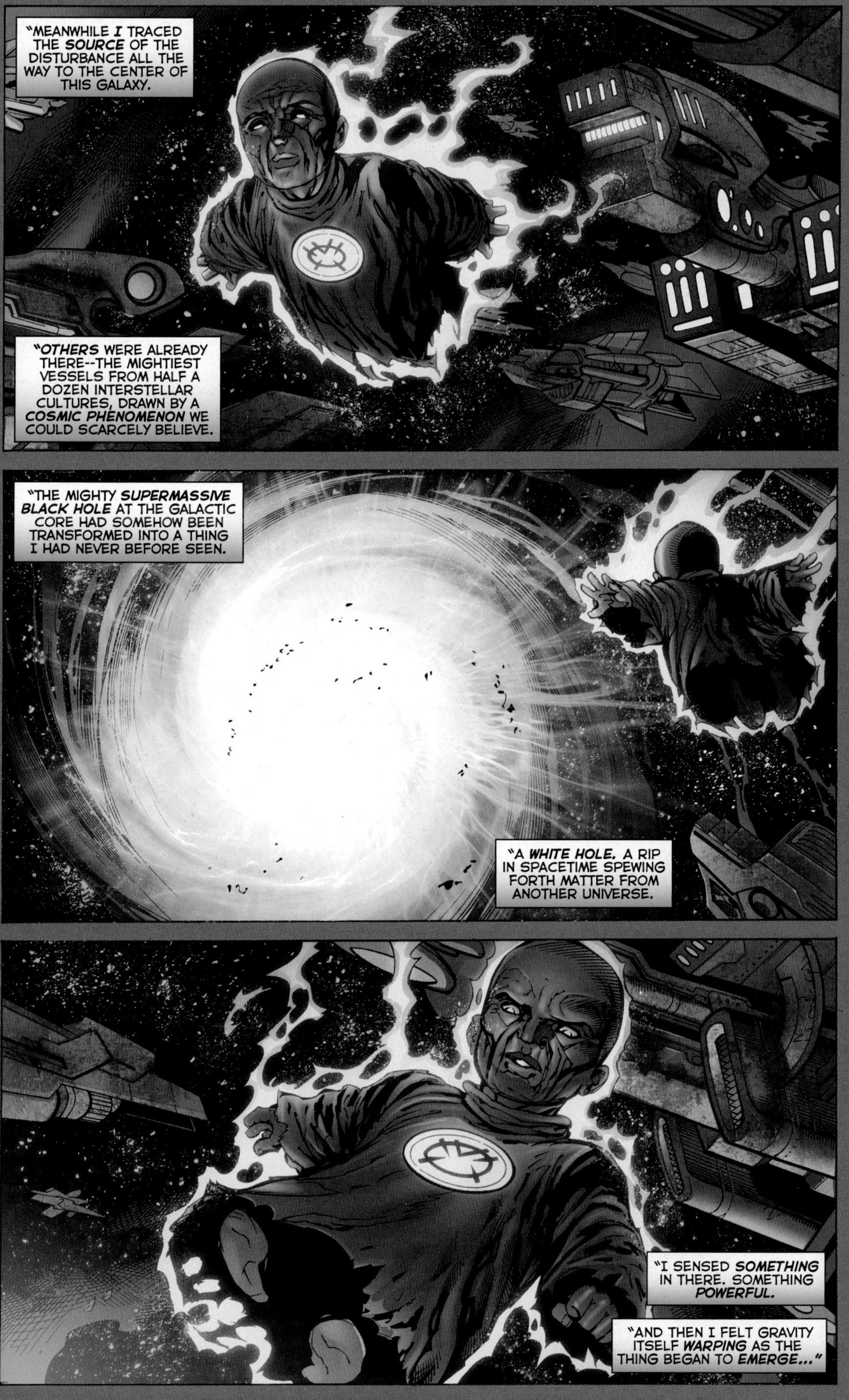

"MEANWHILE I TRACED THE SOURCE OF THE DISTURBANCE ALL THE WAY TO THE CENTER OF THIS GALAXY.
"OTHERS WERE ALREADY THERE--THE MIGHTIEST VESSELS FROM HALF A DOZEN INTERSTELLAR CULTURES, DRAWN BY A COSMIC PHENOMENON WE COULD SCARCELY BELIEVE.
"THE MIGHTY SUPERMASSIVE BLACK HOLE AT THE GALACTIC CORE HAD SOMEHOW BEEN TRANSFORMED INTO A THING I HAD NEVER BEFORE SEEN.
"A WHITE HOLE. A RIP IN SPACETIME SPEWING FORTH MATTER FROM ANOTHER UNIVERSE.
"I SENSED SOMETHING IN THERE. SOMETHING POWERFUL.
"AND THEN I FELT GRAVITY ITSELF WARPING AS THE THING BEGAN TO EMERGE..."

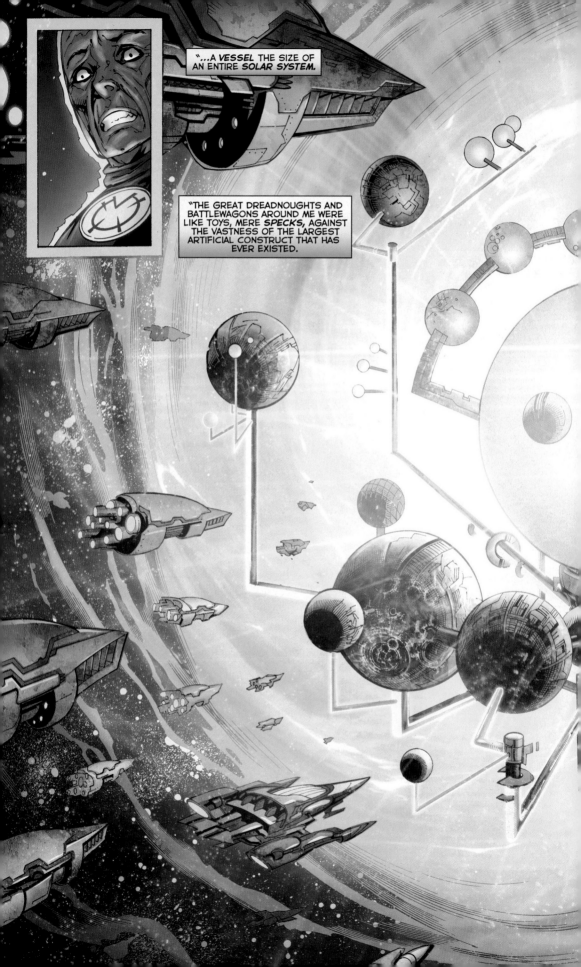

"...A *VESSEL* THE SIZE OF AN ENTIRE *SOLAR SYSTEM.*

"THE GREAT DREADNOUGHTS AND BATTLEWAGONS AROUND ME WERE LIKE TOYS, MERE *SPECKS,* AGAINST THE VASTNESS OF THE LARGEST ARTIFICIAL CONSTRUCT THAT HAS EVER EXISTED.

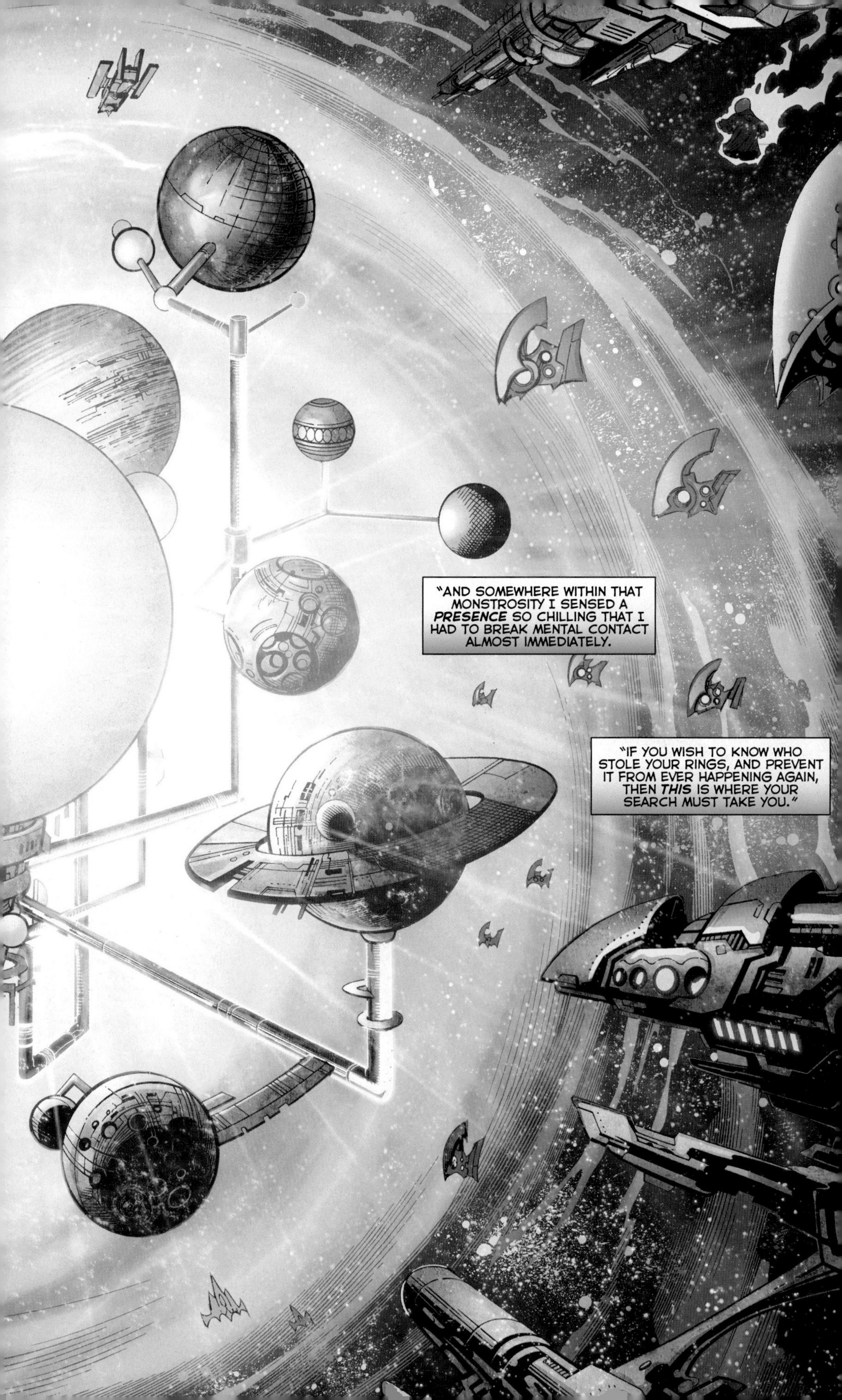
"AND SOMEWHERE WITHIN THAT MONSTROSITY I SENSED A *PRESENCE* SO CHILLING THAT I HAD TO BREAK MENTAL CONTACT ALMOST IMMEDIATELY.
"IF YOU WISH TO KNOW WHO STOLE YOUR RINGS, AND PREVENT IT FROM EVER HAPPENING AGAIN, THEN *THIS* IS WHERE YOUR SEARCH MUST TAKE YOU."

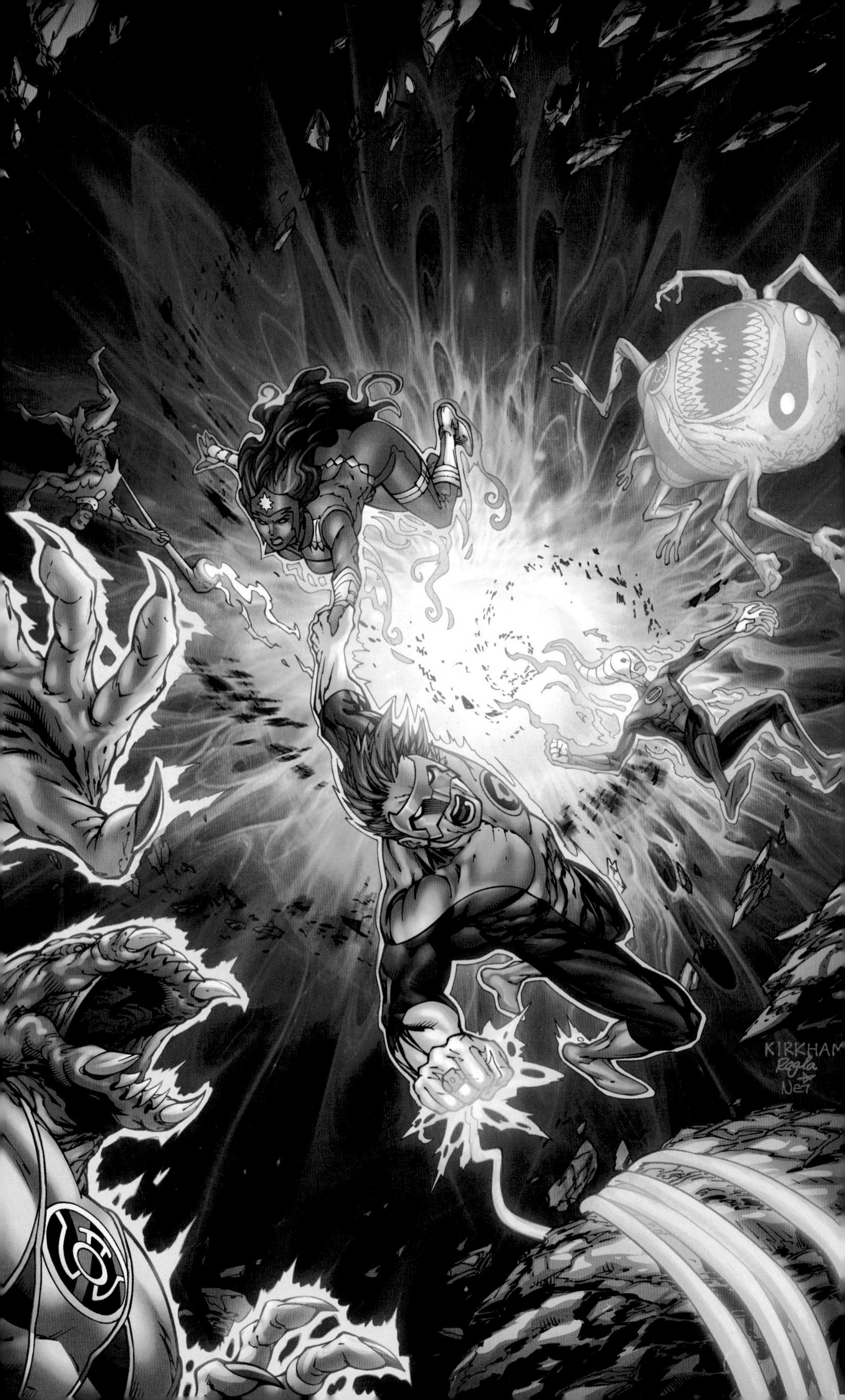
KIRKHAM

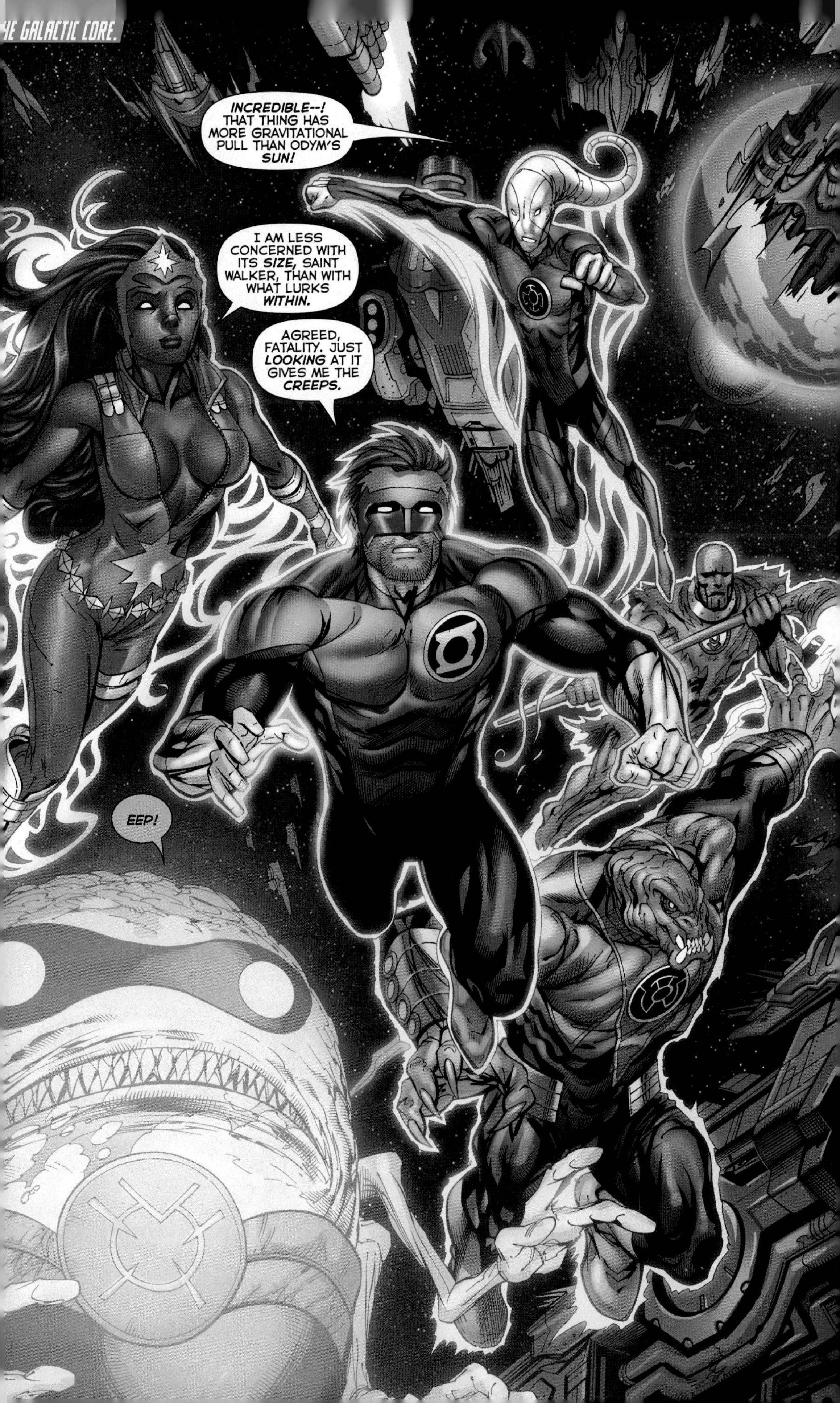

HE GALACTIC CORE.
INCREDIBLE--! THAT THING HAS MORE GRAVITATIONAL PULL THAN ODYM'S SUN!
I AM LESS CONCERNED WITH ITS SIZE, SAINT WALKER, THAN WITH WHAT LURKS WITHIN.
AGREED, FATALITY. JUST LOOKING AT IT GIVES ME THE CREEPS.
EEP!

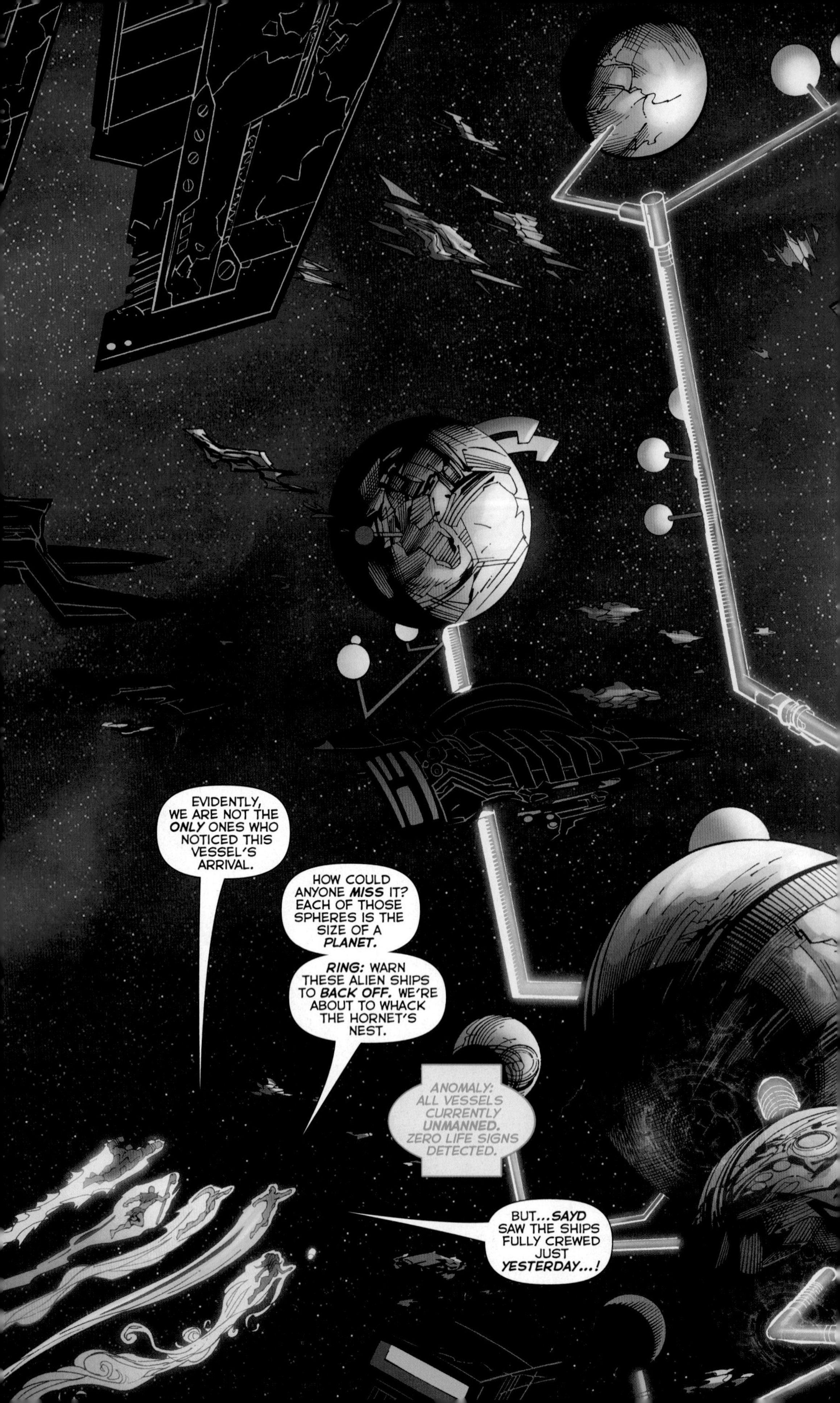

EVIDENTLY, WE ARE NOT THE *ONLY* ONES WHO NOTICED THIS VESSEL'S ARRIVAL.
HOW COULD ANYONE *MISS* IT? EACH OF THOSE SPHERES IS THE SIZE OF A *PLANET.*
RING: WARN THESE ALIEN SHIPS TO *BACK OFF.* WE'RE ABOUT TO WHACK THE HORNET'S NEST.
ANOMALY: ALL VESSELS CURRENTLY *UNMANNED.* ZERO LIFE SIGNS DETECTED.
BUT...*SAYD* SAW THE SHIPS FULLY CREWED JUST *YESTERDAY...!*

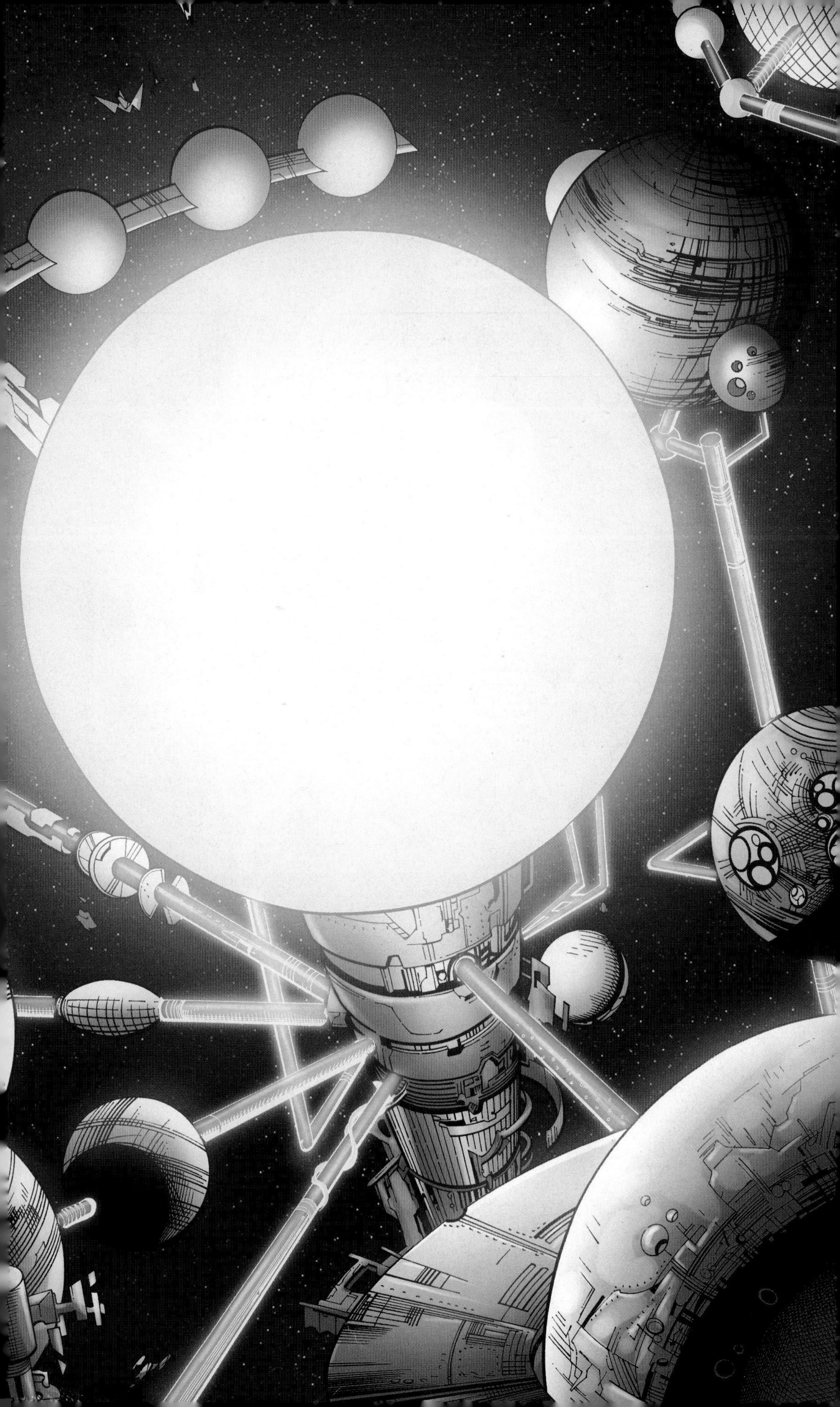

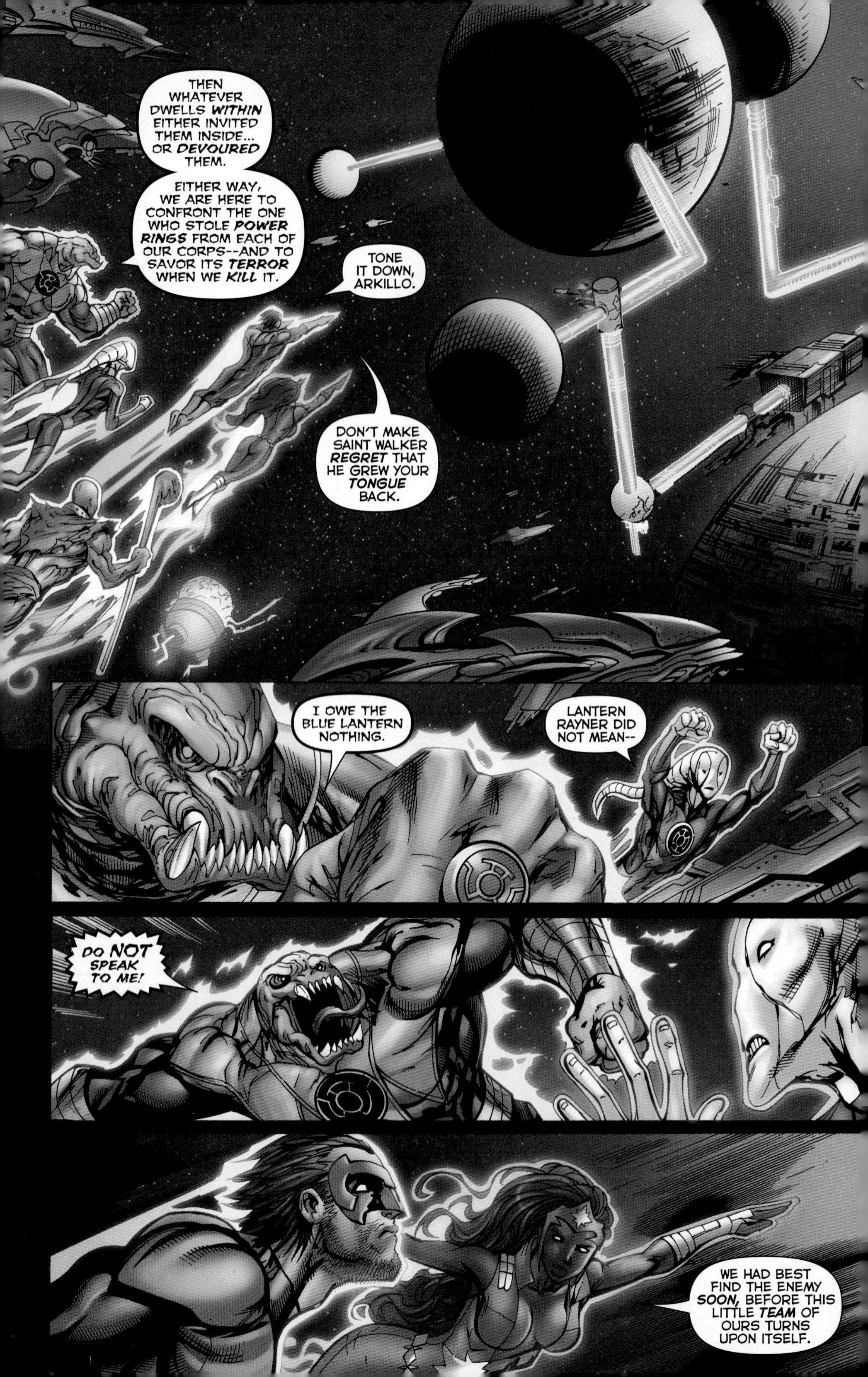
THEN WHATEVER DWELLS WITHIN EITHER INVITED THEM INSIDE... OR DEVOURED THEM.
EITHER WAY, WE ARE HERE TO CONFRONT THE ONE WHO STOLE POWER RINGS FROM EACH OF OUR CORPS--AND TO SAVOR ITS TERROR WHEN WE KILL IT.
TONE IT DOWN, ARKILLO.
DON'T MAKE SAINT WALKER REGRET THAT HE GREW YOUR TONGUE BACK.
I OWE THE BLUE LANTERN NOTHING.
LANTERN RAYNER DID NOT MEAN--
DO NOT SPEAK TO ME!
WE HAD BEST FIND THE ENEMY SOON, BEFORE THIS LITTLE TEAM OF OURS TURNS UPON ITSELF.

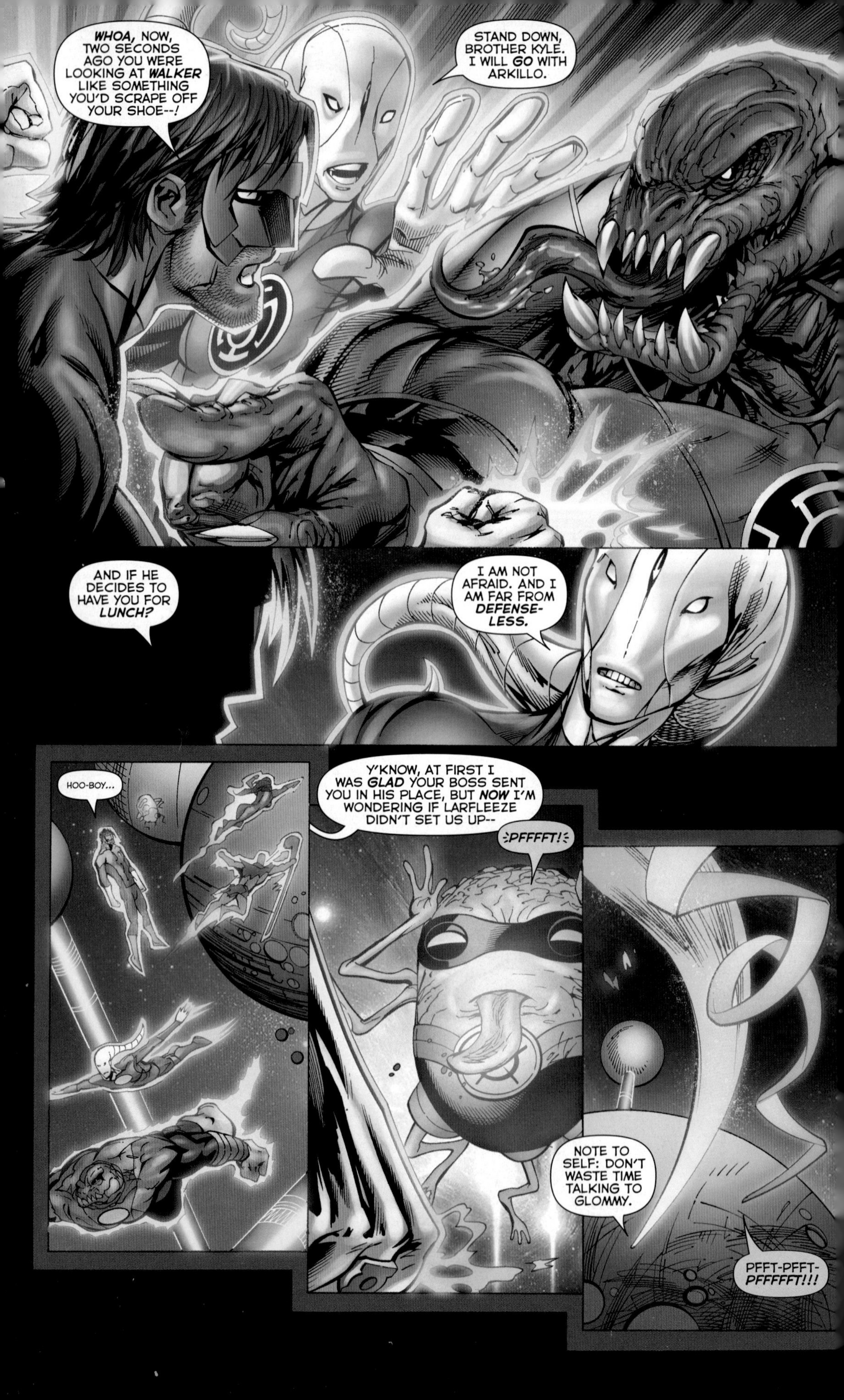
WHOA, NOW, TWO SECONDS AGO YOU WERE LOOKING AT WALKER LIKE SOMETHING YOU'D SCRAPE OFF YOUR SHOE--!
STAND DOWN, BROTHER KYLE. I WILL GO WITH ARKILLO.
AND IF HE DECIDES TO HAVE YOU FOR LUNCH?
I AM NOT AFRAID. AND I AM FAR FROM DEFENSE-LESS.
HOO-BOY...
Y'KNOW, AT FIRST I WAS GLAD YOUR BOSS SENT YOU IN HIS PLACE, BUT NOW I'M WONDERING IF LARFLEEZE DIDN'T SET US UP--
PFFFFT!
NOTE TO SELF: DON'T WASTE TIME TALKING TO GLOMMY.
PFFT-PFFT-PFFFFFT!!!

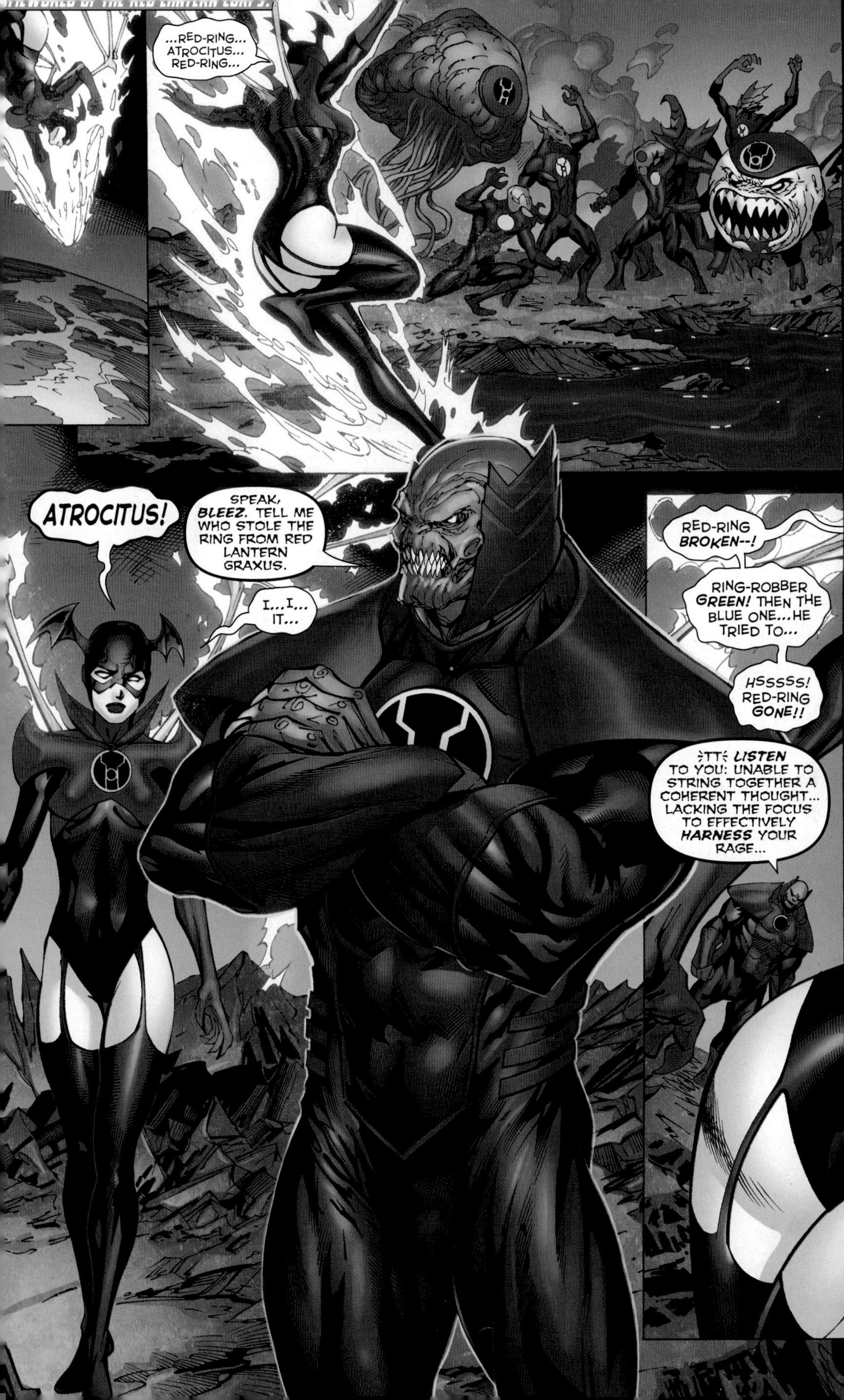
...RED-RING... ATROCITUS... RED-RING...
ATROCITUS!
SPEAK, BLEEZ. TELL ME WHO STOLE THE RING FROM RED LANTERN GRAXUS.
I...I... IT...
RED-RING BROKEN--!
RING-ROBBER GREEN! THEN THE BLUE ONE...HE TRIED TO...
HSSSSS! RED-RING GONE!!
TT LISTEN TO YOU: UNABLE TO STRING TOGETHER A COHERENT THOUGHT... LACKING THE FOCUS TO EFFECTIVELY HARNESS YOUR RAGE...

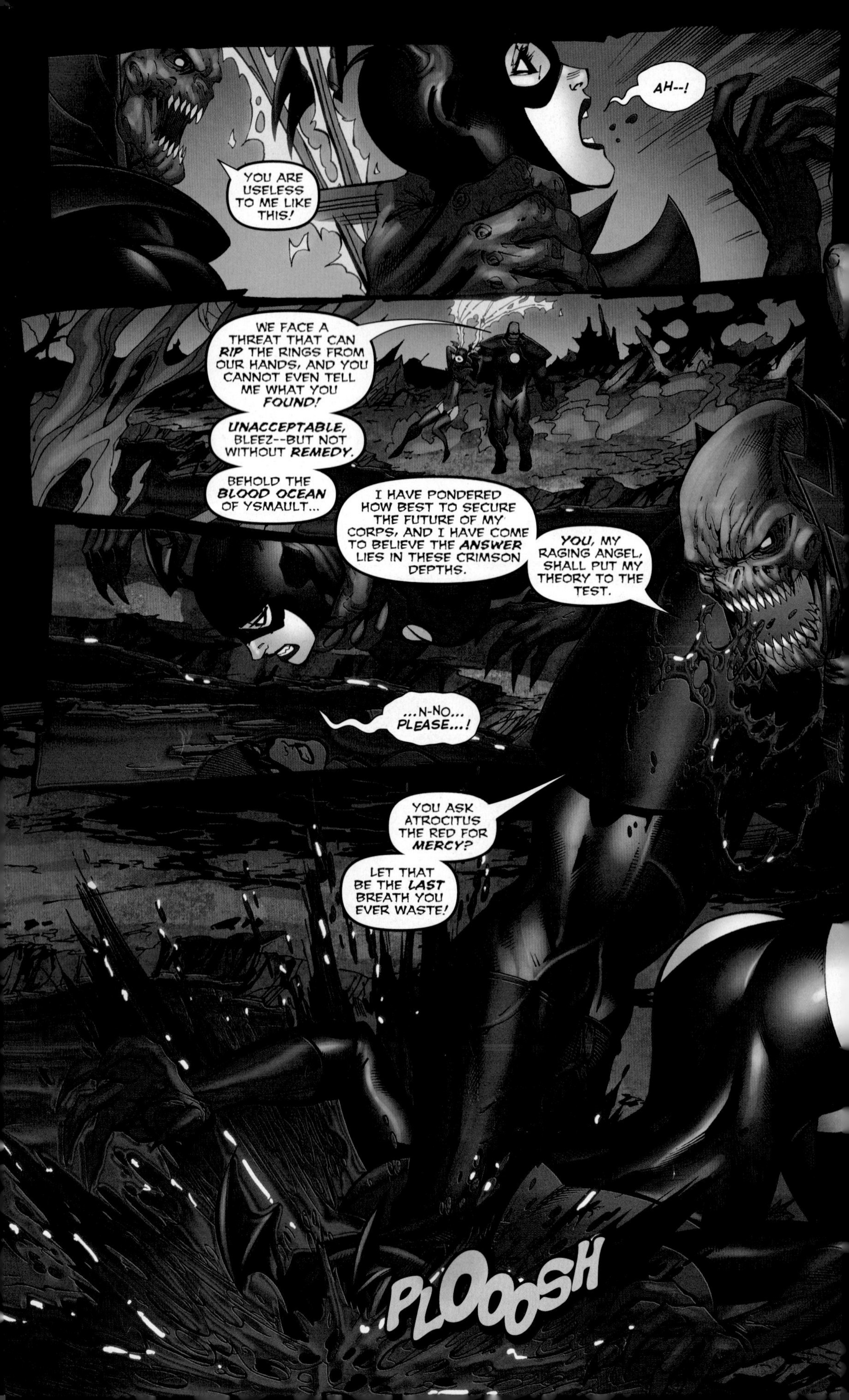
AH--!
YOU ARE USELESS TO ME LIKE THIS!
WE FACE A THREAT THAT CAN RIP THE RINGS FROM OUR HANDS, AND YOU CANNOT EVEN TELL ME WHAT YOU FOUND!
UNACCEPTABLE, BLEEZ--BUT NOT WITHOUT REMEDY.
BEHOLD THE BLOOD OCEAN OF YSMAULT...
I HAVE PONDERED HOW BEST TO SECURE THE FUTURE OF MY CORPS, AND I HAVE COME TO BELIEVE THE ANSWER LIES IN THESE CRIMSON DEPTHS.
YOU, MY RAGING ANGEL, SHALL PUT MY THEORY TO THE TEST.
...N-NO... PLEASE...!
YOU ASK ATROCITUS THE RED FOR MERCY?
LET THAT BE THE LAST BREATH YOU EVER WASTE!
PLOOOOSH

THEY ARE ABOUT TO ENTER THE *ORRERY*, LARFLEEZE...

:MUNCH:... CALL ME *LORD* LARFLEEZE... :CHOMP:... *SOUNDS BETTER*... :ULP:...

YES, OF COURSE. MUSTN'T OFFEND YOUR *DIGNITY.*

MY POINT, *LORD* LARFLEEZE, IS THAT IT WON'T BE LONG BEFORE THEY DISCOVER THE *TRUTH.*

ALL I CARE IS THAT THEY *STOP* HIM...:SHLUP:...*WITHOUT* DAMAGING THAT *WONDERFUL* TOY SOLAR SYSTEM.

I'VE NEVER SEEN *ANYTHING* LIKE IT-- AND I *WANT* IT! :MUNCH:

NOW FETCH ME MORE *RATWAFFLE CHEESE!*

THREE WORDS:

RAT.

WAFFLE.

CHEESE.

YOU UNDERSTAND THAT ONCE THEY ARE INSIDE, I WILL NO LONGER BE ABLE TO MONITOR THEM-- NOT EVEN GLOMULUS...

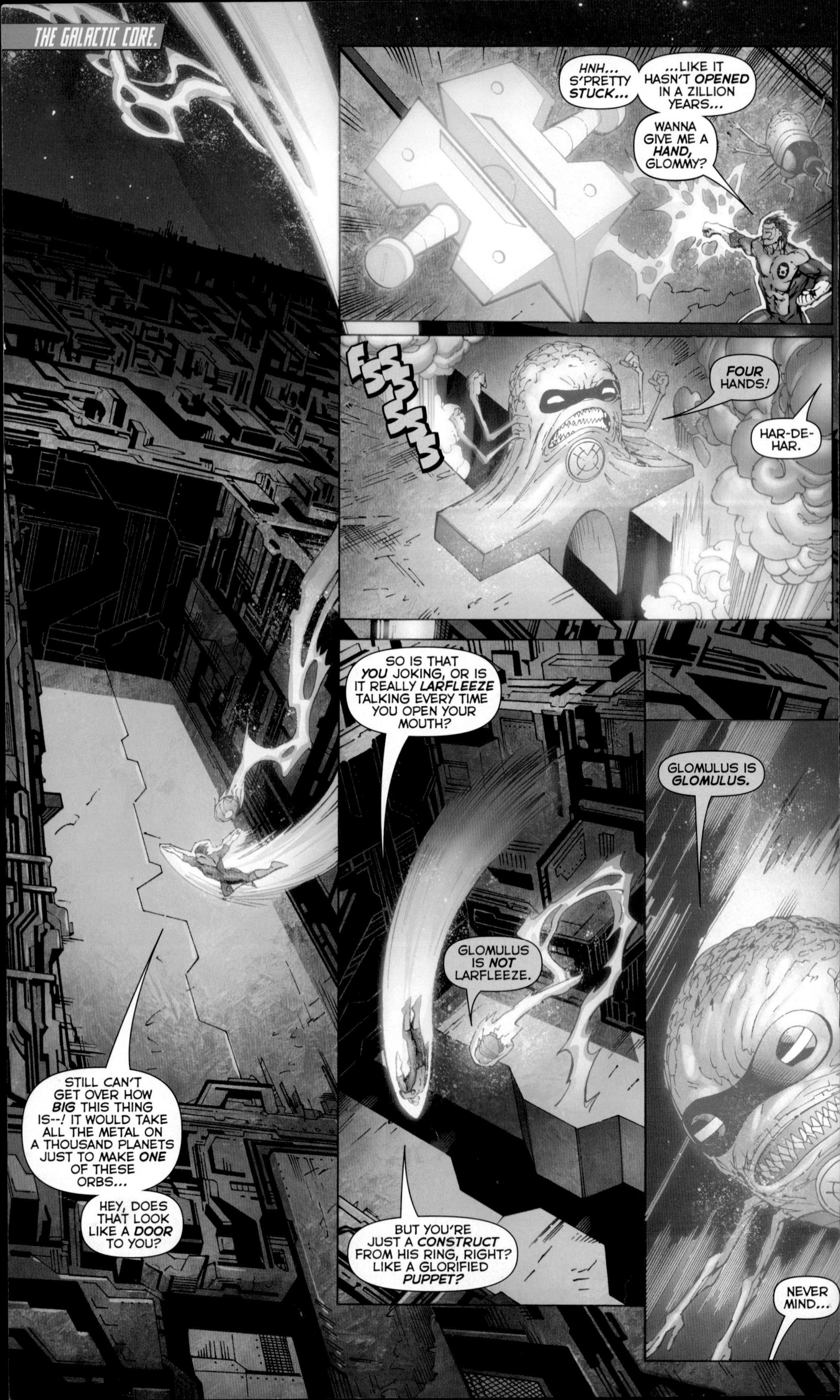
THE GALACTIC CORE.
HNH... S'PRETTY STUCK...
...LIKE IT HASN'T OPENED IN A ZILLION YEARS...
WANNA GIVE ME A HAND, GLOMMY?
FSSSSSS
FOUR HANDS!
HAR-DE-HAR.
STILL CAN'T GET OVER HOW BIG THIS THING IS--! IT WOULD TAKE ALL THE METAL ON A THOUSAND PLANETS JUST TO MAKE ONE OF THESE ORBS...
HEY, DOES THAT LOOK LIKE A DOOR TO YOU?
SO IS THAT YOU JOKING, OR IS IT REALLY LARFLEEZE TALKING EVERY TIME YOU OPEN YOUR MOUTH?
GLOMULUS IS NOT LARFLEEZE.
BUT YOU'RE JUST A CONSTRUCT FROM HIS RING, RIGHT? LIKE A GLORIFIED PUPPET?
GLOMULUS IS GLOMULUS.
NEVER MIND...

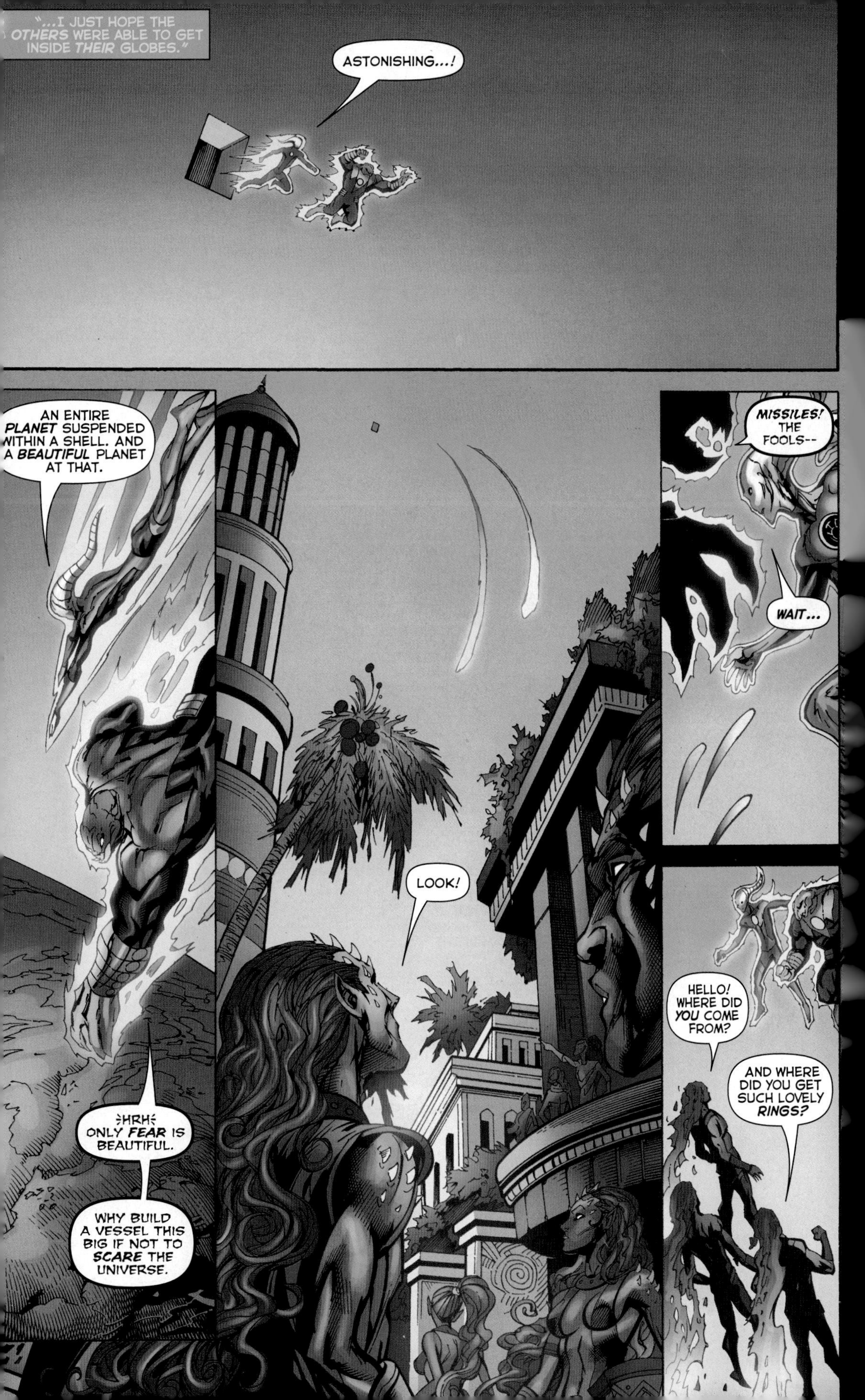

"...I JUST HOPE THE OTHERS WERE ABLE TO GET INSIDE THEIR GLOBES."
ASTONISHING...!
AN ENTIRE PLANET SUSPENDED WITHIN A SHELL. AND A BEAUTIFUL PLANET AT THAT.
HRH ONLY FEAR IS BEAUTIFUL.
WHY BUILD A VESSEL THIS BIG IF NOT TO SCARE THE UNIVERSE.
LOOK!
MISSILES! THE FOOLS--
WAIT...
HELLO! WHERE DID YOU COME FROM?
AND WHERE DID YOU GET SUCH LOVELY RINGS?

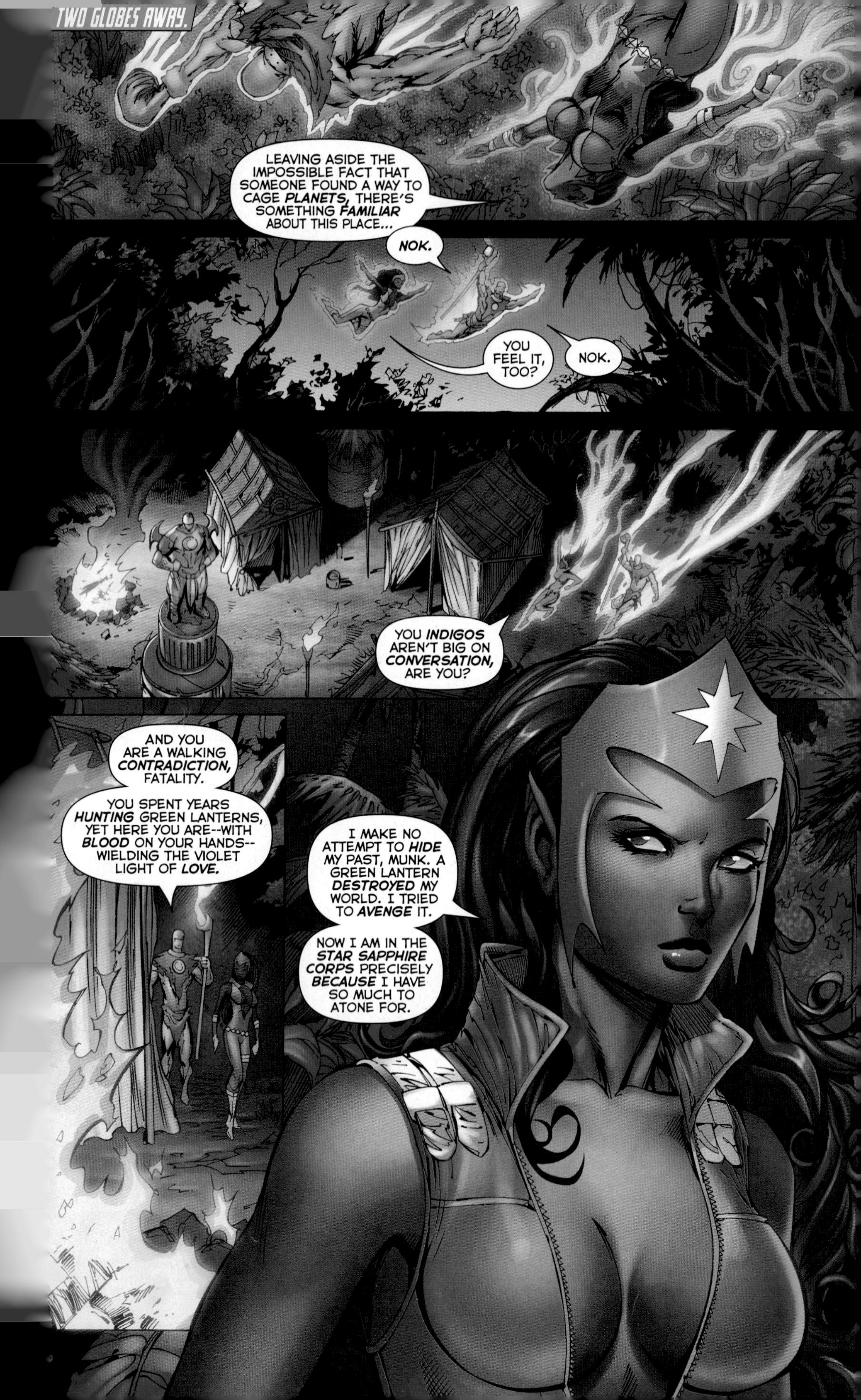
TWO GLOBES AWAY.
LEAVING ASIDE THE IMPOSSIBLE FACT THAT SOMEONE FOUND A WAY TO CAGE PLANETS, THERE'S SOMETHING FAMILIAR ABOUT THIS PLACE...
NOK.
YOU FEEL IT, TOO?
NOK.
YOU INDIGOS AREN'T BIG ON CONVERSATION, ARE YOU?
AND YOU ARE A WALKING CONTRADICTION, FATALITY.
YOU SPENT YEARS HUNTING GREEN LANTERNS, YET HERE YOU ARE--WITH BLOOD ON YOUR HANDS--WIELDING THE VIOLET LIGHT OF LOVE.
I MAKE NO ATTEMPT TO HIDE MY PAST, MUNK. A GREEN LANTERN DESTROYED MY WORLD. I TRIED TO AVENGE IT.
NOW I AM IN THE STAR SAPPHIRE CORPS PRECISELY BECAUSE I HAVE SO MUCH TO ATONE FOR.

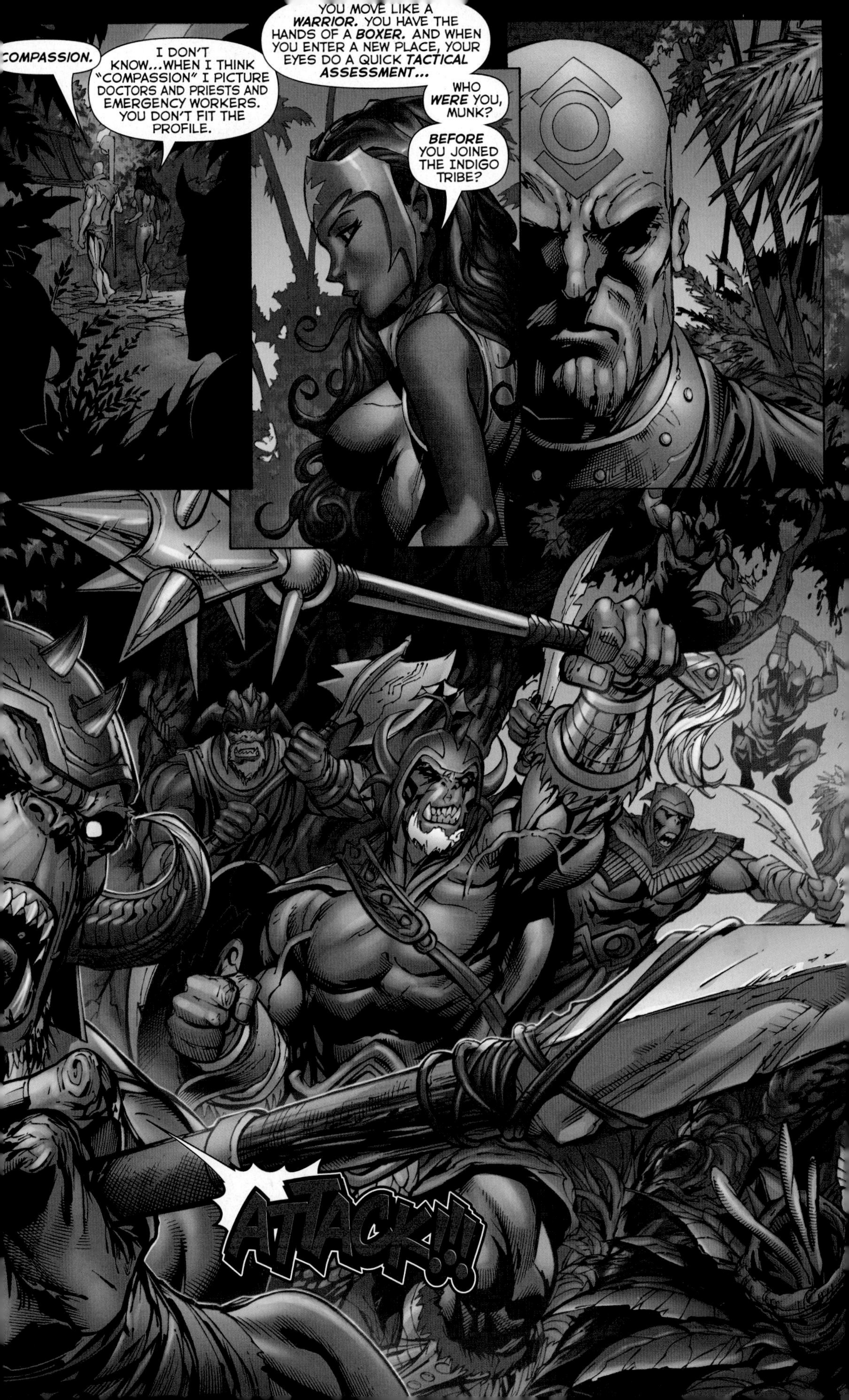
COMPASSION.
I DON'T KNOW...WHEN I THINK "COMPASSION" I PICTURE DOCTORS AND PRIESTS AND EMERGENCY WORKERS. YOU DON'T FIT THE PROFILE.
YOU MOVE LIKE A WARRIOR. YOU HAVE THE HANDS OF A BOXER. AND WHEN YOU ENTER A NEW PLACE, YOUR EYES DO A QUICK TACTICAL ASSESSMENT...
WHO WERE YOU, MUNK?
BEFORE YOU JOINED THE INDIGO TRIBE?
ATTACK!!!

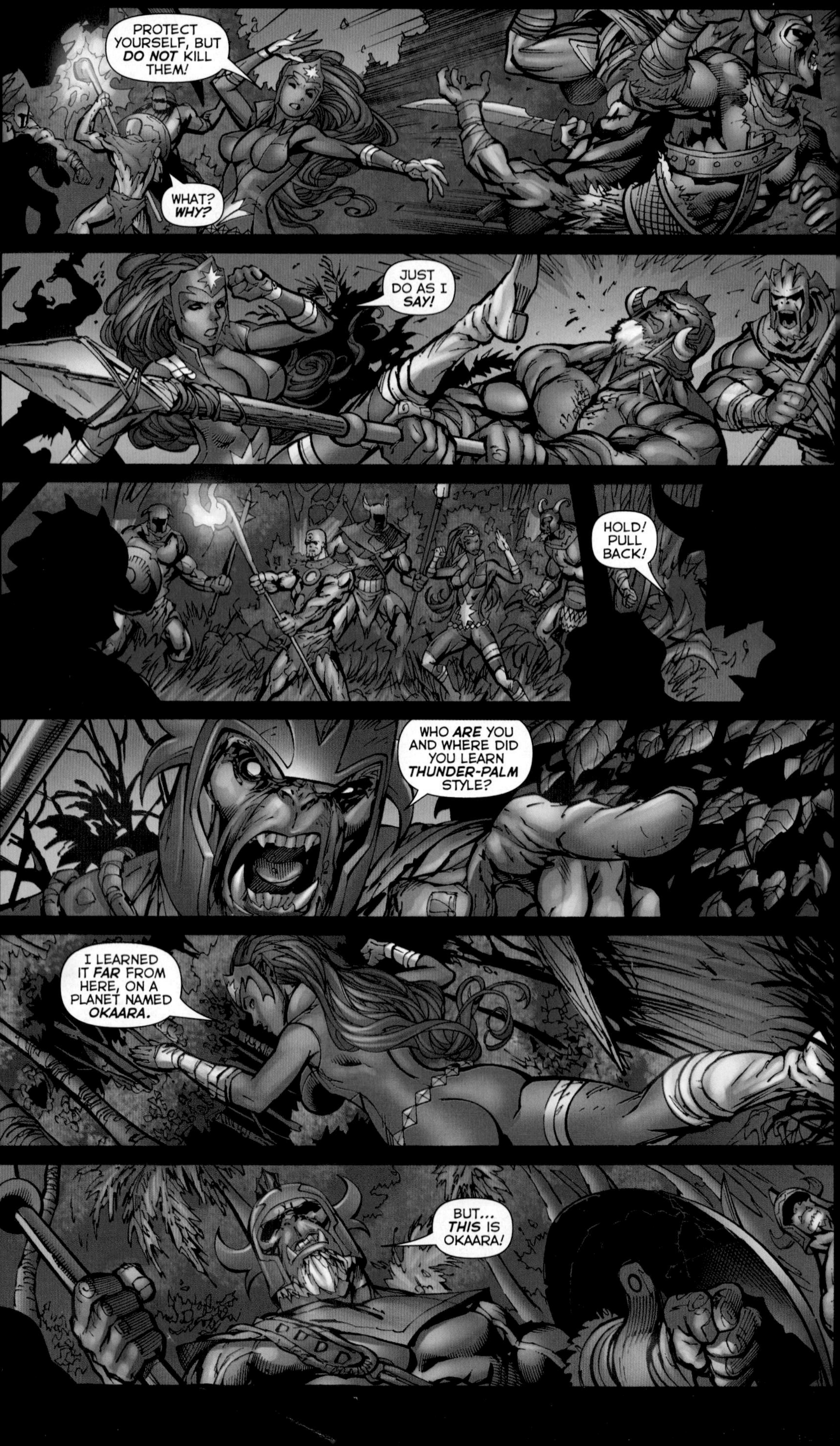
PROTECT YOURSELF, BUT DO NOT KILL THEM!
WHAT? WHY?
JUST DO AS I SAY!
HOLD! PULL BACK!
WHO ARE YOU AND WHERE DID YOU LEARN THUNDER-PALM STYLE?
I LEARNED IT FAR FROM HERE, ON A PLANET NAMED OKAARA.
BUT... THIS IS OKAARA!

BWOMMMMMM BWOMMMMMM

"THE ARCHANGEL *INVICTUS* DWELLS WITHIN THE SUN, WATCHING OVER US ALL.

BWOMMMMMM BWOMMMMMM

"HE *SAFEGUARDS* US AND KEEPS US *FAITHFUL.*

BWOMMMMMM BWOMMMMMM

"WE ARE *ALL* HIS CHILDREN HERE IN THE ORRERY.

BWOMMMMMM BWOMMMMMM

"HE HEARS OUR *PRAYERS.* HE KNOWS OUR *TRIUMPHS* AND OUR *TRESPASSES.*

"AND NOW HE KNOWS *YOURS,* GREEN LANTERN."

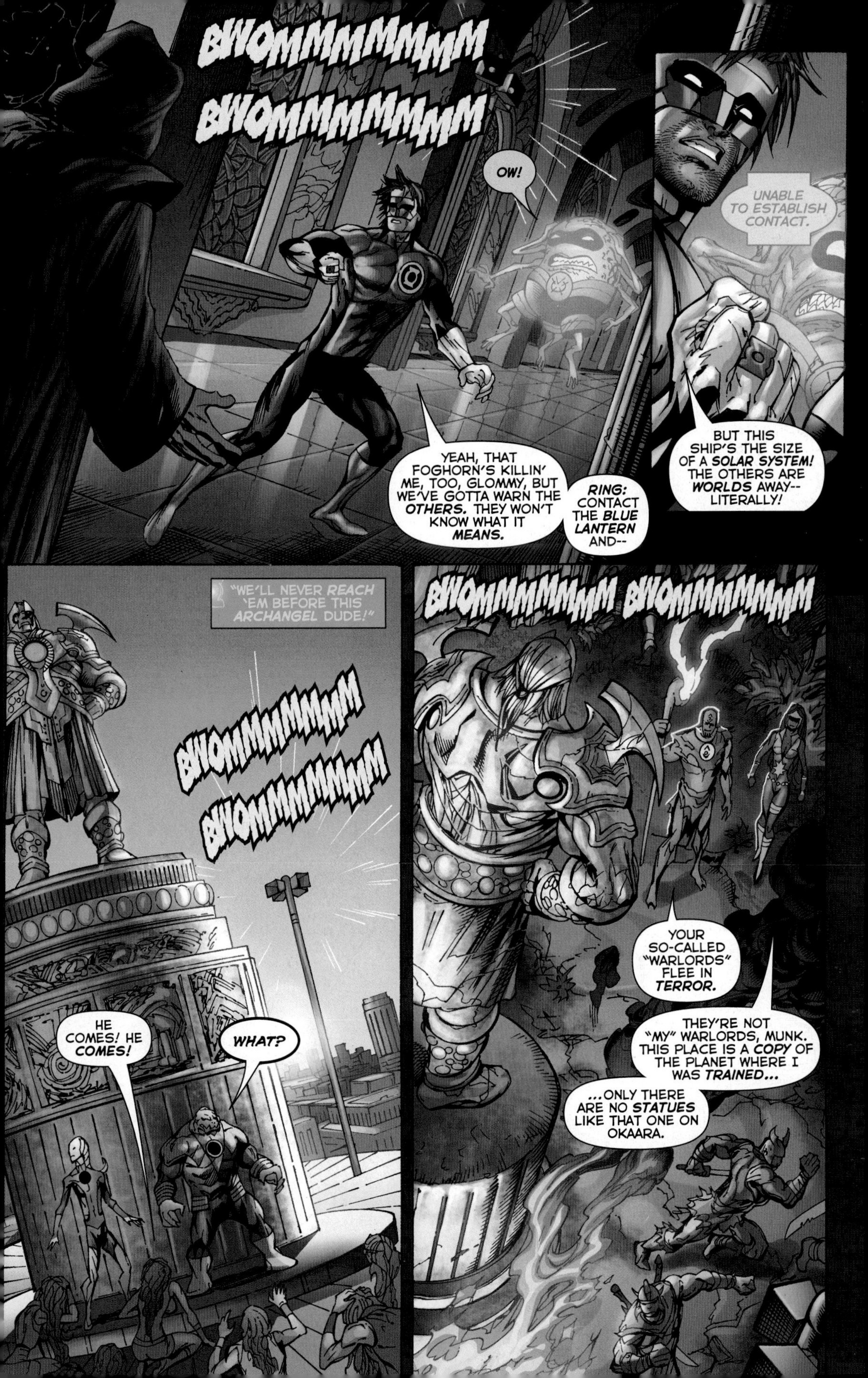
BWOMMMMMMM
BWOMMMMMMM
OW!
YEAH, THAT FOGHORN'S KILLIN' ME, TOO, GLOMMY, BUT WE'VE GOTTA WARN THE OTHERS. THEY WON'T KNOW WHAT IT MEANS.
RING: CONTACT THE BLUE LANTERN AND--
UNABLE TO ESTABLISH CONTACT.
BUT THIS SHIP'S THE SIZE OF A SOLAR SYSTEM! THE OTHERS ARE WORLDS AWAY-- LITERALLY!
"WE'LL NEVER REACH 'EM BEFORE THIS ARCHANGEL DUDE!"
BWOMMMMMMM
BWOMMMMMMM
HE COMES! HE COMES!
WHAT?
BWOMMMMMMM BWOMMMMMMM
YOUR SO-CALLED "WARLORDS" FLEE IN TERROR.
THEY'RE NOT "MY" WARLORDS, MUNK. THIS PLACE IS A COPY OF THE PLANET WHERE I WAS TRAINED...
...ONLY THERE ARE NO STATUES LIKE THAT ONE ON OKAARA.

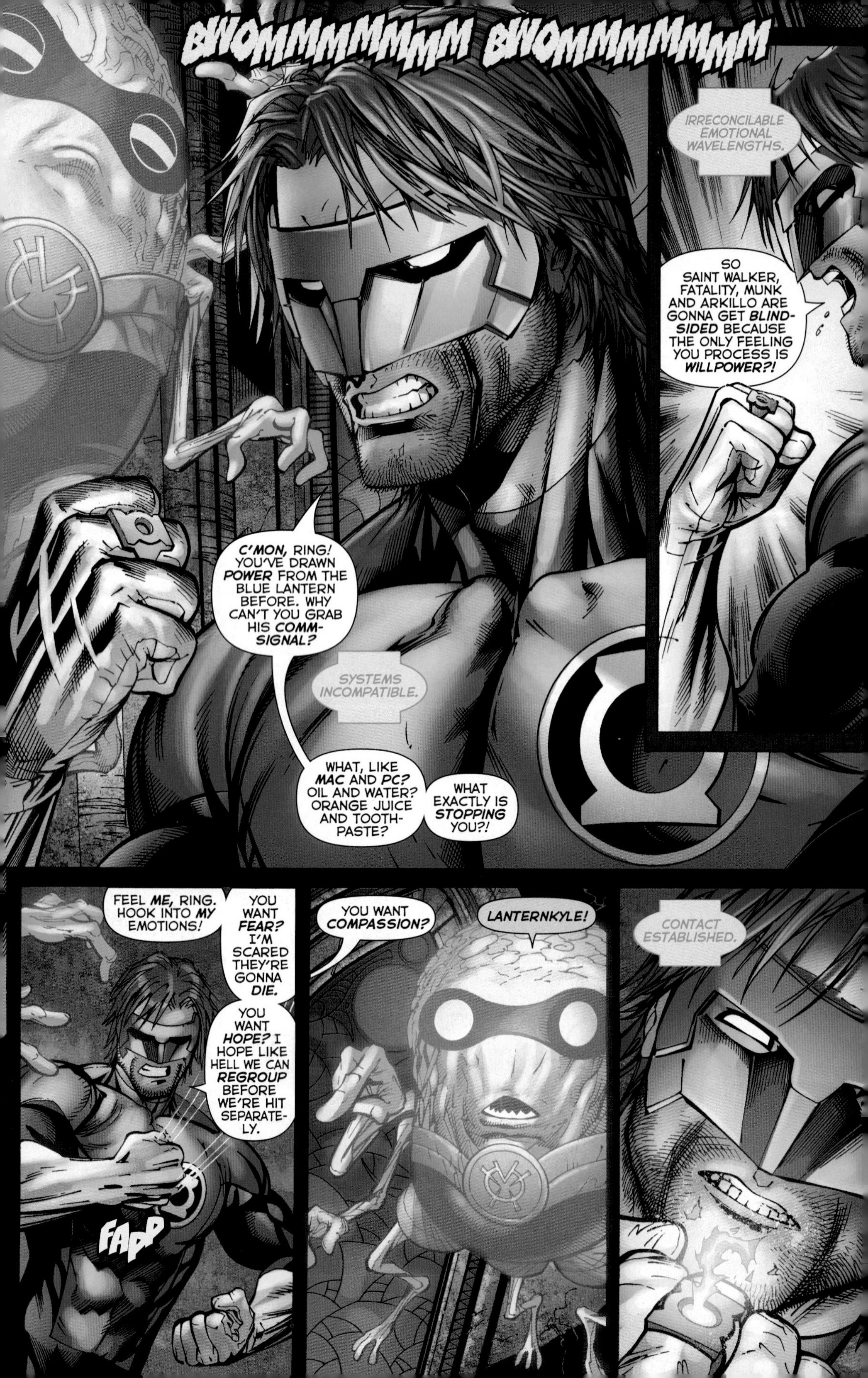

BWOMMMMMMM BWOMMMMMMM
IRRECONCILABLE EMOTIONAL WAVELENGTHS.
SO SAINT WALKER, FATALITY, MUNK AND ARKILLO ARE GONNA GET BLIND-SIDED BECAUSE THE ONLY FEELING YOU PROCESS IS WILLPOWER?!
C'MON, RING! YOU'VE DRAWN POWER FROM THE BLUE LANTERN BEFORE. WHY CAN'T YOU GRAB HIS COMM-SIGNAL?
SYSTEMS INCOMPATIBLE.
WHAT, LIKE MAC AND PC? OIL AND WATER? ORANGE JUICE AND TOOTH-PASTE?
WHAT EXACTLY IS STOPPING YOU?!
FEEL ME, RING. HOOK INTO MY EMOTIONS!
YOU WANT FEAR? I'M SCARED THEY'RE GONNA DIE.
YOU WANT HOPE? I HOPE LIKE HELL WE CAN REGROUP BEFORE WE'RE HIT SEPARATE-LY.
FAPP
YOU WANT COMPASSION?
LANTERNKYLE!
CONTACT ESTABLISHED.

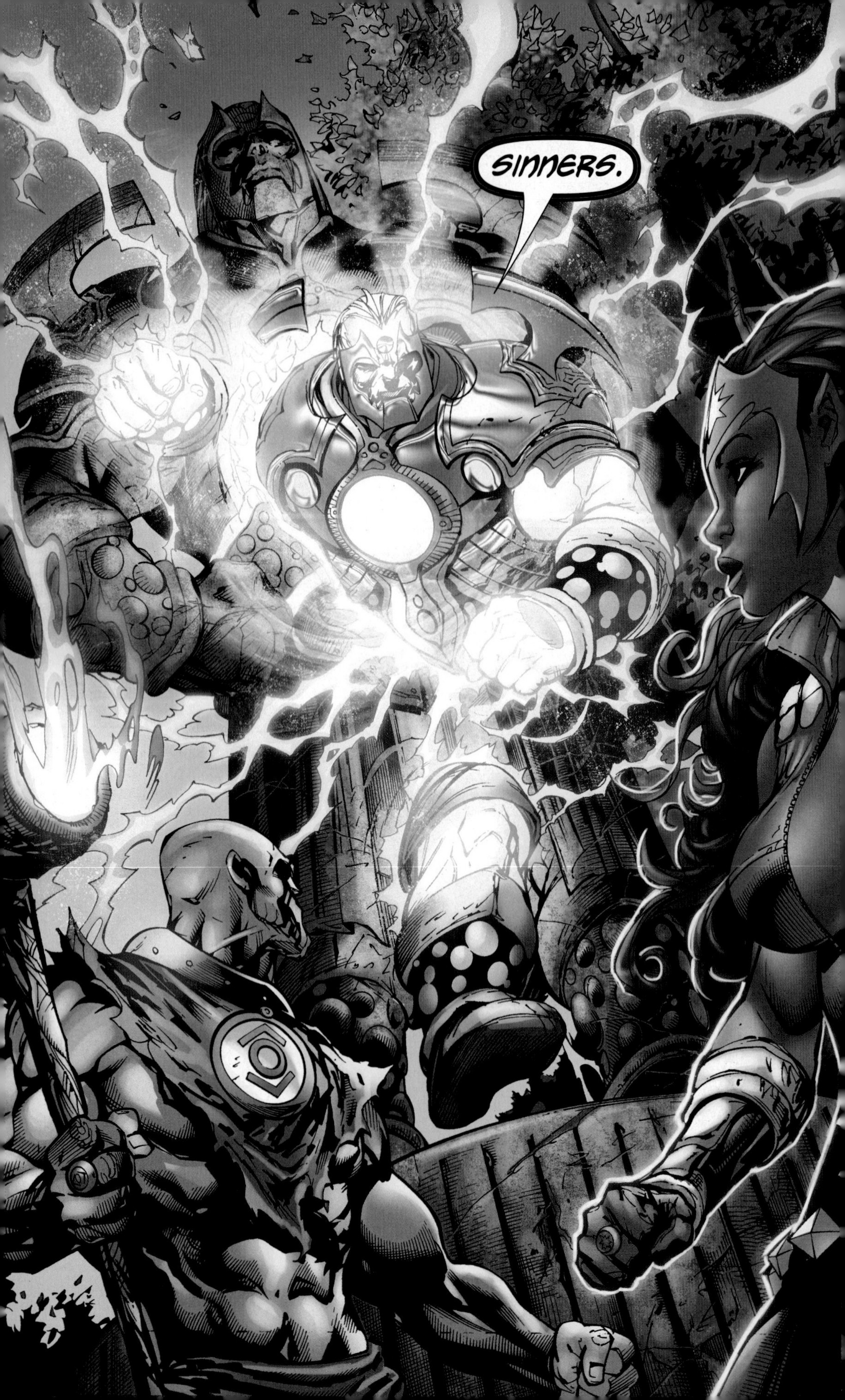
SINNERS.

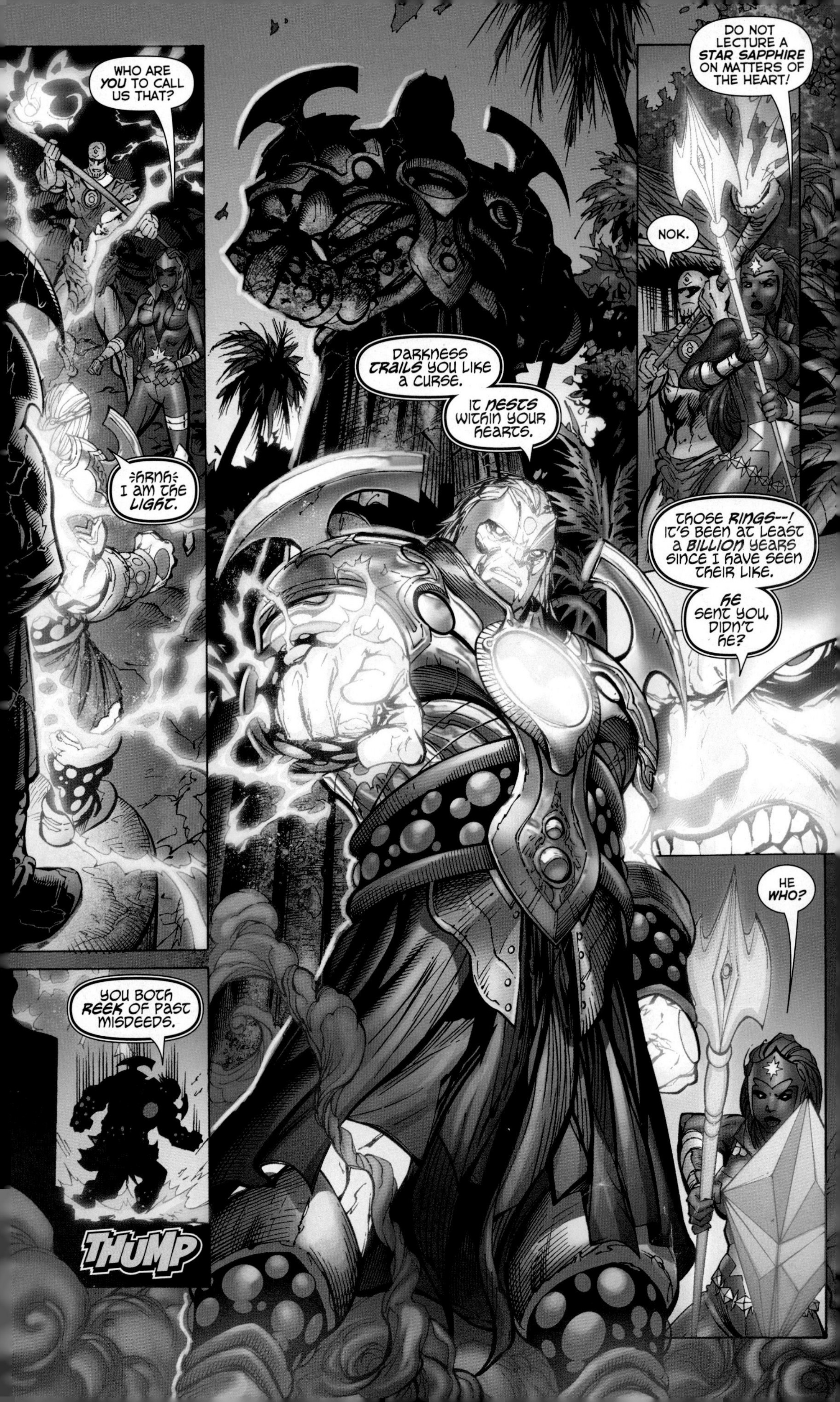
WHO ARE YOU TO CALL US THAT?
NGH I AM THE LIGHT.
DARKNESS TRAILS YOU LIKE A CURSE.
IT NESTS WITHIN YOUR HEARTS.
DO NOT LECTURE A STAR SAPPHIRE ON MATTERS OF THE HEART!
NOK.
THOSE RINGS--! IT'S BEEN AT LEAST A BILLION YEARS SINCE I HAVE SEEN THEIR LIKE.
HE SENT YOU, DIDN'T HE?
HE WHO?
YOU BOTH REEK OF PAST MISDEEDS.
THUMP

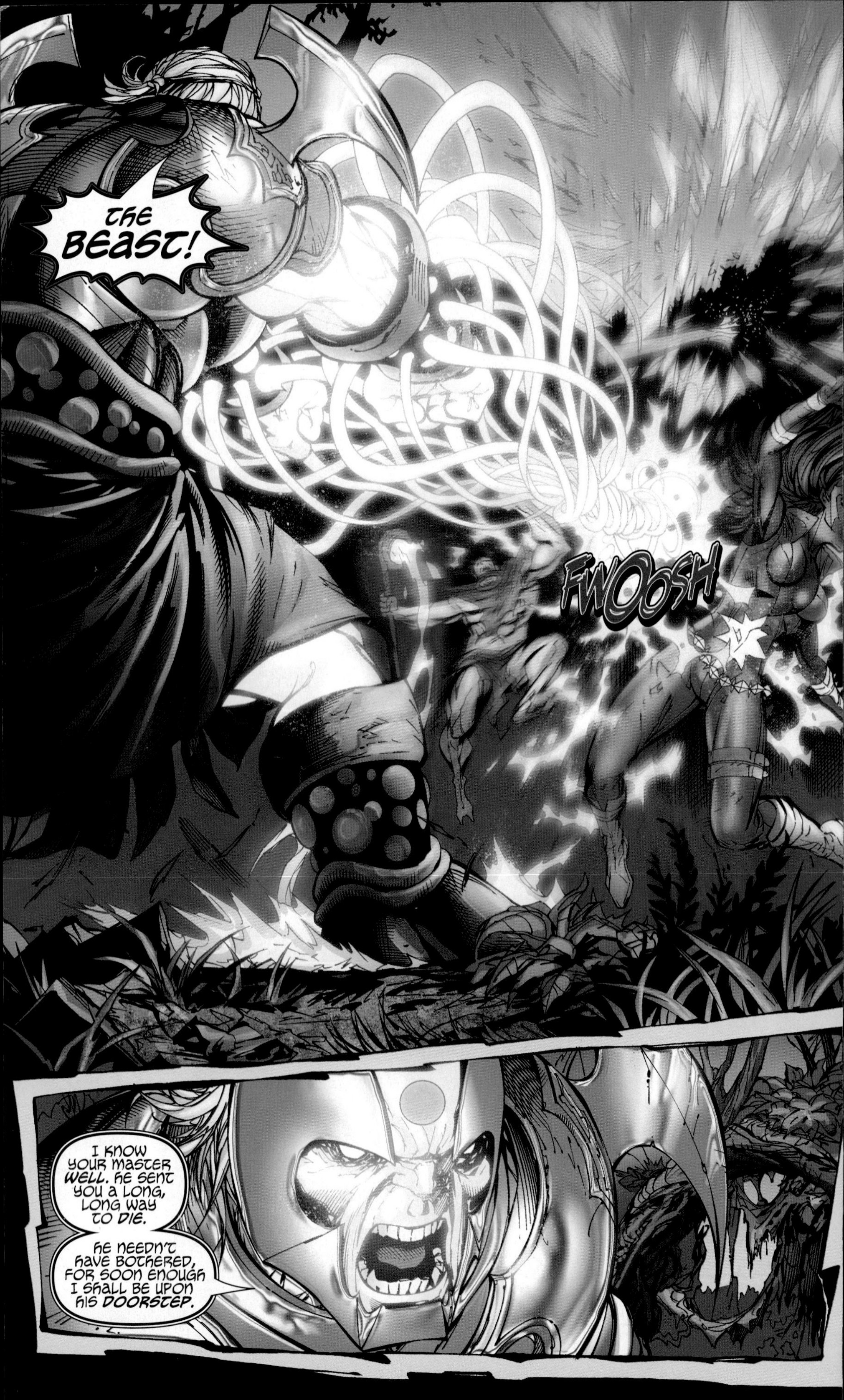
THE BEAST!
FWOOSH!
I KNOW YOUR MASTER WELL. HE SENT YOU A LONG, LONG WAY TO DIE.
HE NEEDN'T HAVE BOTHERED, FOR SOON ENOUGH I SHALL BE UPON HIS DOORSTEP.

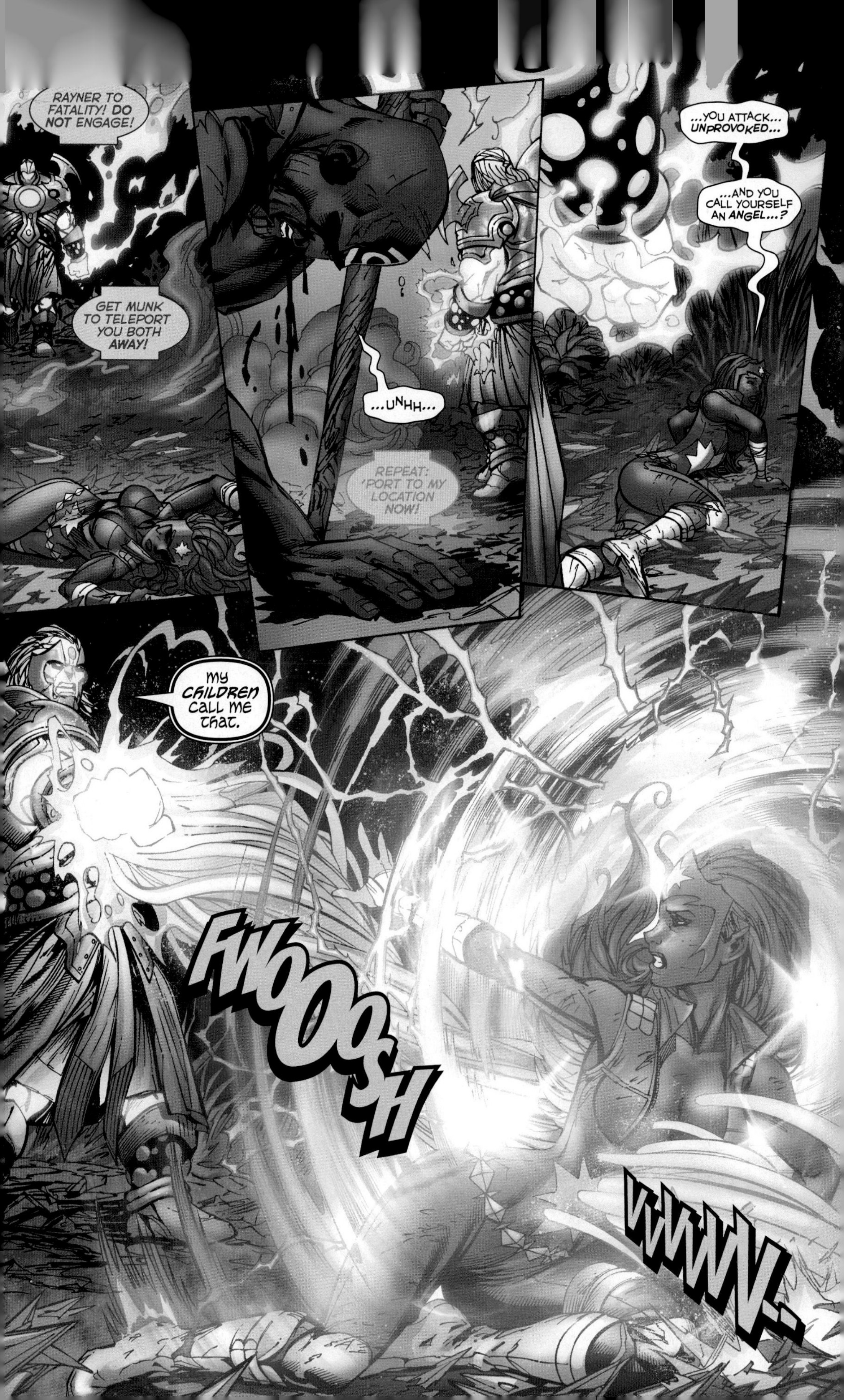
RAYNER TO FATALITY! DO NOT ENGAGE!
GET MUNK TO TELEPORT YOU BOTH AWAY!
...UNHH...
REPEAT: 'PORT TO MY LOCATION NOW!
...YOU ATTACK... UNPROVOKED...
...AND YOU CALL YOURSELF AN ANGEL...?
MY CHILDREN CALL ME THAT.
FWOOOSH
VVVVVV..

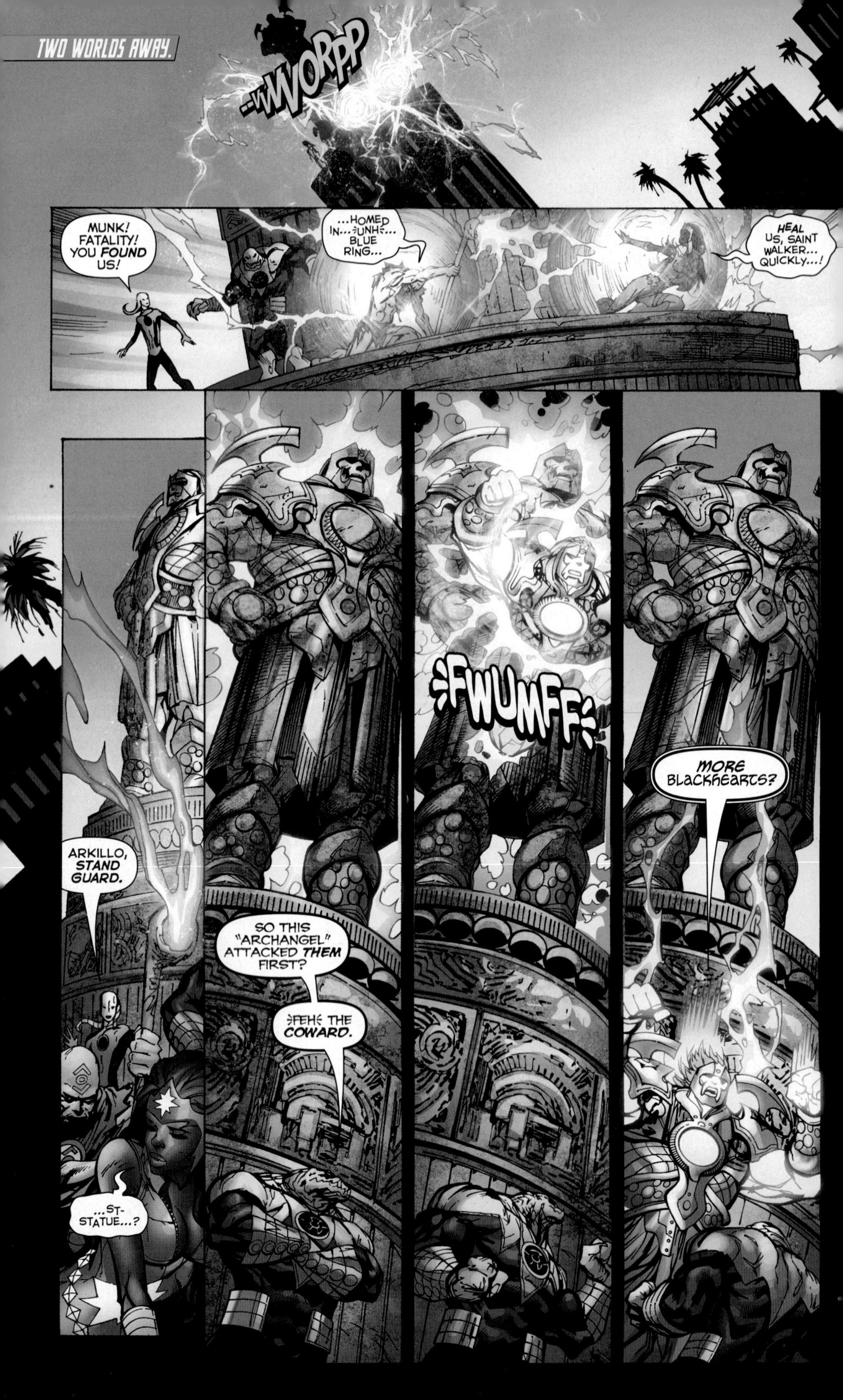
TWO WORLDS AWAY.
-VWVORPP
MUNK! FATALITY! YOU FOUND US!
...HOMED IN...UNH... BLUE RING...
HEAL US, SAINT WALKER... QUICKLY...!
ARKILLO, STAND GUARD.
...ST- STATUE...?
SO THIS "ARCHANGEL" ATTACKED THEM FIRST?
FEH. THE COWARD.
FWUMFF
MORE BLACKHEARTS?

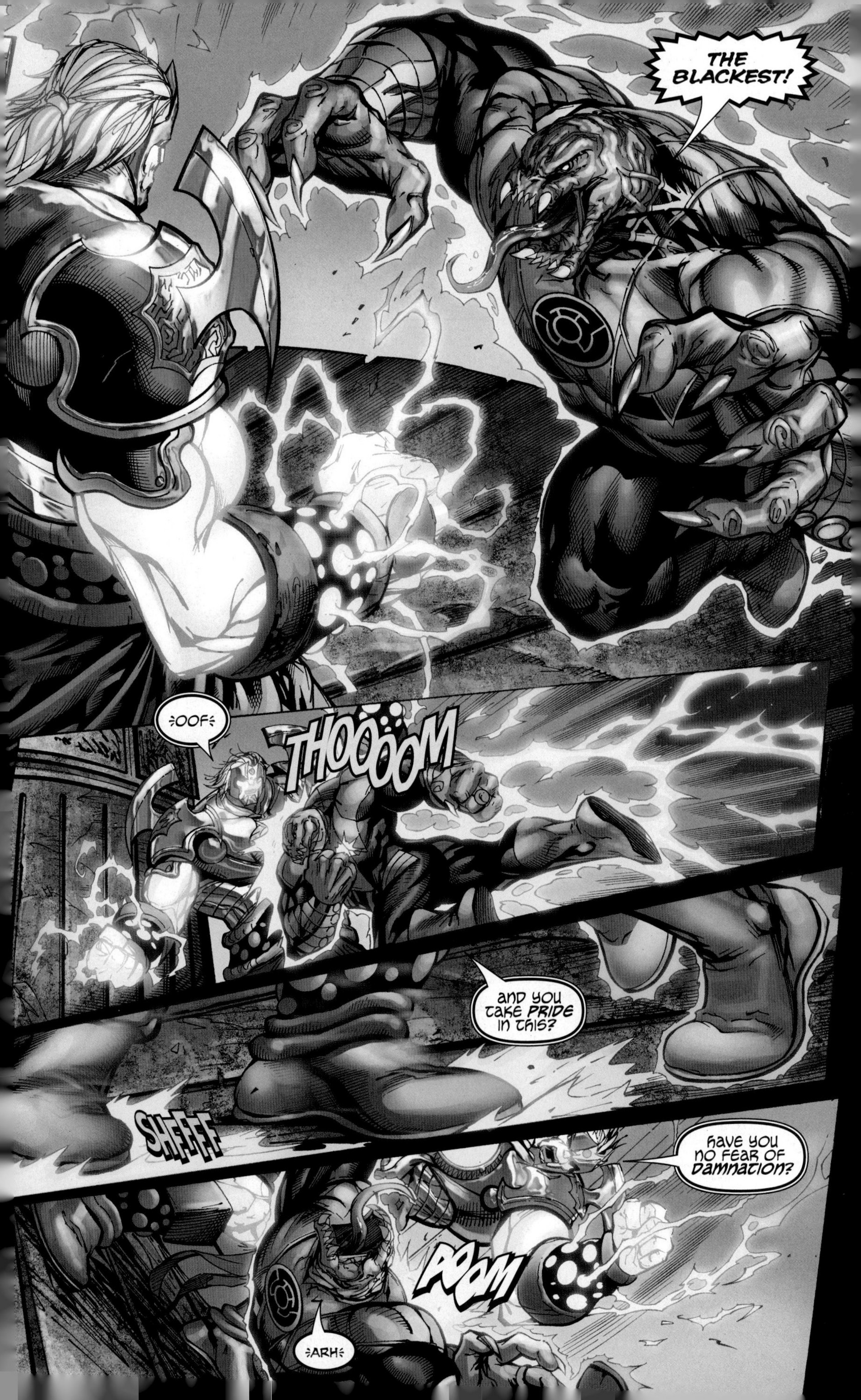
THE BLACKEST!
OOF
THOOOOM
AND YOU TAKE PRIDE IN THIS?
SHFFFF
HAVE YOU NO FEAR OF DAMNATION?
POOM
ARH

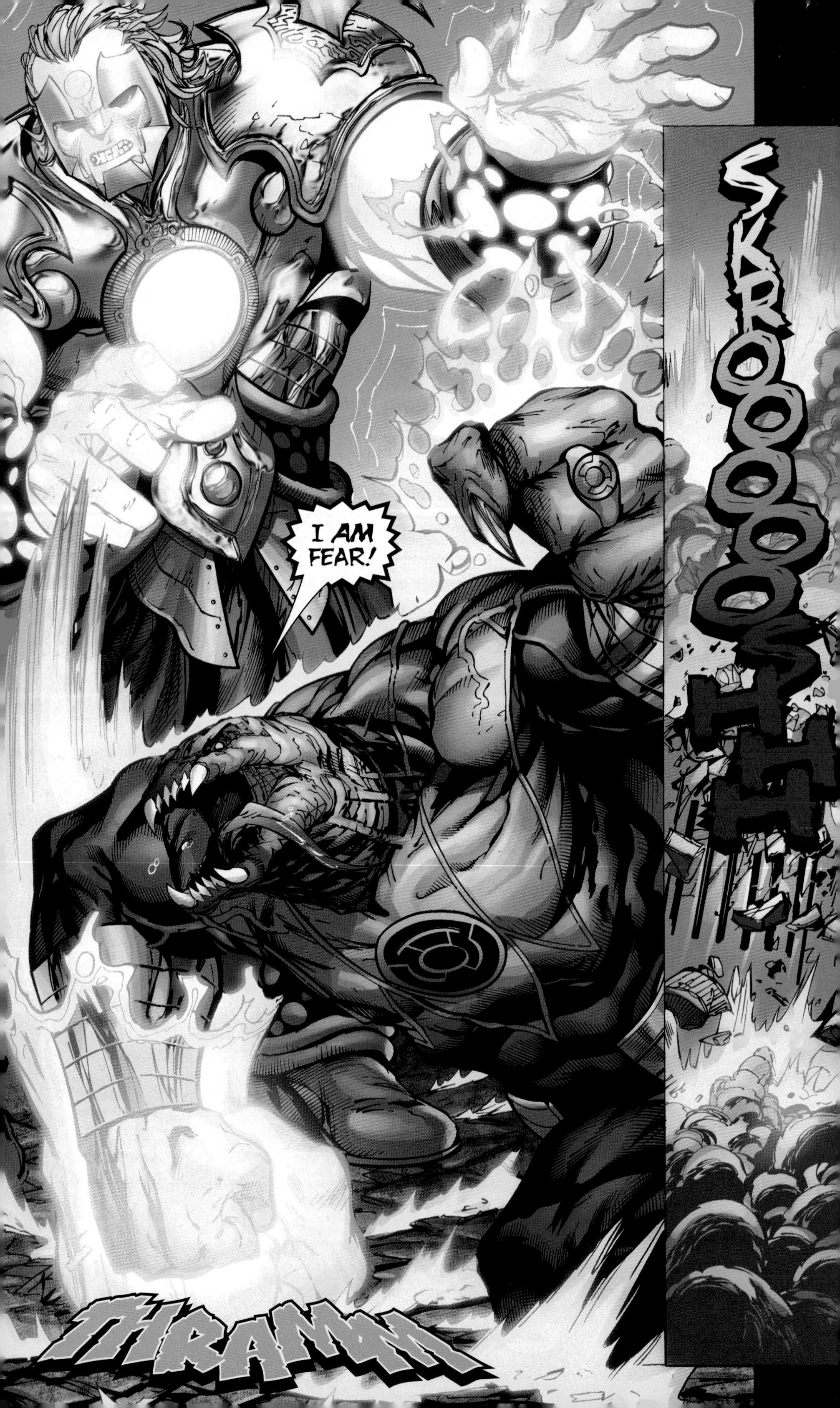

I AM FEAR!
SKROOOOOOSHHH
THRAMM

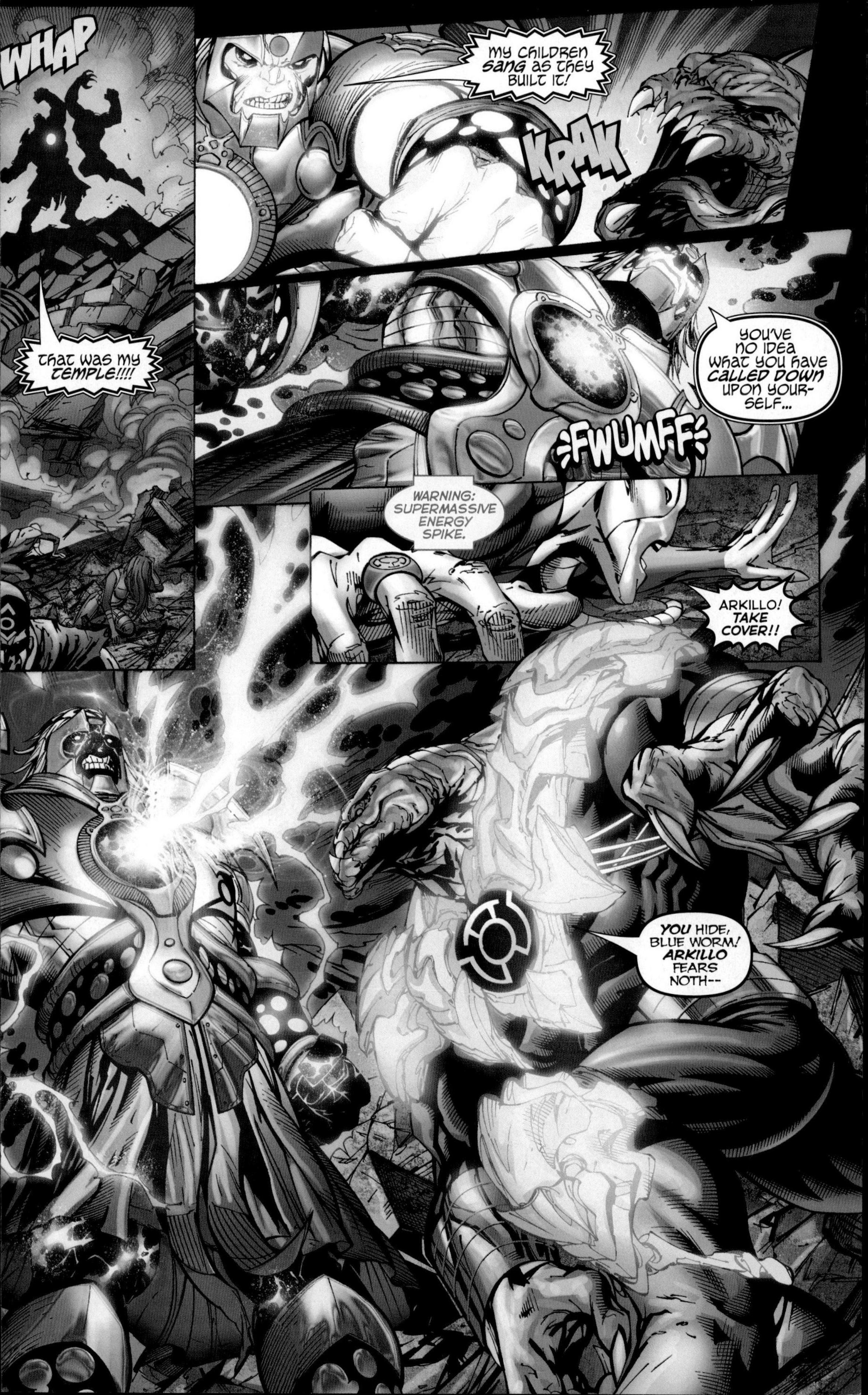
WHAP
MY CHILDREN SANG AS THEY BUILT IT!
KRAK
THAT WAS MY TEMPLE!!!!
YOU'VE NO IDEA WHAT YOU HAVE CALLED DOWN UPON YOUR-SELF...
FWUMFF
WARNING: SUPERMASSIVE ENERGY SPIKE.
ARKILLO! TAKE COVER!!
YOU HIDE, BLUE WORM! ARKILLO FEARS NOTH--

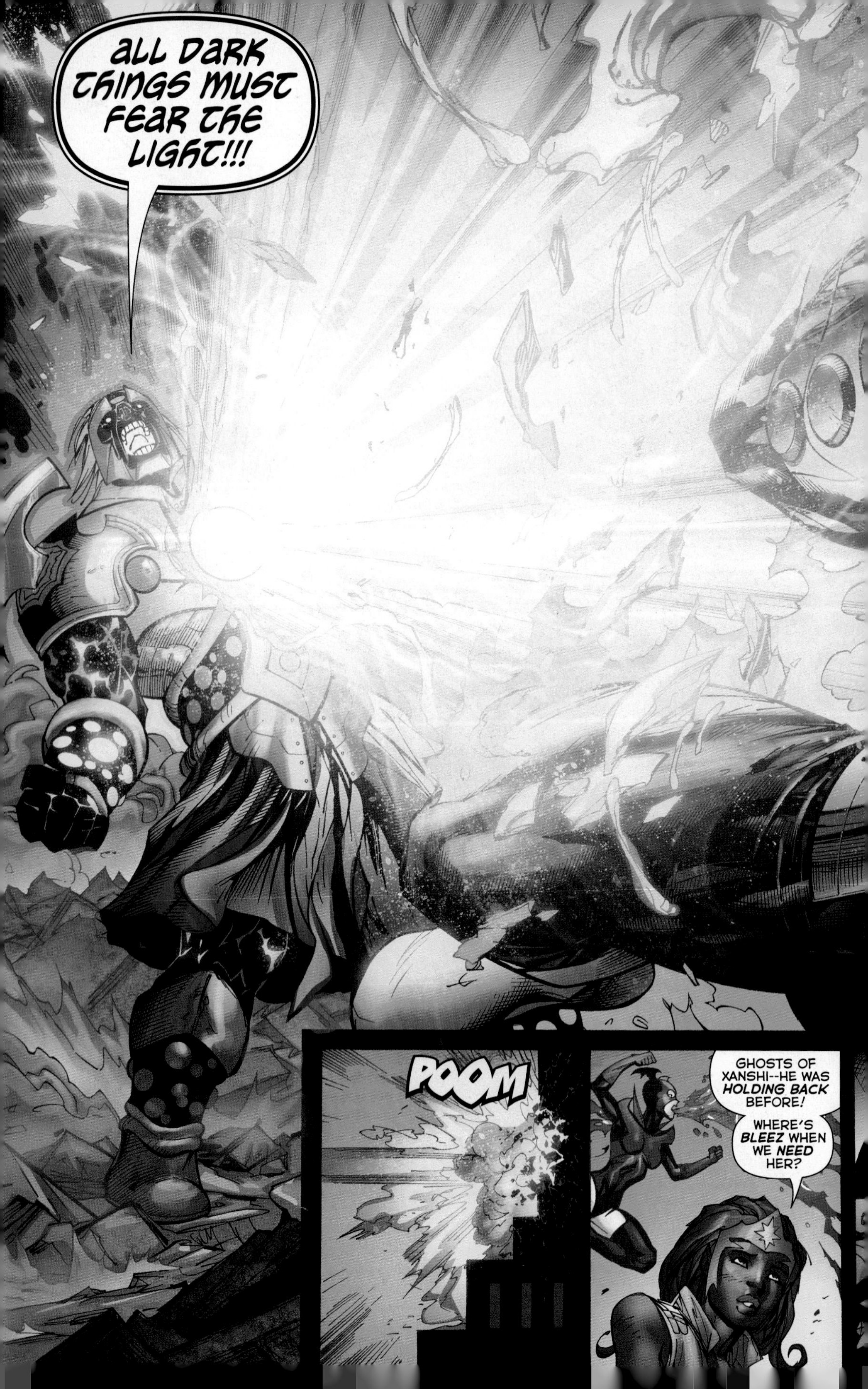

ALL DARK THINGS MUST FEAR THE LIGHT!!!
POOM
GHOSTS OF XANSHI--HE WAS HOLDING BACK BEFORE!
WHERE'S BLEEZ WHEN WE NEED HER?

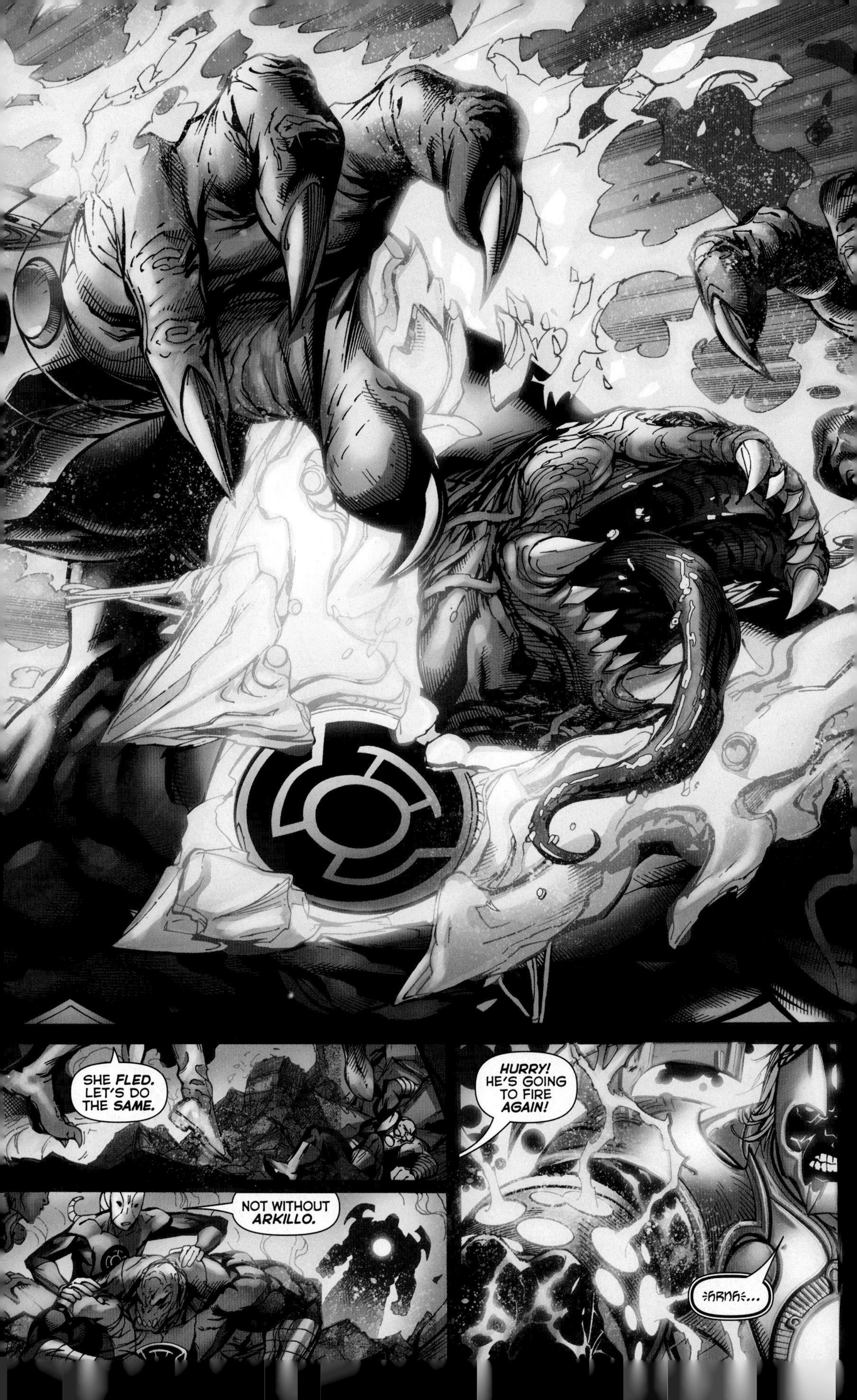

SHE FLED. LET'S DO THE SAME.
HURRY! HE'S GOING TO FIRE AGAIN!
NOT WITHOUT ARKILLO.

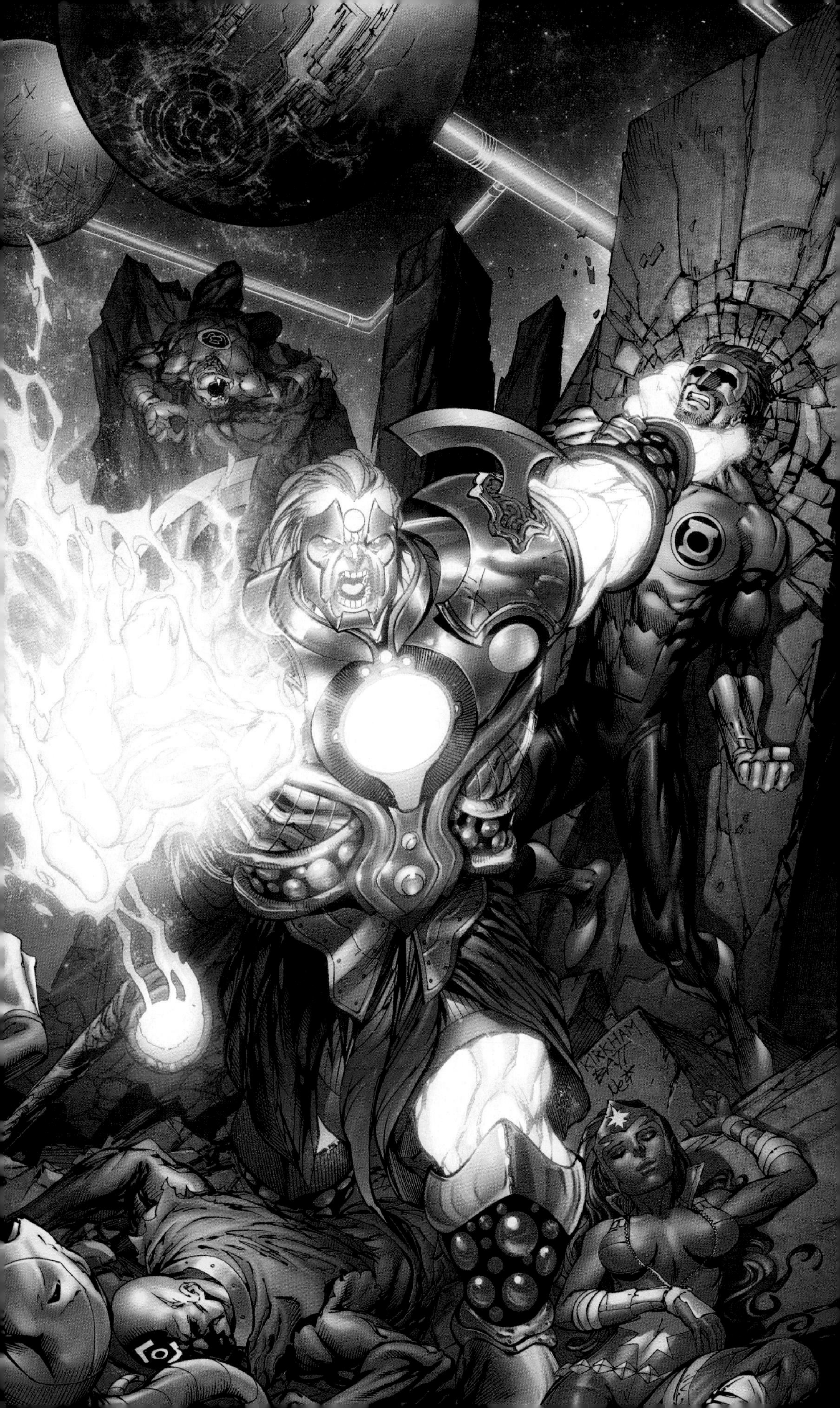
KIRKHAM
BATT

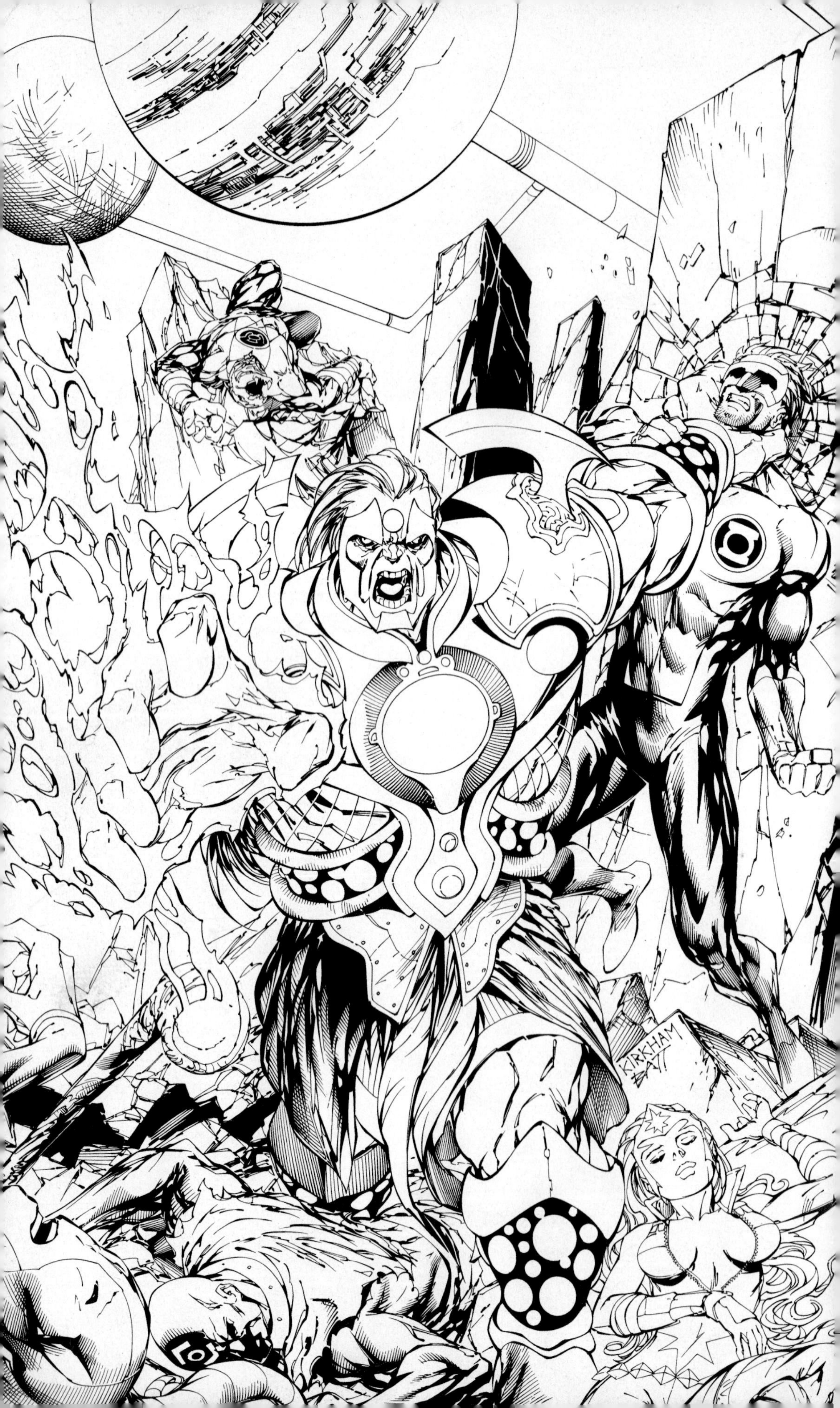
KIRKHAM
BATT

"EONS AGO, MY PEOPLE SAFEGUARDED THE WORLDS THAT ORBIT THE SUN-STAR *VEGA*. IT WAS A DUTY WE GLADLY TOOK ON, YEARNING TO MAKE VEGA A *BEACON OF RIGHTEOUS-NESS* IN A DARK AND LONELY COSMOS.

"FROM THE MEGA-CITIES OF *MALTUS* TO THE JUNGLES OF *OKAARA*...FROM THE MOUNTAINS OF *EUPHORIX* TO THE DESERTS OF *TAMARAN*, WE TAUGHT THEM *ALL* TO EMBRACE THE LIGHT.

"AND WHEN THEY BENT A KNEE, IT WAS TO *THE ANGELS OF VEGA* THAT THEY PRAYED.

"BUT *ONE* SPECIES IN PARTICULAR HAD NO NEED OF OUR ENLIGHTENMENT.

"THE STONE DENIZENS OF CHANGRALYN WERE *BORN* RIGHTEOUS.

"THEY WERE THE GENTLEST, MOST PEACE-LOVING BEINGS I EVER MET.

"UNDER MY GUIDANCE, THEIR SPIRITUAL LEADERS FORMED A *COUNCIL OF VIRTUE* TO SPREAD OUR TEACHINGS ACROSS THE STARS.

"VEGA'S FUTURE SEEMED BRIGHT INDEED."

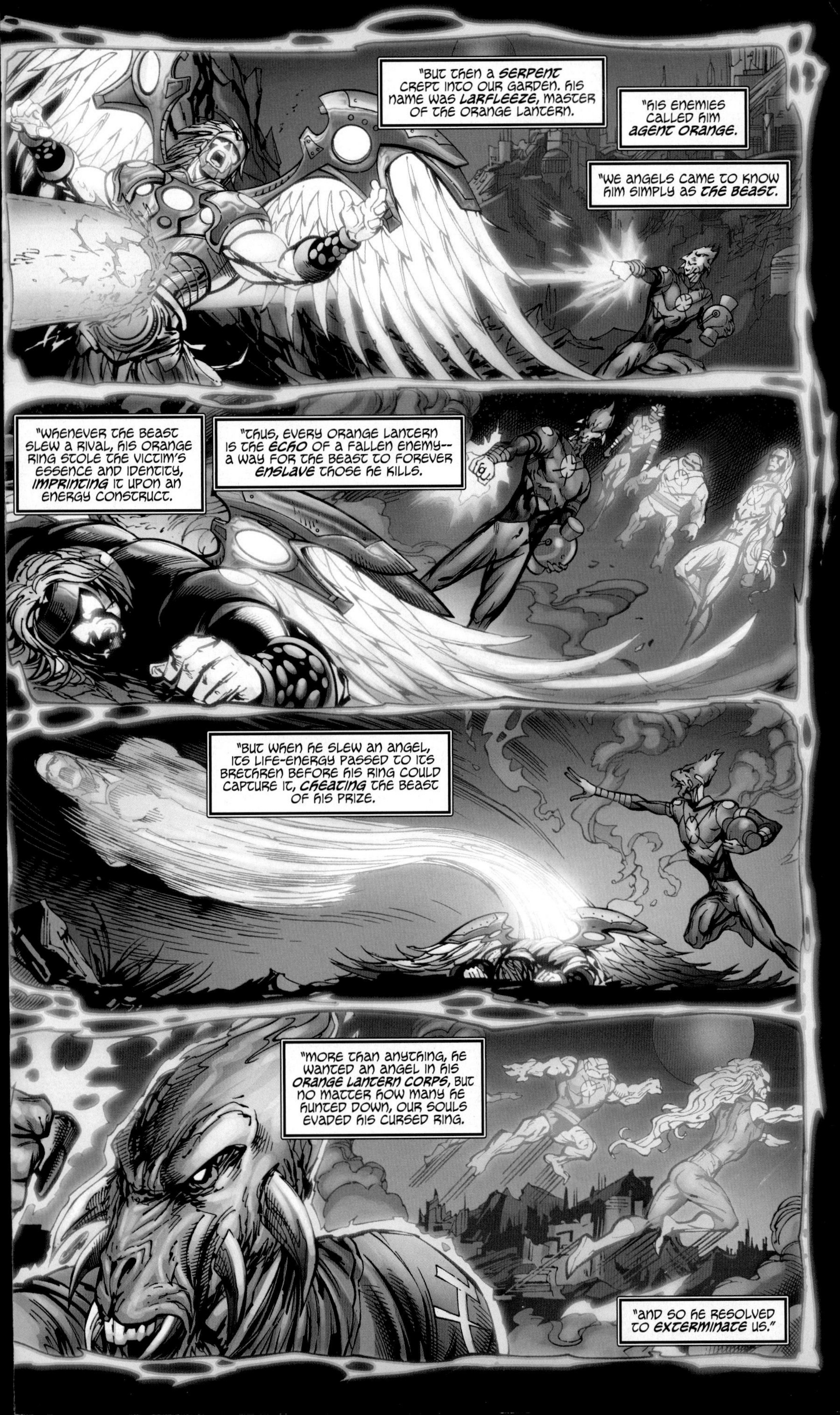
"BUT THEN A SERPENT CREPT INTO OUR GARDEN. HIS NAME WAS LARFLEEZE, MASTER OF THE ORANGE LANTERN.
"HIS ENEMIES CALLED HIM AGENT ORANGE.
"WE ANGELS CAME TO KNOW HIM SIMPLY AS THE BEAST.
"WHENEVER THE BEAST SLEW A RIVAL, HIS ORANGE RING STOLE THE VICTIM'S ESSENCE AND IDENTITY, IMPRINTING IT UPON AN ENERGY CONSTRUCT.
"THUS, EVERY ORANGE LANTERN IS THE ECHO OF A FALLEN ENEMY-- A WAY FOR THE BEAST TO FOREVER ENSLAVE THOSE HE KILLS.
"BUT WHEN HE SLEW AN ANGEL, ITS LIFE-ENERGY PASSED TO ITS BRETHREN BEFORE HIS RING COULD CAPTURE IT, CHEATING THE BEAST OF HIS PRIZE.
"MORE THAN ANYTHING, HE WANTED AN ANGEL IN HIS ORANGE LANTERN CORPS, BUT NO MATTER HOW MANY HE HUNTED DOWN, OUR SOULS EVADED HIS CURSED RING.
"AND SO HE RESOLVED TO EXTERMINATE US."

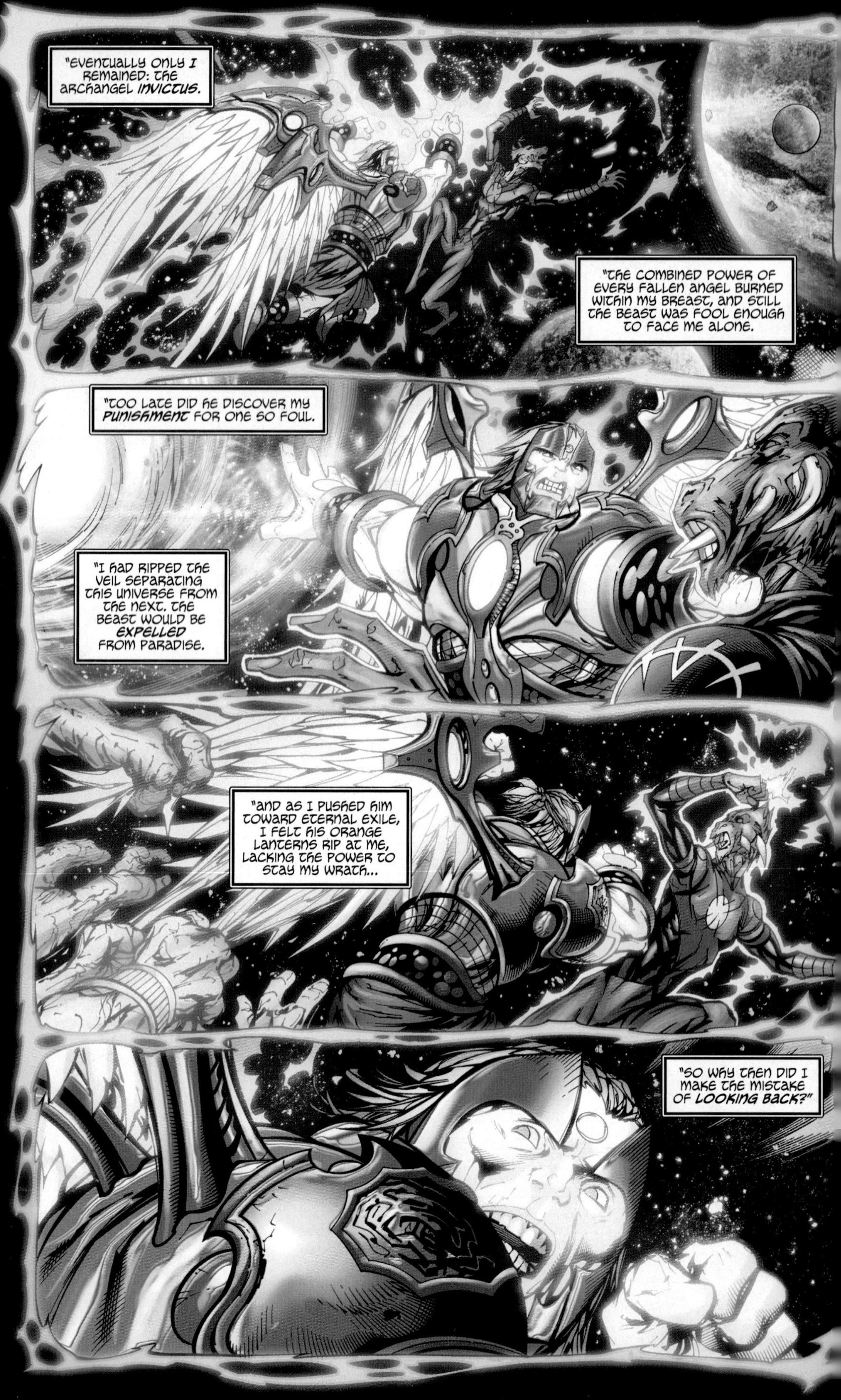
"EVENTUALLY ONLY *I* REMAINED: THE ARCHANGEL *INVICTUS*.
"THE COMBINED POWER OF EVERY FALLEN ANGEL BURNED WITHIN MY BREAST, AND STILL THE BEAST WAS FOOL ENOUGH TO FACE ME ALONE.
"TOO LATE DID HE DISCOVER MY *PUNISHMENT* FOR ONE SO FOUL.
"I HAD RIPPED THE VEIL SEPARATING THIS UNIVERSE FROM THE NEXT. THE BEAST WOULD BE ***EXPELLED*** FROM PARADISE.
"AND AS I PUSHED HIM TOWARD ETERNAL EXILE, I FELT HIS ORANGE LANTERNS RIP AT ME, LACKING THE POWER TO STAY MY WRATH...
"SO WHY THEN DID I MAKE THE MISTAKE OF ***LOOKING BACK?***"

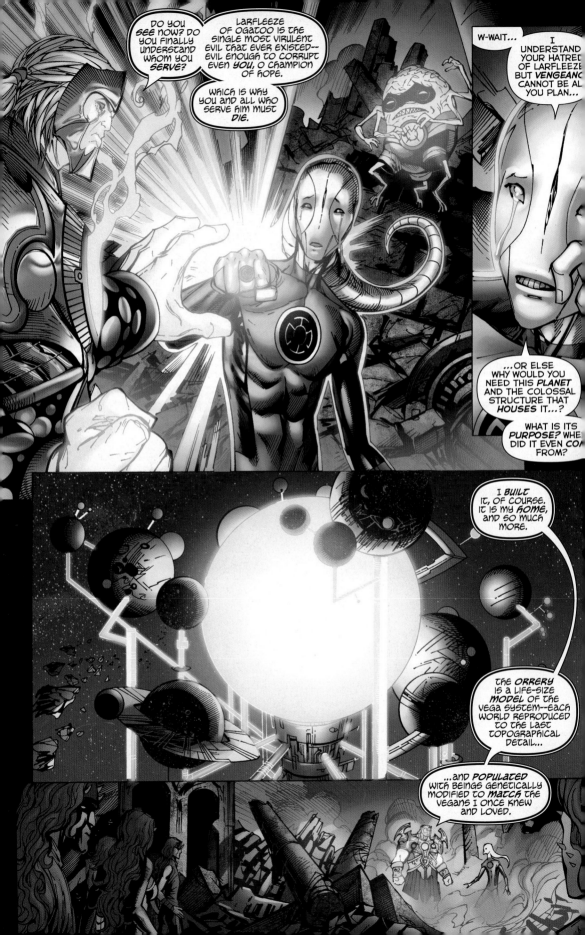

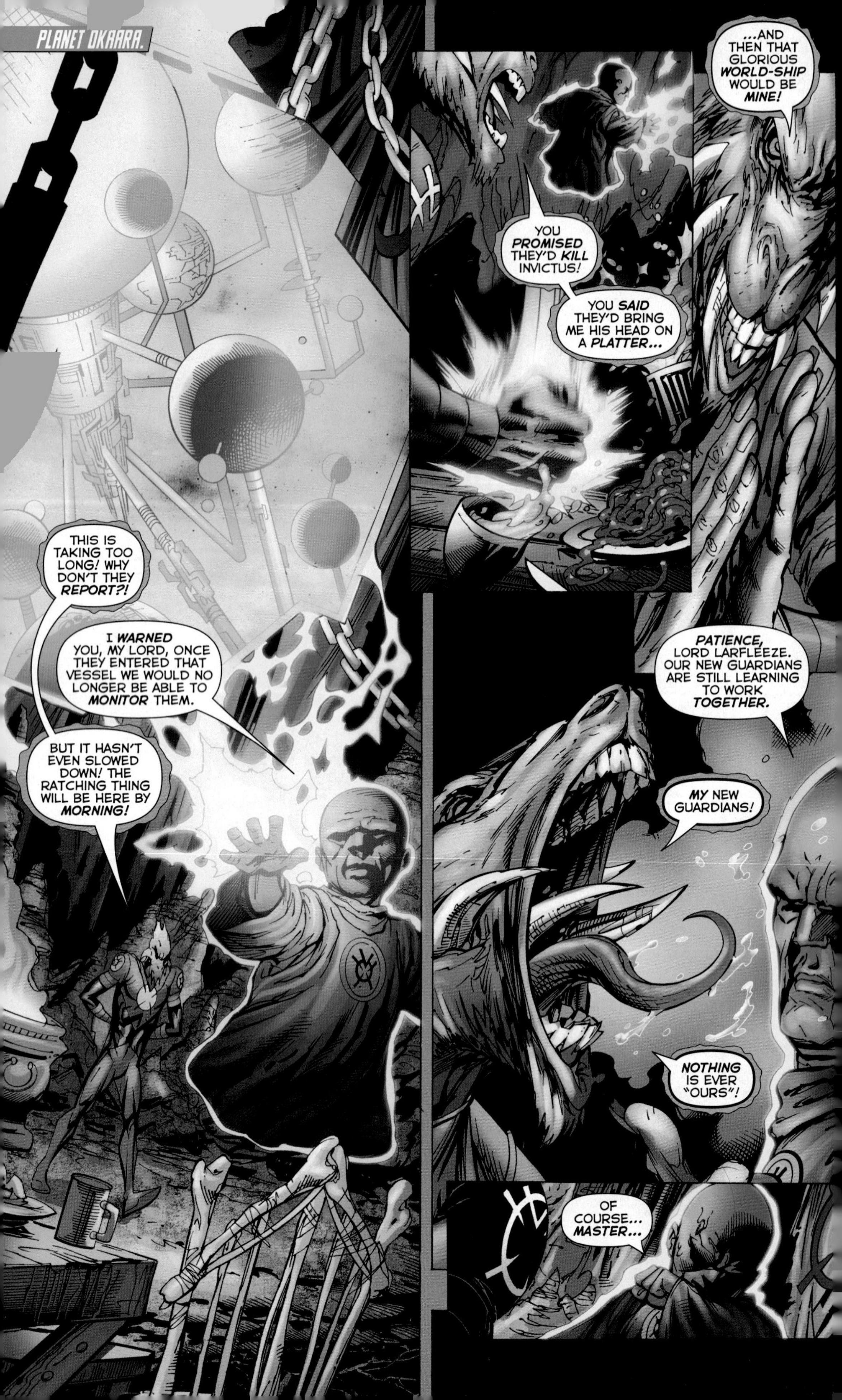
PLANET OKAARA.
THIS IS TAKING TOO LONG! WHY DON'T THEY REPORT?!
I WARNED YOU, MY LORD, ONCE THEY ENTERED THAT VESSEL WE WOULD NO LONGER BE ABLE TO MONITOR THEM.
BUT IT HASN'T EVEN SLOWED DOWN! THE RATCHING THING WILL BE HERE BY MORNING!
YOU PROMISED THEY'D KILL INVICTUS!
YOU SAID THEY'D BRING ME HIS HEAD ON A PLATTER...
...AND THEN THAT GLORIOUS WORLD-SHIP WOULD BE MINE!
PATIENCE, LORD LARFLEEZE. OUR NEW GUARDIANS ARE STILL LEARNING TO WORK TOGETHER.
MY NEW GUARDIANS!
NOTHING IS EVER "OURS"!
OF COURSE... MASTER...

STAY PUT, BLEEZ, OR--

YOUR ARGUMENT *IS* COMPELLING, GREEN LANTERN... BUT I HAVE HEARD HONEYED WORDS BEFORE.

WORDS ARE NOTHING WITHOUT *DEEDS* TO BACK THEM.

THEN LET US *PROVE* TH--

SILENCE!

THUMP

BACK OFF, LOVE-LANTERN. RAGE MAY BE BLIND, BUT IT ISN'T STUPID.

YOU WILL *INDEED* PROVE YOURSELVES TO ME. I RATHER *LIKE* THE THOUGHT OF DESTROYING MY ENEMY WITH HIS OWN WEAPON.

H-HOW DO YOU MEAN?

I MEAN I SHALL LET YOU LEAVE HERE ALIVE--ON *ONE* CONDITION:

YOU, GREEN LANTERN, SHALL SLAY LARFLEEZE FOR ME.

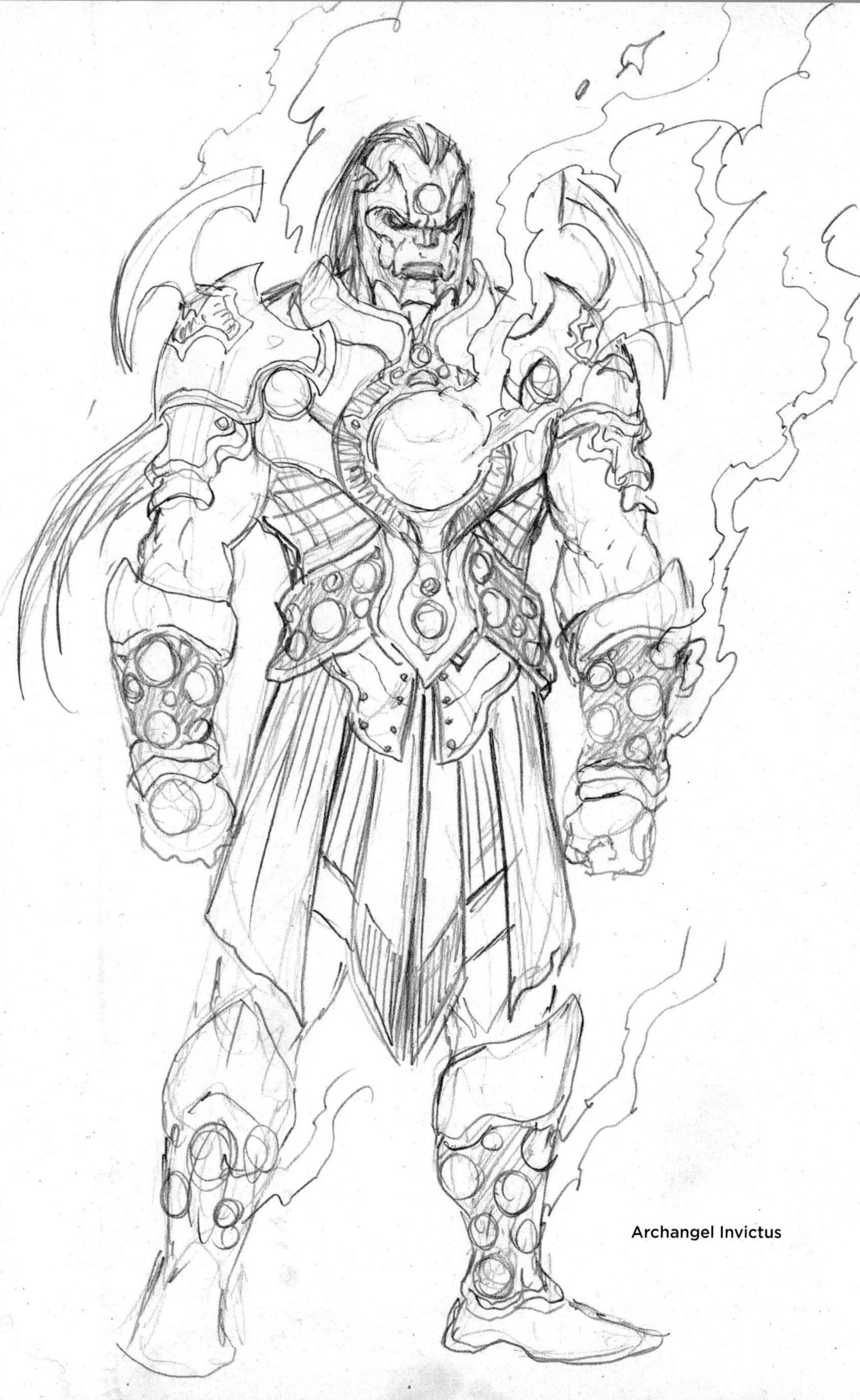

Archangel Invictus

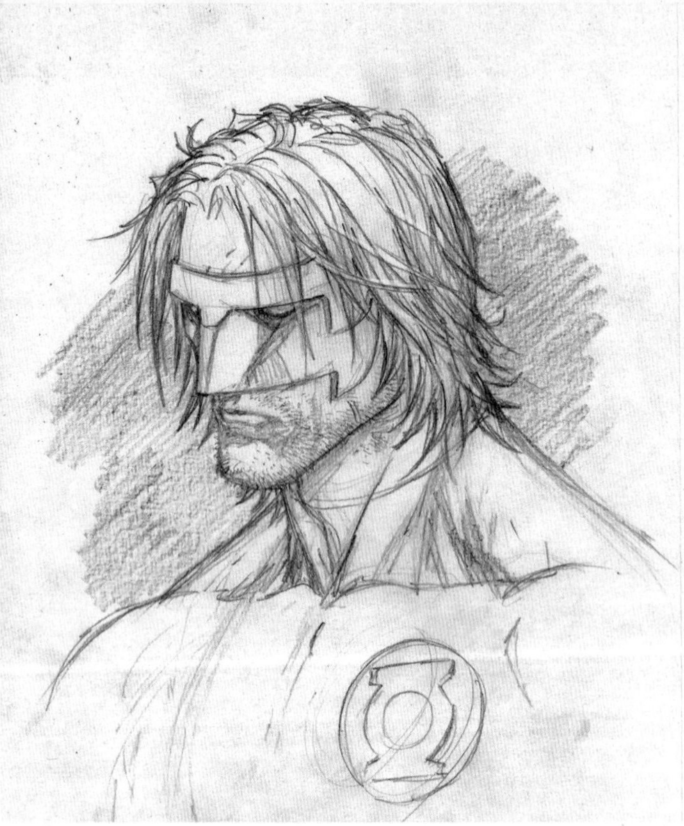

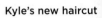

Kyle's new haircut

Fatality's redesign

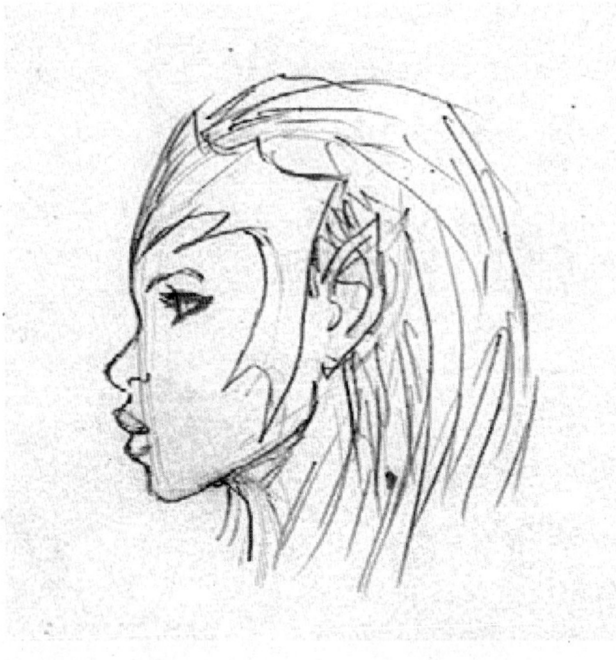

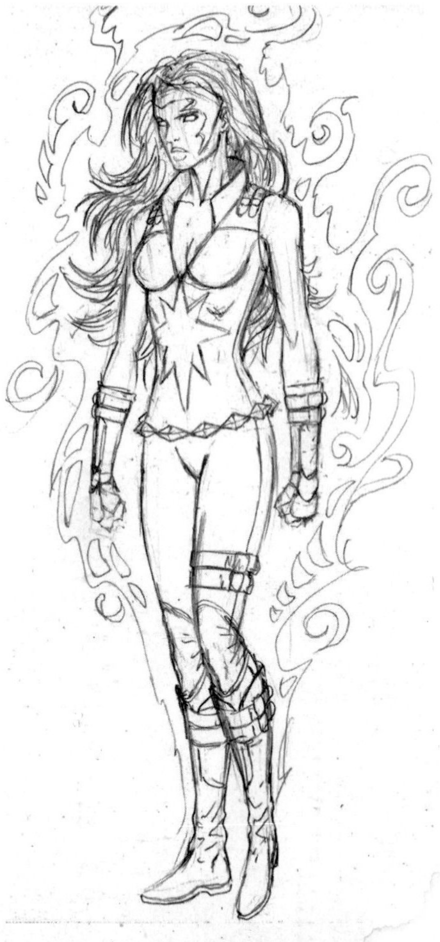